CRIMINOLOGICAL THEORIES

Introduction and Evaluation

Second Edition

Ronald L. Akers
University of Florida

Roxbury Publishing Company
Los Angeles, California

Library of Congress Cataloging-in-Publication Data

Akers, Ronald L.
  Criminological theories: introduction and evaluation/
Ronald L. Akers—2nd ed.
    p. cm.
    Includes bibliographical references and index.
    ISBN 0-935732-51-9
    1. Criminology. I. Title.
    HV6018.A38 1997
    364—dc20   96-19834
                                                        CIP

CRIMINOLOGICAL THEORIES:
INTRODUCTION AND EVALUATION (Second Edition)

Publisher and Editor: Claude Teweles
Copy Editor: Anton Diether
Project Editor: Dawn VanDercreek
Proofreading: Joyce Rappaport
Production: James Ballinger
Cover Design: concept by Caroline and Levi Akers; production
  art by Allan Miller and Marnie Deacon
Typesetting: Synergistic Data Systems

Printed on acid-free paper in the United States of America. This book meets the standards of recycling of the Environmental Protection Agency.

ISBN 0-935732-51-9

ROXBURY PUBLISHING COMPANY
P.O. Box 491044
Los Angeles, California 90049-9044
(213) 653-1068
Email: roxbury@crl.com

This book is dedicated

to the precious memory of my father

**Charles E. Akers
(1920-1993)**

and to my loving mother

Thelma Louise Akers

PREFACE TO THE SECOND EDITION

The purposes of this book are to review the basic concepts and principles of criminological theories and to evaluate their adequacy as explanations of criminal and deviant behavior or of the criminal law and justice system. While not exhaustive, the coverage of theories is comprehensive. I have included all the major theories that have been the subject of nine out of ten theory-testing articles in the leading criminological journal over the past three decades (Stitt and Giacopassi, 1992).

The first goal in presenting each theory is to give a concise and clear exposition of its central concepts, assertions, and hypotheses. The intent is to provide an accurate, understandable introduction for readers who are not familiar with the theory and a review for those who are. In each case, an effort has been made not only to present the classic or original statements of a theory but to show modifications and revisions of it, including the most recent and significant developments.

The second goal is to evaluate the theory. In Chapter 1, I review the main criteria by which the merits of a theory can be judged—logical consistency, scope, parsimony, applicability to policy, testability, and empirical validity. All these are invoked at various points, but the central focus of the evaluation of each theory is the *empirical validity* of the theory. I review the research relevant to the theory and assess how well the findings support or contradict the main assertions of the theory. Before the empirical adequacy of a theory can be evaluated, of course, it must be testable, and a considerable amount of attention is given to questions of tautology and measurement. The last chapter (Chapter 11) is devoted to the topic of theoretical rivalry and integration. Recent examples of conceptual and propositional integration are reviewed and evaluated.

This Second Edition contains several significant changes from the First Edition. The chapter sequence and structure have been changed. The distinction between theories that explain the making and enforcing of law and theories that explain criminal and delinquent behavior has been retained, but the Second Edition is not divided, as was the First Edition, into two parts to reflect this distinction. In the First Edition, conflict, Marxist, and feminist theories were split between chapters at the beginning and at the end of the book. One chapter combined Marxist and feminist views on law and criminal justice, and one chapter combined these two with conflict theory of crime. In the Second Edition, Chapter 8 (Conflict Theory), Chapter 9 (Marxist and Critical Theories), and Chapter 10 (Feminist Theory) are new chapters that present separate, more unified, and clearer introductions and evaluations of these theories, both as explanations of criminal justice and as explanations of crime. Recent developments in critical, constitutive, left realist, and peacemaking criminology are included, along with advances in feminist theory. Each of the other chapters has also been updated and substantially revised in light of recent research and important changes in the theories.

The book's breadth of coverage combined with its modest length allows its adoption either as the principal or supplemental text in courses on theories of crime, delinquency, and deviance. It would also be useful as a supplemental text or one of several reading assignments in criminology, juvenile delinquency, deviance, criminal behavior, and similar courses.

While writing with a student audience in mind, I have not hesitated to draw upon the contemporary research literature and have not shied away from addressing central issues and controversies in the field. The text citations to the theoretical and research literature and the list of references are thorough and extensive. Therefore, I believe that other readers will find some value in the book. It should be useful to criminal justice practitioners looking for validated theoretical principles and relevant literature on which to build or enhance programs and policy. Theoreticians and researchers will find some original analysis and insights that may be of interest.

ACKNOWLEDGMENTS

I acknowledge the personal encouragement and highly competent help of Claude Teweles, president and publisher of Roxbury Publishing Company. I appreciate very much his unfailing interest and attention to the project, from the first discussions about the new edition to the final stage of publication. Anton Diether did the copy editing and proofing. His alert editing saved me from many awkward and cloudy sentences, and I thank him for it.

I am grateful for the collegial insights and suggestions from the many instructors who adopted the First Edition. Their encouraging responses to the book and their professional judgment in making suggestions for improvement were invaluable to me. I am grateful to Marcia Marcionette, one of my doctoral students at the University of Florida, who was of great help in my literature searches and reference checking.

It is a joy to thank my family publicly for their unconditional love that always sustains me: my wife Caroline, my sons Ron and Levi, my daughter Tamara, and her husband Lee Phillips. The debt I owe Caroline and Levi extends to their specific contributions to this book. They collaborated on the concept and design of a prototype for the front cover of both editions of the book.

TABLE OF CONTENTS

CHAPTER 3
BIOLOGICAL AND PSYCHOLOGICAL THEORIES

CHAPTER 4
SOCIAL LEARNING THEORY

CHAPTER 5
SOCIAL BONDING AND CONTROL THEORIES

CHAPTER 6
LABELING THEORY

CHAPTER 7
SOCIAL DISORGANIZATION,
ANOMIE, AND STRAIN THEORIES

CHAPTER 8
CONFLICT THEORY

CHAPTER 11
INTEGRATING CRIMINOLOGICAL THEORIES

CHAPTER 1

INTRODUCTION TO CRIMINOLOGICAL THEORY

What Is Theory?

To many students, criminal justice practitioners, and other people, theory has a bad name. In their minds, the word "theory" means an irrelevant antonym of "fact." Facts are real, while theories seem to involve no more than impractical mental gymnastics. Theories are just fanciful ideas that have little to do with what truly motivates real people. This is a mistaken image of theory in social science in general and in criminology in particular. Theory, if developed properly, is about real situations, feelings, experience, and human behavior. An effective theory helps us to make sense of facts that we already know and can be tested against new facts.

Consider the situation of a young girl's child abuse and her later involvement in prostitution. What about the relationship between the limited opportunities for legitimate work and the selection of a career in crime? Think about the fact that members from a significant proportion of immigrant groups have become successively involved in organized crime, such as Jews, Irish, and Italians, and now Puerto Ricans, African Americans, and Latinos. Or consider the fact that some kinds of behavior are legally defined as criminal, while others are not. Theories are tentative answers to the commonly asked questions about such events and behavior. Why? By what process? How does it work? The answers may provide explanations of one set of events by referring to other events.

> In general, scientific theories make statements about the relationship between two classes of phenomena. (Vold and Bernard, 1986:4)

> Theories, then, are really generalizations of a sort; they explain how two or more events are related to each other. (Williams and McShane, 1988:2)

1

A theory is a set of interconnected statements or propositions that explain how two or more events or factors are related to one another. (Curran and Renzetti, 1994:2)

Note that these and other definitions of theory (see Gibbs, 1990) refer to statements about relationships between actual events; about *what is* and *what will be.* They are not answers to questions of *what ought to be,* nor are they philosophical, religious, or metaphysical systems of beliefs and values about crime and society.

❧ Criminological theories are abstract, but they entail more than ivory-tower or arm-chair speculations. They are part of the broader social science endeavor to explain human behavior and society. Understanding why people conform to or deviate from social and legal norms is an integral part of a liberal education. Moreover, such understanding is vital for those who plan to pursue specialized careers in the law or criminal justice. Virtually every policy or action taken regarding crime is based on some underlying theory or theories of crime. It is essential, therefore, to comprehend and evaluate the major theories of criminology, not only for the academic or research criminologist, but also for the educated citizen and the legal or criminal justice professional.

Types of Criminological Theories

Edwin H. Sutherland (1947) defined criminology as the study of the entire process of *law-making, law-breaking,* and *law-enforcing.* This definition provides us with a starting point for classifying criminological theories. One such major type of theory addresses the first and third part of this process: the making and enforcing of the law. Theories of this kind attempt to account for why we have laws and why the criminal justice system operates the way it does. Another major type of theory explains law-breaking. Such theories account for criminal and delinquent behavior. They are usually extended to explain any deviant behavior that violates social norms, whether or not such behavior also violates the law.

There are not as many different theories of the first kind (theories of law and criminal justice) as there are of the second kind (theories of criminal and deviant behavior). Therefore, while both are important, more attention will be paid here to the second type of theory. Conflict, labeling, Marxist, and feminist theories are examples of theories that attempt to shed light on both criminal behavior and the law.

Theories of Making and Enforcing Criminal Law

Theories of making and enforcing criminal law (also herein referred to as theories of law and criminal justice) offer answers to questions of how or why certain behavior and people become defined and are dealt with as criminal in society. Why is a particular conduct considered illegal and what determines the kind of action to be taken when it occurs? How is it decided, and who makes the decision, that such conduct is criminal? And how are the resources of the public and state brought to bear against it? Theories try to answer these questions by proposing that social, political, and economic variables affect the legislation of law, administrative decisions and rules, and the implementation and operation of law in the criminal justice system.

This does not refer to philosophies regarding what kind of legal system we should have; nor is it a theoretical statement, for instance, to argue that we *should* have a fair, just, and effective criminal justice system. Such a statement offers desirable social goals that citizens may debate and vote on, but it provides no scientific explanation of law and criminal justice. Arguments over the goals and purposes of the system—such as whether it should focus on crime control rather than due process, should provide just deserts for law violators or only take actions that deter crime, or should rehabilitate or severely punish serious offenders—are not theoretical arguments. Philosophical and pragmatic debates over society's control of crime may be informed by theory or have relevance to the application of theory, but they are not *themselves* theoretical explanations of why laws are formulated and enforced. Theories attempt to explain the behavior of the participants in the legal system and the operation of the system itself. They produce hypotheses about the factors that account for legal and criminal justice actions and decisions. Theories do not tell us what are the correct, proper, and desirable values that should be exemplified in the system.

This is not to imply that the theorists themselves are totally unaffected by philosophical and value judgments. There is a significant relationship between theories of crime and criminal justice and philosophies that define the desirable goals of a just, effective, and well-managed criminal justice system. Such goals partially direct which theories will be considered important, and those theories will help to develop strategies to reach these goals.

For example, one of the reasons that conflict theory is important in criminology is that its theoretical propositions about the operation of the system are relevant to the political and moral debate over the justness of that system. The goal of a just system is to treat everyone equitably based on legally relevant factors such as the nature of the criminal act and the laws relating to it. Conflict theory hypothesizes that actions taken in the criminal justice system may be decided differentially based on such factors as the race, class, and gender of offenders, rather than on the type of crime. The decisions of a criminal justice system that relies more on such social characteristics than on the nature of the crime is not a just system. Therefore, the extent to which conflict theory is supported or refuted by research evidence is critical to the debate over the fairness of the criminal justice system.

Theories of Criminal and Deviant Behavior

Theories of criminal and deviant behavior try to answer the question of why social and legal norms are violated. This question has two interrelated parts: (1) Why are there variations in group rates of crime and deviance, and (2) why do some individuals come to commit criminal and deviant acts?

The first question poses the problem of trying to make sense of the differences in the location and proportion of deviant and criminal behavior in various groups and societies. For example, why does the United States have such a high rate of crime compared to Japan and most of the Western European countries? Why do males as a group commit so many more violent and criminal acts than females? How do we explain the differences in homicide and drug use among different classes and groups within the same society?

The second question raises the issue of explaining differences among individuals in committing or refraining from criminal acts. Why are some individuals more likely to break the law than others? By what process or under what circumstances do people typically, and not just in a specific, individual case, reach the point of obeying or violating the law? Why does one person commit a crime, given a certain opportunity, while another does not, given the same opportunity? Why are some people more likely than others to commit frequent crimes or pursue criminal careers?

The first set of questions focuses on societal and group patterns, the second on individual differences. A theory that addresses broader questions about differences across societies or major groups in society is called a "macro" theory. Conversely, one that focuses specifically on small group or individual differences is referred to as operating on the "micro" level of analysis (Orcutt, 1983; Alexander et al., 1987). Other terms have also been used to make a similar distinction between theories. Cressey (1960) refers to "epidemiology" (the prevalence and distribution of crime across groups and societies) and "individual conduct." Akers refers to such different theories as social *structural* or *processual* (Akers, 1968; 1985). These distinctions between macro and micro, structural and processual, refer not only to questions about groups and individual behavior, but also to the kinds of answers a theory offers. For example, a theory that tries to answer the question of the differences between male and female crime rates by relying on innate biological differences between men and women would still be operating on the micro level.

In actuality, the two major questions of group and individual behavior are really just subtypes of the same general question: *Why do or do not people commit crime and deviance?* This is why theories of criminal behavior are neither strictly structural nor processual, although each will emphasize one or the other. Theories emphasizing social structure propose that the proportion of crimes among groups, classes, communities, or societies differ because of variations in their social or cultural make-up. Most structural theories, however, also include implicit or explicit statements regarding the process by which these structural conditions produce high or low crime rates. Processual theories assert that an individual commits criminal acts because he or she has experienced a particular life history, possessed a particular set of individual characteristics, or encountered a particular situation. Such theories also consider the deviancy-producing structures that an individual must encounter in order to increase the probability of his or her committing a crime.

There are other ways to classify criminological theories. One common way is to refer not just to micro or macro, but to several levels of explanation that ascend from the smallest to the largest unit of analysis. Such a classification typically categorizes the theories according to the general scientific discipline from which the explanatory variables are drawn. The most common classifications are: *biological* theories that explain crime with one or more genetic, chemical, neurological, or physiological variables; *psychological* theories based on personality, emotional maladjustment, mental retardation, psychic disturbance, or psychological traits; *social psychological* theories that account for crime by reference to behavior, self, and cognitive variables in a group context; and *sociological* theories that explain crime with cultural, structural, and socio-demographic variables. (See Nettler, 1984; Gibbons, 1979; Vold and Bernard, 1986; Liska, 1987; Williams and McShane, 1988; Shoemaker, 1990; Jensen and Rojek, 1992.)

Just as the categories of structure and process overlap to some extent, some theories will draw from two or more disciplines. For instance, contemporary biological theories do not rely exclusively on genetic or biochemical factors, but also draw from psychological or sociological variables as well. Other theories, such as social learning, are clearly social-psychological, utilizing both sociological and psychological variables.

The theories are arranged in the following chapters in an order that draws roughly from both the structure-process distinction and the classification of theories as biological, psychological, and sociological. Chapter 2 introduces the classical and contemporary statements of deterrence theory. Chapter 3 surveys early and recent biological and psychological theories. The remaining chapters review the major sociological theories of crime. Social learning theory (Chapter 4), control theories (Chapter 5), and labeling theory (Chapter 6) are the more social-psychologically oriented of these sociological theories. Chapter 7 (anomie/strain theories) and Chapter 8 (conflict), Chapter 9 (Marxist), and Chapter 10 (feminist theories) discuss those theories that draw the most heavily from social structure and culture. Labeling, conflict, Marxist, and feminist perspectives are both theories of criminal justice and theories of criminal behavior. The final chapter examines the extent to which the differences and commonalities in theories can be reconciled and integrated.

Whatever the classification of theory that may be used, there will be some kind of overlap, shortcomings, and loose ends. No special case will be made here for the order in which the various theories are presented. The focus here is not on how best to classify each theory but rather on introducing what each theory proposes and on evaluating its validity.

Criteria for Evaluating Theory

How do we know if a theory offers a sound explanation of crime or criminal justice? The various theories that will be explored provide different, sometimes contradictory, explanations of crime. How do we judge which explanation is preferable over another, or which is the best amongst several theories? The weakest reason for accepting or rejecting a theory of crime is how well it conforms to one's own beliefs, ideologies, or preferred policies.

If criminological theories are to be scientific, then they must be judged by scientific criteria. The most important of these is empirical validity, the extent to which a theory can be verified or refuted with carefully gathered evidence. But there are several other major criteria by which theories can be assessed. These include internal *logical consistency, scope and parsimony, testability, empirical validity, and usefulness and policy implication.* (For discussions of the criteria for evaluating criminological theories, see Schrag, 1962; Gibbons, 1979:14-16; Vold and Bernard, 1986:340-363; Liska, 1987: 14-25; Shoemaker, 1990: 3-11; Barlow and Ferdinand, 1992:189-99; Tittle, 1995:17-53).

Logical Consistency, Scope, and Parsimony

The basic prerequisite for a sound theory is that it has clearly defined concepts and that its propositions are logically stated and internally consistent. For example, a theory which proposes that criminals are biologically deficient and that deficiency explains their criminal behavior cannot also claim that family socialization is the basic cause of criminal behavior.

The scope of a theory refers to the range of phenomena which it proposes to explain. For instance, a theory that accounts only for the crime of check forgery may be accurate, but it is obviously very limited in scope. A better theory is one which accounts for a wide range of offenses including check forgery. A theory of juvenile delinquency that does not relate as well to adult criminality is more restricted than one that accounts for both juvenile delinquency and adult crime. A theory that explains only the age distribution of crime has a more limited scope than one that explains the age, race, sex, and class distributions of crime.

Parsimony, the conciseness and abstractness of a set of concepts and propositions, is also a desirable characteristic in a scientific theory. Scope and parsimony are interrelated, in that a theory which explains a wide scope of events with a few, succinct statements is scientifically preferable to one which relies on a complex set of propositions and variables that accounts for only a small range of events. The principle of parsimony is to use as few propositions as possible to explain the widest range of phenomena. For example, a theory which proposes that *all* crime and delinquency is caused by low self-control is much more parsimonious than a theory that requires a different set of multiple hypotheses to explain crime and delinquency, depending upon the type of offense and the age, sex, or race of the offender.

Testability

A scientific theory must be testable by objective, repeatable evidence. If a theory cannot be tested against empirical findings, it has no scientific value. Gibbons (1979:14) argues that, "In the final analysis, the acid test of a scientific theory is testability; that is, the extent to which it can either be verified or disproved by appropriate empirical evidence." It is not enough for a theory to fit known facts about crime or contain empirical evidence consistent with its propositions. It must also be possible to subject the theory to empirical falsification; in other words, it must be open to evidence that may counter or disprove its hypotheses with negative findings. If it is not *falsifiable* in this sense, it is not testable (Stinchcombe, 1968).

A theory may be untestable because the definitions of its concepts and its propositions are stated as a *tautology*. A tautology is a statement or hypothesis that is true by definition or involves circular reasoning. If, for example, one begins with the definition of low self-control as the failure to refrain from crime then proposes low self-control as a cause of law violation, then one's proposition is tautological. Given the definition of low self-control, the proposition can never be proven false, because self-control is defined by the very thing it is hypothesized to explain. It simply says that a person who has low self-control has low self-control, or that a person who violates the law violates the law. A variation on a tautology that is true by definition is seen in the practice of placing a label on some behavior, then using that label to explain the same behavior. For instance, one may label serial killers as psychopaths, then assert that people commit serial murders because they are psychopathic. Such a statement does no more than repeat the label. Similarly, we may observe that a person drinks excessively and has problems with alcohol, so we theorize that the person overdrinks because he is an alcoholic. How do we know he is an alcoholic? We know because he drinks excessively and has problems with alcohol. We have come full circle.

Another way in which a theory may be untestable is that its propositions are so open-ended that any contradictory empirical evidence can be interpreted or re-interpreted to support the theory. For example, a theory may propose that males who rob banks are motivated by an irrational and unconscious impulse to resolve their guilt over their childhood sexual attraction towards their own mothers. This is a testable explanation of male bank robbery because it is not true by definition. If research finds enough bank robbers who fit this description, then the theory is supported. If research uncovers other cases where bank robbers claim their only motive is money and they have no such feelings towards their mothers, then that can be taken as falsifying the theory. However, the theory cannot be falsified if the claims of the latter bank robbers are dismissed by asserting that their very denial of these feelings in effect *supports* the theory, because the same unconscious impulse that motivated them to rob banks also rendered them unconscious of their true motivations. Similarly, a theory may contend that criminal laws always serve the interests of the ruling capitalist elite. Even if laws are enacted to serve the interest of the working class, one could always re-interpret them with the argument that such laws only appear to serve the working class but in fact serve the ruling class. There is no way to falsify the theory. Hence, a theory that can never be proven wrong, regardless of the findings, is not a testable theory.

A theory may also be untestable because its concepts are not measurable by observable and reportable events. A theory's concepts and propositions identify the explanatory events or *independent variables* that account for variations in the *dependent variables*, which are events or behavior to be explained. Even a non-tautological theory cannot be tested if it is not possible to find observable events that can be taken as objective and repeatable measures of these concepts. Without such measures, the hypothesized relationships cannot be checked against actual events. If a theory proposes that people commit crimes because they are possessed by invisible demons, there is no way to prove whether or not such demons are responsible for the crime. If we cannot measure the existence of demons separately from the occurrence of criminal behavior, we may simply assume the existence of the demons from the existence of the crimes. We have a similar tautology if the dependent and independent variables are measured by the same events. For example, it is tautological to explain delinquent behavior as the result of social disorganization, if one of the indicators of social disorganization is the delinquency rate itself. Both the events to be explained and the events used to explain them are the same thing. It is tautological to interpret an event as the cause of itself.

Not all concepts must be directly measurable for a theory to be testable, but one must be able to relate them in a logical and clear way to measurable phenomena. For instance, one part of social learning theory proposes that an individual's exposure to admired models who are involved in deviant or delinquent behavior will increase the chances that person will imitate those same behaviors. Imitation is defined as one engaging in acts after he or she has watched them being engaged in by others. It is quite possible to directly observe the behavior of adult or peer models whom adolescents are in a position to imitate, or to ask adolescents to report exposure to such models then observe the extent to which their behavior matches that of the models. The concept of imitation refers to observable, measurable events; therefore, propositions about modeling are testable.

Empirical Validity

This is the most important criterion for judging a theory. Empirical validity simply means that a theory has been supported by research evidence. For a theory to be logical, parsimonious, and non-tautological means little if it turns out to be false. It is seldom the case, however, that a theory is found to be entirely true or entirely false. Falsifiable theories may encounter some negative evidence without being judged as wholly invalid. The question is, what degree of empirical support does the theory have? Do the findings of research provide weak or strong support? Does the preponderance of evidence support or undermine the theory? How does its empirical validity compare with that of other theories?

For instance, deterrence theory proposes in part that offenders will not repeat their crimes if they have been caught and given severe legal punishment. If research finds that this is true for only a small minority of offenders or that punished offenders are only slightly less likely to repeat crimes than unpunished offenders, then the theory has some, but not much, empirical validity. Labeling theory, on the other hand, proposes that the experience of being caught and processed by the criminal justice system labels offenders as criminal. Hence, the label promotes their self-identity as criminals and makes them more likely, rather than less likely, to repeat their crimes. If research finds that, other things being equal, apprehended offenders are more likely to recidivate than those who have not been caught, then labeling theory has more empirical validity than deterrence theory.

Empirical Validity and the Concept of Causality and Determinism

Notice the terms "more likely" and "less likely." Empirical validity does not mean that a theory must identify variables that always cause criminal behavior to occur or always explain the decision to arrest an offender. The traditional concept of causality in science is that cause X must precede and produce effect Y. To be a cause, X must be both a "necessary condition," the absence of which means that Y will not occur, and a "sufficient condition," so that Y always occurs in the presence of X. No criminological theory can meet these two traditional causation criteria of necessary and sufficient conditions. But that makes little difference, since a probabilistic concept of causality is more appropriate for assessing the empirical validity of criminological theories. The probabilistic concept of causation simply asserts that the presence of X renders the occurrence of Y more probable. That is, contemporaneous variations or changes in criminal behavior are associated or correlated with variations or changes in the explanatory variables identified in the theory. The presence of the variables specified in the theory precede the occurrence of crime and delinquency, thereby predicting when they are more likely to occur or re-occur. The stronger the correlations and associations, the greater the theory's empirical validity.

Interpreting correlations as causation even in the probabilistic sense remains a problem, because the direction of the relationship between two correlated variables may not be the same as specified in the theory. For instance, a theory may hypothesize that an adolescent engages in delinquent conduct as a result of associating with other adolescents who are already delinquent. Finding a correlation between one's own delinquent behavior and the delinquency of one's friends, therefore, could be taken as evidence in support of the theory. But the relationship may exist for converse reasons; that is, the adolescent first becomes delinquent and then seeks out delinquent associates. Thus, the association with other delinquents may be the dependent variable, resulting from one's own prior delinquency, rather than the independent variable that increases the probability that the adolescent will commit delinquency. Further research would be needed to find out which direction the relationship typically runs.

The probabilistic concept of causality suggests that human behavior is neither completely determined by external forces nor completely an outcome of the unfettered exercise of free will choices. Rather, behavior is best understood from the middle-ground perspective of "soft determinism" (Matza, 1964). Soft determinism recognizes that various factors influence and limit actions but leave room for individual choices that cannot be completely predicted. Increasingly, criminological theorists have come to adopt this view.

> . . .[B]iological, sociocultural, and developmental factors may influence—*but not determine*—behavior because the systematic processes underlying criminal behavior are complex, dynamic, and self-reinforcing. A key reason for the effective unpredictability of these and similar nonlinear systems is their extreme sensitivity to initial conditions. (Vila, 1994:329)

> Numerous theorists, however, have come to advance similar arguments in recent years. Versions of soft determinism or indeterminism are now advocated by control theorists, rational choice theorists, social learning theorists, conflict theorists, and others. . . . [P]eople may transcend previous experience through reflective thought—altering their preferences and developing unexpected and sometimes novel strategies for acting on those preferences. (Agnew, 1995:83, 88)

Usefulness and Policy Implications

Finally, the value of a criminological theory can be further evaluated by its usefulness in providing guidelines for effective social and criminal justice policy and practice. Every criminological theory implies a therapy or a policy. The basic assumption in theory-guided practice is that the better the theory explains the problem, the better it is able to guide efforts to solve the problem.

All major criminological theories have implications for, and have indeed been utilized in, criminal justice policy and practice. Every therapy, treatment program, prison regimen, police policy, or criminal justice practice is based, either explicitly or implicitly, on some explanation of human nature in general or criminal behavior in particular. Every recommendation for changes in our legal and criminal justice system has been based on some underlying theory that explains why the laws have been enacted, why the system operates as it does, and why those who are in the system behave as they do.

The question, then, is not whether policy can be or should be based on theory—it already is guided by theory—but rather, how well is policy guided by theory and how good is the theory on which the policy is predicated? In most public discourse about criminal justice policy, the underlying theoretical notions are ill-stated and vaguely understood. A policy may be adopted for political, economic, or bureaucratic reasons, then a theoretical rationale is formulated or adopted to justify the policy. Typically, the theoretical underpinnings of a program are not a single coherent and tested theory, but rather a hybrid mixture of several, sometimes conflicting, theoretical strands. This understandably results from the effort to try any number of things to see what works. Utility and effectiveness, not theoretical purity, is the standard in policy and practical application. However, this often leads to adopting theories without close regard to how well they meet the criteria for a good theory.

A clear, parsimonious, non-tautological, and empirically valid theory has even more to recommend it if it can also guide programs and practices. If a program guided by that theory is instituted and is successful in achieving its goals, we gain additional confidence in the validity of the theory. However, this is an indirect and imprecise way to judge the empirical validity of a theory. The program may be a poor adaptation of the theoretical principles to the actual situation. There may be practical or ethical roadblocks against carrying out the actions that the theory implies are needed to change criminal behavior, reduce recidivism, or make the system operate better. There may be political or economic factors that come into play to enhance or retard the effectiveness of the program that have nothing to do with the validity of the theory.

Empirical Validity as the Primary Criterion

This brings us back again to the primary standard for judging a theory—its verification or refutation by empirical research (Gibbs, 1990). Reference will be made, where appropriate, to tautologies, applications to policy, and other criteria for evaluating criminological theories. But the emphasis in this book will be on: (1) introducing the central concepts and propositions of criminological theories, and (2) evaluating their empirical validity.

Summary

Criminological theories are both theories of the making and enforcing of criminal law and theories of breaking the law. The former attempts to explain the content of the laws and the behavior of the criminal justice system; the latter tries to explain the commission, occurrence, and patterns of criminal and deviant behavior. Structural or macro theories focus on differences in group and societal rates of crime, while processual or micro theories address individual differences and social processes. The aim of criminological theory is to gain an understanding of crime and criminal justice. Theories are useful for addressing the issues of which policies are more or less likely to work, but they are not philosophical statements about what ought to be done.

A theory may be evaluated, either on its own or by comparison with other theories, on the criteria of clarity and consistency, scope and parsimony, testability, practical usefulness, and empirical validity. Of these the most important is empirical validity. To what extent is the theory supported by empirical findings or more supported than alternative theories? That is the criterion to which most of the attention will be given in the following chapters.

CHAPTER 2

DETERRENCE AND RATIONAL CHOICE THEORIES

Classical Criminology and the Deterrence Doctrine

Classical criminology refers primarily to the eighteenth century writings of Cesare Beccaria in Italy and Jeremy Bentham in England.[1] Both were utilitarian social philosophers who were primarily concerned with legal and penal reform rather than with formulating an explanation of criminal behavior. In doing so, however, they formulated a theory of crime that remains relevant to criminology today.[2]

The system of law, courts, and penalties of the day that the classical criminologists wanted to change was marred in most European countries by arbitrary, biased, and capricious judicial decisions. It was common to use torture to coerce confessions and to inflict cruel punishments, including whipping, public hanging, and mutilation. The classical criminologists were intent on providing a philosophical rationale for reforming the judicial and legal system to make it more rational and fair. Their ideas converged with the developing interests of the rising middle classes of merchants and the economic philosophy promoting trade, commerce, and industry. They promoted reforms which many of the leading intellectuals of the day were advocating. Their arguments also fit well with developing political movements seeking greater citizen participation and democratic control of government. Many of the law reforms proposed by classical utilitarian philosophers, such as doing away with cruel and unusual punishment and instituting the right to a speedy trial, were incorporated into the Constitution of the United States in its Bill of Rights amendments. Others, such as a legislatively fixed scale of punishment for each type and degree of crime, were incorporated into the new legal codes of France in 1791, following the French Revolution.

Deterrence: Certainty, Severity, and Celerity of Punishment

Severity and Fitting the Punishment to the Crime

The basic premise in classical criminology is that actions are taken and decisions are made by persons in the rational exercise of free will. All individuals choose to obey or violate the law by a rational calculation of the risk of pain versus potential pleasure derived from an act. In contemplating a criminal act, they take into account the probable legal penalties and the likelihood that they will be caught. If they believe that the legal penalty threatens more pain than the probable gain produced by the crime, then they will not commit the crime. Their calculation is based on their own experience with criminal punishment, their knowledge of what punishment is imposed by law, and their awareness of what punishment has been given to apprehended offenders in the past. (See the discussion of specific and general deterrence below.)

A legal system that is capricious and uncertain does not guarantee sufficient grounds for making such rational decisions. Such a system is not only unjust, it is also ineffective in controlling crime. In order to prevent crime, therefore, criminal law must provide reasonable penalties which are applied in a reasonable fashion to encourage citizens to obey rather than violate the law. The primary purpose of criminal law is deterrence. It should not be used simply to avenge the wrongs done to the state or the victim. The legislators enact laws that clearly define what is unlawful, prescribe punishment for law violation sufficient enough to offset the gain from crime, and thereby deter criminal acts by citizens. Judges should do no more than determine guilt or innocence and should use no discretion to alter penalties provided for by law.

The punishment must "fit the crime." This may be interpreted as retribution: an eye for an eye, a tooth for a tooth. But to Bentham and Beccaria, fitting the punishment to the crime meant more than making the punishment proportional to the harm caused to society. It meant that the punishment must be tailored to be just severe enough to overcome the gain offered by crime. Punishment that is too severe is unjust, and punishment that is not severe enough will not deter.

The assumption behind this argument is that the amount of gain or pleasure derived from committing a particular crime is approximately the same for everyone. Therefore, making the punishment fit the crime stands in contrast to the punishment fitting the individual. The law should strictly apply the penalty called for a particular crime, and the penalty should not vary by the characteristics or circumstances of the offender. The argument also assumes that the more serious or harmful the crime, the more the individual stands to gain from it; therefore, the more serious the crime, the more severe the penalty should be to deter it. In classical criminology, this concept of proportionality meant that the legislature should enact an exact scale of crimes with an exact scale of threatened punishment, without regard to individual differences. This was later modified to consider that age and mental capacity may affect one's ability to reason rationally.

Certainty and Celerity of Punishment

The deterrence doctrine does not rest on the severity of legal penalties alone. It further determines that, in order to deter, punishment for crime must be swift and certain. Celerity refers to the swiftness with which criminal sanctions are applied after the commission of crime.

> The more immediately after the commission of a crime a punishment is inflicted, the more just and useful it will be. . . . An immediate punishment is more useful; because the smaller the interval of time between the punishment and the crime, the stronger and more lasting will be the association of the two ideas of crime and punishment. (Beccaria, 1972:18-19)

Certainty refers to the probability of apprehension and punishment for a crime. If the punishment for a crime is severe, certain, and swift, the citizenry will rationally calculate that more is to be lost than gained from crime and will be deterred from violating the law. Both Beccaria and Bentham saw a connection between certainty and severity of punishment. Certainty is more effective in deterring crime than severity of punishment. The more severe the punishment, the less likely it is to be applied; and the less certain the punishment, the more severe it must be to deter crime.

Specific and General Deterrence

There are two ways by which deterrence is intended to operate. First, apprehended and punished offenders will refrain from repeating crimes if they are certainly caught and severely punished. This is known as "specific deterrence" or "special deterrence." Second is "general deterrence," in which the state's punishment of offenders serves as an example to those in the general public who have not yet committed a crime, instilling in them enough fear of state punishment to deter them from crime (Zimring, 1971; Zimring and Hawkins, 1973).

Modern Deterrence Theory

Studies of Deterrence

The principles of certainty, severity, and celerity of punishment, proportionality, and specific and general deterrence remain at the heart of modern deterrence theory (Zimring and Hawkins, 1973; Gibbs, 1975; Wright, 1993b). Furthermore, the deterrence doctrine remains the philosophical foundation for modern Western criminal law and criminal justice systems. The policy implications of deterrence theory evolved from the interest in changing the judicial and penal policy of the eighteenth century, and the theory continues to attract many adherents today because of its direct applicability to policy on law enforcement, courts, and imprisonment. The most common policy reaction to crime problems is to call for increased penalties, more severe sentences, additions to the police force so more arrests can be made, and the increased certainty of conviction and sentencing. These trends are directly related to all the efforts by legislators to make criminal penalties more certain and severe, to reduce the recidivism of already punished offenders, and to deter new offenders. A policy of longer sentences, especially when selectively applied to habitual offenders, may also be based on the premise that imprisonment, even when it does not deter, will at least incapacitate offenders for a period of time (Blumstein et al., 1978). But the deterrence potential is always behind the policy on all criminal sanctions, from the death penalty on down.

In spite of the long history and continuing importance of deterrence theory, empirical research designed to test it was rare until the late 1960s. Prior to that, most discussions of deterrence revolved around the humanitarian, philosophical, and moral implications of punishment rather than the empirical validity of the theory (Ball, 1965; Toby, 1964; Gibbs, 1975). Since 1970, however, deterrence has been one of the most frequently discussed and researched theories in criminology (see Gibbs, 1975; Tittle, 1980; Wright, 1993b; Stitt and Giacopassi, 1992).

The first studies on deterrence consisted primarily of comparisons between states which provided capital punishment for first-degree homicide and those which had no death penalty. The early studies also examined homicide rates in states before and after they abolished capital punishment. These studies found that the provision or absence of the death penalty in state statutes had no effect on the homicide rate (Sellin, 1959; Bedau, 1964). Research by Gibbs (1968), Tittle (1969), and Chiricos and Waldo (1970) set the stage for many of the studies that followed and have continued to this day. Their studies moved beyond the effects of the death penalty to test the deterrent effect of certainty and severity of punishment on a whole range of criminal and delinquent offenses. They did not include measures for celerity of punishment, however, and it has seldom been included in deterrence research ever since.

Objective Measures of Deterrence

Deterrence research measures the severity and certainty of criminal penalties in two ways. The first approach is to use *objective* indicators from official criminal justice statistics. The certainty or risk of penalty, for instance, is measured by the arrest rate (the ratio of arrests to crimes known to the police) or by the proportion of arrested offenders who are prosecuted and convicted in court. The severity of punishment may be measured by the maximum sentence provided by law for an offense, by the average length of sentence for a particular crime, or by the proportion of convicted offenders sentenced to prison rather than to probation or some other non-incarceration program. Deterrence theory predicts an inverse or negative relationship between these official measures of legal penalties and the official crime rate measured by crimes known to the police. When the objective certainty and severity of criminal sanctions are high, according to the theory, official crime rates should be low (Gibbs, 1968; 1975; Tittle, 1969; 1980; Chiricos and Waldo, 1971; Ross, 1982).

Perceptual Measures of Deterrence

The second approach is to measure individuals' subjective *perceptions* of legal penalties. The objective threat of legal punishment means nothing if citizens are not aware of the official sanctions or do not believe that there is any high risk of penalty if they were to commit a crime. In fact, most people have a very limited knowledge of what the legal penalties actually are and often make very inaccurate estimations of the true odds of apprehension and incarceration. But a person's fear of punishment should have a deterrent effect on his or her decision to violate the law, even if that fear has no connection with objective reality. Ultimately, deterrence theory proposes that it is what people believe about the certainty, severity, and swiftness of punishment, regardless of its true risks, that determines their choice of conformity or crime.

Recognizing this crucial cognitive dimension of deterrence, researchers have utilized "subjective" measures of the risks and severity of legal penalties as perceived by individuals. This is measured, for example, by asking respondents on questionnaires or in interviews questions such as, "How likely is it that someone like you would be arrested if you committed X?" Most research on deterrence since the 1970s has used these perceptual measures, typically relating individuals' perceptions of risk and severity of penalties to their self-reported delinquency and crime.[3] The higher the risks of apprehension and the stiffer the penalties for an offense perceived by individuals, the theory predicts, the less likely they are to commit that offense.

Do Criminal Sanctions Deter?

If there were no criminal justice system and no penalties provided by law for harmful acts against others and society, it would be obvious that laws prohibiting certain behavior would carry no threat for violation. The laws could maintain some moral suasion, and most would probably still obey the law and refrain from predatory acts. But lawlessness would be more rampant than it is now. Indeed, a formal control system of laws and government is essential to social order in a modern political state. In this sense, the mere existence of a system that provides punishment for wrongdoing deters an unknown amount of crime. This effect of the chance of punishment versus no punishment at all has been referred to as *absolute deterrence* (see Zimring and Hawkins, 1973; Gibbs, 1975; see also Wright, 1993b).

However, absolute deterrence is not the relevant issue in deterrence research. Most people, most of the time and under most circumstances, conform to the law because they adhere to the same moral values as those embodied in the law, not because they are worried about imprisonment. We do not steal and kill because we believe it is morally wrong. We have been educated and socialized to abhor these things. Our socialization comes from the family, church, school, and other groups and institutions in society; and partly from the *educative effect* of the law itself, simply by its formal condemnation of certain acts (Andenaes, 1971; see Gibbs, 1975, for a review of other preventive effects of law beyond deterrence). Therefore, the important question that research on deterrence attempts to answer is, does the actual or perceived threat of formally applied punishment by the state provide a significant *marginal deterrent* effect beyond that assured by the informal control system? (Gibbs, 1975; Zimring and Hawkins, 1968)

The best answer seems to be yes, but not very much. Studies of both objective and perceptual deterrence often do find negative correlations between certainty of criminal penalties and the rate or frequency of criminal behavior, but the correlations tend to be low. Severity of punishment has an even weaker effect on crime, whether among the main body of criminal offenders (Smith and Akers, 1992) or among a special category such as those convicted of white-collar offenses (Weisburd et al., 1995). Neither the existence of capital punishment nor the certainty of the death penalty has ever had a significant effect on the rate of homicides. Findings show that there is some deterrent effect from the perceived certainty of criminal penalties, but the empirical validity of deterrence theory is limited.

Deterrence and the Experiential Effect

Paternoster et al. (1983; 1985) take a more critical stance toward deterrence theory. They maintain that even a conclusion of modest support for deterrence theory is a misinterpretation of the findings of negative correlations between the perceptions of sanctions and the deterrence of offenses. They support their argument by referring to the fact that much of deterrence research is "cross-sectional." Cross-sectional research means that the perceptions of risk and the self-reported offenses are measured during the same time period. Indeed, in some studies, the respondents have been asked about current perceptions of deterrence, while questions about offenses have included violations that occurred in the past. Consequently, this research often does not ascertain whether the respondents' perceptions of risk came before or after they committed the offenses. Sometimes, the offenses preceded the reported perceptions of risk.

Paternoster et al.'s own longitudinal study, which measured perceptions of the certainty of legal punishment before and after offenses, was able to show that "the effect of prior behavior on current perceptions of the certainty of arrest, the *experiential effect*, is stronger than the effect of perceptions of certainty on subsequent behavior, the deterrent effect" (Paternoster et al., 1983:471; emphasis added). Those respondents with "little prior experience in committing an offense have higher estimates of the certainty of punishment than those with experience" (Paternoster et al., 1985:429). In other words, the more frequently respondents have been involved in law violations in the past, the lower their perceived risk of sanctions in the present. Paternoster et al. (1983) concluded that findings of negative associations between perceived risks and criminal behavior reflect more the "experiential" effect of behavior on the perceptions of risk than the "deterrent" effect.

Paternoster et al. (1983) are correct in concluding that the correlation they found between the perceptions of risk and subsequent offenses are too weak to validate deterrence theory. They fail to recognize, however, that their findings on the experiential effect may not in fact contradict the principle of specific deterrence. If respondents had previously committed offenses, but had not been punished for them, the principle of specific deterrence would subsequently predict a low level of perceived certainty. Individuals who are involved in repeated crimes without suffering punishment should have lower perceptions of risk, since they have gotten away with it so often. This in turn should be related to repeating offenses in the future (Stafford and Warr, 1993). Specific deterrence is supposed to operate based on persons getting caught and punished for criminal acts. If they are not, the theory argues, then they will come to believe that the certainty of punishment is low. In this sense, then, deterrence theory predicts the very experiential effect that Paternoster et al. found.

It would be contrary to the principle of specific deterrence if the research had found that respondents who reported frequent arrests in the past still had perceptions of a low risk of criminal sanctions. Paternoster et al. asked only about prior behavior. They did not measure past experience with arrest and punishment, so we do not know the extent to which their finding of an experiential effect contradicts deterrence theory.

Modifications and Expansions of Deterrence Concepts

Another aspect of this study by Paternoster et al. (1983; 1985) points to the movement by many researchers to expand deterrence concepts beyond legal penalties. Paternoster et al. included variables from social bonding theory (i.e., moral beliefs and attachment to parents and peers) and social learning theory (i.e., the perceived risk of informal sanctions from family and friends and association with offenders). (See Chapters 4 and 5.) When these other variables are taken into account, the already weak relationship between the perceptions of risk of legal penalties and offense behavior virtually disappears.

The research by Paternoster et al. followed up previous studies (Anderson et al., 1977; Akers et al., 1979; Grasmick and Green, 1980) in which the concept of deterrence is expanded beyond the strictly legal or formal sanctions to include "informal deterrence." Informal deterrence means the actual or anticipated social sanctions and other consequences of crime and deviance that prevent their occurrence or recurrence. This research has found that the perceptions of informal sanctions, such as the disapproval of family and friends or one's own conscience and moral commitments, do have deterrent effects. Indeed, they have more effect on refraining from law violations than the perceived certainty of arrest or severity of penalties (Green, 1989; Grasmick and Bursik, 1990).

Zimring and Hawkins (1973) have argued that formal punishment may deter most effectively when it "sets off" or provokes these informal social sanctions. An adolescent may refrain from delinquency, not only merely out of fear of what the police will do, but of what his or her parents will do once they learn of his or her arrest. Williams and Hawkins (1989) expand on this notion of the deterrent effects of informal sanctions that may be triggered by the application of formal criminal justice sanctions. They found in their study that the arrest of an abusing husband or boyfriend may have a deterrent effect, in part because of a concern over the negative reactions of friends, family, neighbors, or employers toward him based on their knowledge that he has been arrested. In this instance, fear of arrest may be a deterrent, not only because of the negative experience of the arrest itself, but because of other negative consequences invoked by the arrest. These may include the informal costs of severed relationships, damage to one's reputation, and the possible loss of current or future employment. Williams and Hawkins argue that the general concept of deterrence should be expanded to include these informal negative sanctions. Subsequent research by Nagin and Paternoster (1991b) does not support this argument, however, when it is applied to delinquency. They find a very small deterrent effect from the perceptions of formal sanctions, and this effect is not increased at all as a result of informal costs that may be related to the formal sanction. Instead, the informal sanctions have an independent effect on delinquent behavior that is stronger than the effect of perceived formal sanctions.

That the informal sanction system may be more effective in controlling crime than legal sanctions should come as no surprise. But does research evidence that informal sanctions on criminal and delinquent behavior have a deterrent effect on crime increase the empirical validity of deterrence theory? In my opinion, it does not. Deterrence theory refers only to the threat of legal punishment.

> [T]he proper definition [of deterrence]...is narrow. In a legal context, the term "deterrence" refers to any instance in which an individual contemplates a criminal act but refrains entirely from or curtails the commission of such an act because he or she perceives some risk of legal punishment and fears the consequences. (Gibbs, 1986:325-36)

There is no room in deterrence theory for variations in the rewards for crime, the social consequences of actions, individual or group propensities toward crime, and the whole range of other variables. The question to be answered about deterrence theory is not whether punishment of any kind from any source deters, but whether the threat of punishment *by law* deters. The more the deterrence theory is expanded to include informal sanctions and other aspects of the social environment beyond the law, the less it remains a deterrence theory and the more it begins to resemble other theories that already include these variables. It is more appropriate, therefore, to interpret positive findings on informal sanctions and similar variables as supporting the other theories (e.g., social learning and social bonding), from which the variables have been borrowed, than it is to conclude that such findings support an expanded deterrence theory.

Rational Choice Theory

Deterrence and Expected Utility

The expansion of the concept of deterrence has been most associated with the introduction into criminology in the 1980s of "rational choice" theory.[4] Rational choice theory is based on the "expected utility" principle in economic theory. The expected utility principle simply states that people will make rational decisions based on the extent to which they expect the choice to maximize their profits or benefits and minimize the costs or losses. This is the same general assumption about human nature made in classical criminology.

The obvious affinity between deterrence and rational choice theories stems from the fact that they both grew out of the same utilitarian philosophy of the eighteenth century (see Gibbs, 1975). The former was applied to the law, and the latter to the economy. Despite this long historical connection, rational choice theory of crime has only recently been introduced in criminology. Except for the use of such concepts as "aleatory risk" in delinquency research by sociologists (Short and Strodtbeck, 1965), rational choice was introduced to criminology primarily through the analyses of crime by economists (see Becker, 1968; Heineke, 1978; Crouch, 1979). Gibbs (1975:203) notes that "shortly after the revival of interest in the deterrence question among sociologists, economists were drawn to the subject in large number."

Some criminologists, who had been conducting deterrence research for some time, began in the 1980s to refer to the economic model of rational choice as an expansion of the deterrence doctrine beyond legal punishment. However, rational choice theorists claim much more than just an expansion of deterrence theory. The theory is proposed as a general, all-inclusive explanation of both the decision to commit a specific crime and the development of, or desistance from, a criminal career. The decisions are based on the offenders' expected effort and reward compared to the likelihood and severity of punishment and other costs of the crime (Cornish and Clarke, 1986).

Research on Rational Choice Theory

(Do offenders calculate that the effort and costs of crime are less than the expected reward before the act in the way predicted by rational choice theory? The answer depends on whether one believes this theory assumes that pure or partial rationality operates in crime. Does the theory hypothesize that each person approaches the commission of a crime with a highly rational calculation of pleasure versus pain before acting on or refraining from the crime? Does an offender choose to commit a crime with full knowledge and free will, taking into account only a carefully reasoned, objectively or subjectively determined set of costs and benefits? If it is this kind of pure rationality that rational choice theory assumes, then the theory has virtually no empirical validity. The purely rational calculation of the probable consequences of an action is a rarity even among the general conforming public. Moreover, even offenders who pursue crime on a regular, business-like basis typically do not operate through a wholly rational decision-making process.)

For instance, in a study of repeat property offenders, Tunnell (1990; 1992) found that the threat of re-imprisonment did not deter their recommission of crimes. Offenders thought that they would gain income from their crimes and would not be caught, or they believed that they would not serve much prison time if they did get caught. Furthermore, they were not afraid to serve time in prison because life in prison was not threatening to them. These findings would seem to be in line with rational choice theory, since the expected benefits were perceived as outweighing the expected costs of the crime; hence, the decision was made to commit the crime. However, the process whereby offenders reached a decision to attempt another crime did not fit the model of a purely rational calculation of costs and benefits. They did try to avoid capture, but their actions and assessments of the risks were very unrealistic, even to some extent irrational. They were unable to make reasonable assessments of the risk of arrests, did little planning for the crime, and were uninformed about the legal penalties in the state where their crimes were committed. Moreover, all of the offenders in the study:

> [R]eported that they (and nearly every thief they knew) simply do not think about the possible legal consequences of their criminal actions before committing crimes. . . . Rather than thinking of possible negative consequences of their actions, those offenders reported thinking primarily of the anticipated positive consequences. . . . They simply believed that they would not be caught and refused to think beyond that point.

> The decision-making process appears *not* to be a matter of rational evaluation or calculation of the benefits and risks . . . [R]isks (1) are thought about only rarely or (2) are considered minimally but are put out of their minds. (Tunnell, 1990:680-81)

Similarly, in an ethnographic study of burglars, Paul Cromwell and his associates found that "a completely rational model of decision making in residential burglary cannot be supported" (Cromwell et al., 1991:43). Rather, professional burglars engage in only partially rational calculation of gains and risks before deciding to burglarize a house, and "research reporting that a high percentage of burglars make carefully planned, highly rational decisions based upon a detailed evaluation of environmental cues may be in error" (Cromwell et al., 1991:42).

> Most of our burglar informants could design a textbook burglary. . . . [T]hey often described their past burglaries as though they were rationally conceived and executed. Yet upon closer inspection, when their previous burglaries were reconstructed, textbook procedures frequently gave way to opportunity and situational factors (Cromwell et al., 1991:42).

The empirical validity of a purely rational explanation of crime may not be important, however, because rational choice theorists seldom put forth such pure models. Instead, they have developed models of partial rationality that incorporate limitations and constraints on choices through lack of information, moral values, and other influences on criminal behavior. Although rational choice theorists often refer to the "reasoning criminal" and the "rational component" in crime, they go to great length to point out how limited and circumscribed reasoning and rationality are. The empirically verified models in the literature are based on the assumptions of a fairly minimal level of rationality.

(See, for example, Piliavin et al., 1986; Cornish and Clarke, 1986; Bennett, 1986; Carroll and Weaver, 1986; Harding, 1990.)

Proponents often contrast rational choice theory with what they label "traditional criminology." They believe that this theory differs from other theories because, in their view, all other criminological theories assume that criminal behavior is irrational. But they are mistaken about other criminological theories. In reality, except for psychoanalytic theory and some versions of biological theory (see Chapter 3), all other criminological theories assume no more or less rationality in crime than do most rational choice models.

Furthermore, the rational choice models that have been supported by research evidence do not stick strictly with measures of expected utility. They incorporate various psychological and sociological background and situational variables taken from other theories, to such an extent that there is little to set them apart from other theoretical models. In fact, some of the studies purporting to find evidence favoring rational choice theory actually test models that are indistinguishable from other, supposedly non-rational choice theories. The clearest example of this is the research by Paternoster (1989a; 1989b). He tested the effect on delinquent behavior of several variables in what he calls a "deterrence/rational choice" model. This model consists of the following variables: affective ties, costs of material deprivation, social groups and opportunities, informal social sanctions, perceptions of formal legal sanctions, and moral beliefs about specific delinquent acts. There is nothing in this set of variables that distinguishes it as a rational choice model. All the variables are taken from social learning and social bonding theories. Paternoster's finding that these variables are related to delinquent behavior, therefore, tells us little about the empirical validity of rational choice theory. However, it does tell us about the validity of social learning and social bonding theories.

The broadening of rational choice theory has the same consequence as the expansion of deterrence theory—it becomes a different theory. When rational choice theory is stated in its pure form, it does not provide an adequate explanation of criminal behavior. It provides a more empirically verified explanation of crime when it is expanded to include variables beyond rationally expected utility. However, when rational choice theory is modified in this way, the level of rationality it assumes is indistinguishable from that expected in other theories, and it incorporates explanatory variables from them. When the modifications reach this point, it is no longer appropriate to call the result rational choice theory (Akers, 1990).

Routine Activities Theory

Felson and Cohen: Offenders, Targets, and Guardians

Elements of deterrence and rational choice are also found in routine activities theory.[5] In order for a personal or property crime to occur, there must be at the same time and place a perpetrator, a victim, and/or an object of property. The occurrence can be facilitated if there are other persons or circumstances in the situation that encourage it, or it can be prevented if the potential victim or another person is present who can take action to deter it. Lawrence Cohen and Marcus Felson (1979) have taken these basic elements of time, place, objects, and persons to develop a "routine activities" theory of crime events. They do so by placing these elements into three categories of variables which increase or decrease the likelihood that persons will be victims of "direct contact" predatory (personal or property) crime.

The three main categories of variables identified by Cohen and Felson are: (1) *motivated offenders*, (2) *suitable targets* of criminal victimization, and (3) *capable guardians* of persons or property. The main proposition in the theory is that the rate of criminal victimization is increased when there is a "convergence in space and time of the three minimal elements of direct-contact predatory violations" (Cohen and Felson, 1979:589). That is, the likelihood of crime increases when there is one or more persons present who are motivated to commit a crime, a suitable target or potential victim that is available, and the absence of formal or informal guardians who could deter the potential offender. The relative presence or absence of these elements is variable, and "the risk of criminal victimization varies dramatically among the circumstances and locations in which people place themselves and their property" (Cohen and Felson, 1979:595). The theory derives its name from the fact that Cohen and Felson begin with the assumption that the conjunction of these elements of crime are related to the normal, legal, and "routine" activities of potential victims and guardians. "[T]he spatial and temporal structure of routine legal activities should play an important role in determining the location, type, and quantity of illegal acts occurring in a given community or society" (Cohen and Felson, 1979:590).

Routine activities are defined by Cohen and Felson as "recurrent and prevalent activities which provide for basic population and individual needs . . . formalized work, as well as the provision of standard food, shelter, sexual outlet, leisure, social interaction, learning, and child-bearing" (Cohen and Felson, 1979:593). They hypothesize that changes in daily activities related to work, school, and leisure since World War II have placed more people in particular places at particular times which both increase their accessibility as targets of crime and keep them away from home as guardians of their own possessions and property.

In recent applications of the theory, Felson (1994) downplays the significance of formal guardians because "crime is a private phenomenon largely impervious to state intervention." Rather, he emphasizes the crime prevention and deterrence that naturally occurs in the informal control system, the "quiet and natural method by which people prevent crime in the course of daily life. This control occurs as people interact and bring out the best in one another" (Felson, 1994:xii-xiii). The police are not the only capable guardians. Indeed, guardians who prevent or deter crime are more likely to be ordinary citizens, oneself, friends, family, or even strangers. The vulnerability of property to theft is affected by a number of physical features, such as its weight and ease of mobility and how much physical "target hardening" (e.g., installing better locks) has been done. But sights and sounds, being in dangerous and risky places, routines of the family and household, and one's personal characteristics have an effect on the risk of victimization for both violent and property crime. Felson also extends the theory beyond predatory crimes to such offenses as illegal consumption and sales of drugs and alcohol.

Felson's emphasis on the informal control system does not distinguish routine activities theory from the general sociological view (discussed above and in Chapter 8) that conformity to the law comes more from the informal system of socialization and control than from the formal control system. This general sociological view has also been applied to drug use. "The general reduction in drug use in American society [from the late 1970s to the early 1990s] may be the result of changes in social norms and the informal control system unrelated to conscious and deliberate prevention, treatment, or law enforcement efforts" (Akers, 1992:183). The validity of routine activities theory, therefore, does not rest on the relative importance of the informal and formal control systems in crime but on how well hypotheses about the effect of the three main elements of the theory on crime are supported.

Empirical Validity of Routine Activities Theory

Cohen and Felson argue that a change in any one of these elements would change the crime rates, but that the presence of all three would produce a multiplier effect on crime rates. Their research (Cohen and Felson, 1979), however, focused on only two of the three elements: suitable targets and the absence of capable guardians. They do not rule out that the "routine activity approach might in the future be applied to the analysis of offenders and their inclinations as well" (Cohen and Felson, 1979:605).

They present data on post-war trends (into the 1970s) in family activities, consumer products, and businesses that seem to be compatible with the trends in type and rate of crimes in the United States. Their main findings, however, relate crime rates to a "household activity ratio," the percentage of all households that are not husband-wife families or where the wife is employed in the labor force. Such households are more vulnerable to crime victimization because their members are away from home more and less able to function as guardians of their property. They are more likely to possess more desirable goods to be stolen, and they are more exposed to personal crime away from home. Controlling for age composition and unemployment, Cohen and Felson found that the changes in household activity were correlated with changes in the rates of all major predatory violent and property crimes. They recognize that these were not the direct measures of the concepts in the theory, but they conclude that the findings are consistent with the theory.

Cohen et al. (1981) present the theory in a more formalized fashion, renaming it "opportunity" theory and testing its propositions with data from the national crime victimization surveys. The formal theory refers to exposure, proximity, guardianship, and target attractiveness as variables that increase the risk of criminal victimization. But these are not measured directly. They are assumed from variations in age, race, and income, household composition, labor force participation, and residence in different areas of the city. Although inconclusive on some, their findings are consistent with most of the hypotheses; consequently, they conclude that the theory is supportable.

Messner and Tardiff (1985) use the routine activities approach to interpret their findings on the correlations between the social characteristics of Manhattan homicide victims, the time and location of the homicides, and the relationship between victims and offenders. They do not attempt to account for the rate or number of homicides, but only for the place and type of homicide. They contend that "sociodemographic and temporal characteristics structure routine activities and, in so doing, affect both the location of potential victims in physical space and the 'pool' of personal contacts from which offenders are ultimately drawn" (Messner and Tardiff, 1985:243). These sociodemographic and temporal variables should be related to where and with whom one carries out the normal round of activities. When one's routine activities are concentrated in and around the home, victims and offenders are less likely to interact; whereas, spending more time away from the house increases the chances of victimization by strangers. Messner and Tardiff found weak support for the expectations about family versus stranger homicides, but no relationship between time and location of homicides.

Sherman et al. (1989) also report findings consistent with routine activities theory in their study of the "hot spots" of predatory crime. They note that prior research on routine activities used data on the characteristics of individuals or households as measures of lifestyles that affect the convergence of victim, offender, and guardians. Their research focused on the "criminology of place" by using Minneapolis police "call data" (i.e., crimes reported to the police by telephone) in Minneapolis to locate concentrations (i.e., hot spots) of such calls at certain addresses, intersections, parks, and hospitals. They found that most crime reports came from only 3 percent of all the locations in the city and that reports of each of the major types of predatory crime were concentrated only in a few locations. Sherman et al. do not know what it is about these places that make them hot spots, but they believe that there is something about them that relates to the convergence of victims and offenders in the absence of guardians.

Kennedy and Forde (1990) also reported support for routine activities theory based on both property and violent crime data from a telephone victimization survey. They found that victimization varies by age, sex, and income, but also varies by the extent to which persons stay at home or go out at night to bars, work, or school. They concluded from this that the routine activity of leaving home at this time renders these persons more vulnerable as victims and less capable as guardians over their property.

Findings from qualitative research on the responses of the formal and informal control systems to the devastation of Hurricane Andrew in Florida in 1992 are generally consistent with routine activities theory. The natural disaster temporarily increased the vulnerability of persons and property as crime targets. For a short time, there was nearly a complete loss of formal guardianship in the form of police protection in some of the neighborhoods. Motivated offenders with previous records were attracted to the areas in the aftermath of the storm, and some local people took criminal advantage of the situation. However, there was little looting in the neighborhoods and crime rates actually went down during the time when the community was most vulnerable (but then increased again after the initial impact period). This was most likely the result of stepping into the void by competent guardians in the form of neighbors watching out for neighbors, citizens guarding their own and others property (sometimes with firearms), citizen patrols, and other steps taken to aid one another in the absence of government and formal control (Cromwell et al., 1995).

The fact that some may be motivated to commit crime when targets are made vulnerable by such events as natural disasters raises questions about the concept of motivated or likely offender. Does the concept of motivated offender in routine activities theory refer only to someone with a pre-existing set of crime-prone motivations or does it include anyone who is enticed by the opportunity for quick gain itself, even though he or she may not have previously existing criminal intentions? In the former case, the situation provokes motivation to action but does not create it; in the latter, the situation both creates and provokes the motivation. Since all persons are thus potentially motivated to commit crime, can the presence of a motivated offender simply be assumed from the presence of any person? If so, how does the theory distinguish between circumstances in which a motivated offender is present and those in which one is not? There is ambiguity on this point in routine activities theory (Akers et al., 1994).

Jensen and Brownfield (1986) point to another variable which is seldom controlled for in studies of routine activities: the deviant or non-deviant nature of the activities in which victims are engaged. They found that the activities most strongly related to adolescents becoming victims of crime are not the normal conforming routine activities (dating, going out at night, shopping, or going to parties), but rather the deviant activity of committing offenses. In other words, those who commit crimes are more likely to be victims of crime. Engaging in offense behavior itself, of course, does not fit Cohen and Felson's definition of "routine" activity. Moreover, as Jensen and Brownfield (1986) point out, since criminal behavior is correlated with victimization, variables taken from theories that explain criminal behavior should also be correlated with victimization.

> In fact, most of the variables in the opportunity [routine activities] model of victimization have appeared in one form or another in traditional etiological theories of crime or delinquency. Exposure and proximity to offenders is central to differential association and social learning theories of criminality. Cohen et al. propose that exposure and proximity to offenders increase the risk of victimization, while differential association and social learning theories propose that the same variables increase the chances of criminal behavior. . . . In short, "victimogenic" variables have been introduced in earlier theories as "criminogenic." (Jensen and Brownfield, 1986)

Even though it draws upon etiological theories, routine activities theory is only indirectly a theory of the commission of criminal behavior. It is primarily a theory of criminal victimization. That is, it does not offer an explanation of why some persons are motivated to develop a pattern of crime or commit a particular crime. It simply assumes that such persons exist and that they commit crimes in certain places and times at which the opportunities and potential victims are available. Routine activities theory does not explain why informal crime precautions may or may not be exercised by individuals in their homes or elsewhere, nor does it explain formal control exercised by law and the criminal justice system. It simply assumes that, if informal or formal guardians are not present or able to prevent crime, then crime will occur.

We have long known that vulnerability to criminal victimization is related to social characteristics such as age, sex, and race, and that unguarded or easily available property is more apt to be stolen or vandalized. Ordinary precautions, of course, decrease the chances of victimization. Common sense tells us that, if one is sitting at home watching television rather than out on the streets, one's home is not likely to be burglarized and one has a zero chance of being the victim of a street mugging. Possessing social characteristics correlated with a higher-risk lifestyle obviously makes one more vulnerable as a crime victim. But Felson and others have taken these common sense and empirical realities and woven them into a coherent framework for understanding the variations in criminal victimization by time and place. The theory is well-stated, logically consistent, and has clear policy implications and powerful potential for understanding the impact of normal, even desirable, social structural changes on predatory crime.

Its empirical validity has not yet been well-established, however. As we have seen, several researchers have reported findings that are consistent with routine activities theory (see also Stahura and Sloan, 1988; Massey et al., 1989; Miethe et al., 1987; Cromwell et al., 1991). But that research has not really tested full models of the theory. With a few exceptions (Stahura and Sloan, 1988), researchers have not measured variations in the motivation for crime or variations in the presence of motivated offenders. Thus, at least one of the three major categories of variables in this theory is usually omitted. Even when included, offender motivation is not directly measured, but rather assumed from variations in the demographic correlates of crime.

Similarly, the other two major categories of suitable targets of crime and absence of capable guardians are usually not directly measured. The original research by Cohen, Felson, and associates used no direct measures of the routine activities of victims or suitable guardians. They were only assumed from labor force participation, household composition, and so on. In subsequent research, victim vulnerability and guardianship have usually been assumed from the social characteristics of victims, although some activities of victims (e.g., their presence at home or their going out at night) have been directly measured (Kennedy and Forde, 1990). As Sherman et al. noted, "most tests of routine activities theory lack independent measures of the lifestyles in question and substitute presumed demographic correlates for them" (Sherman et al., 1989:31). The research on routine activities has reported numerous findings that are consistent with the assumptions in routine activities theory. More work needs to be done to devise direct empirical measures of its key concepts.

Summary

Deterrence theory states that if legal penalties are certain, severe, and swift, crime will be deterred. In empirical studies severity is seldom found to have a deterrent effect on crime. Neither the existence of capital punishment nor the certainty of the death penalty have had an effect on the rate of homicides. A negative correlation between objective or perceived certainty and illegal behavior is a common research finding, but the correlation tends to be weak.

There is more empirical support when deterrence concepts are expanded to take into account the informal social processes of reward, punishment, and moral beliefs. Rational choice theory is another type of expansion or modification of deterrence theory. When rational choice theory is stated in its pure form, it does not stand up well to empirical evidence. However, when this theory is modified so that a relatively low level of rationality is assumed and explanatory variables from other theories are added, it is more likely to be upheld by the data. When deterrence and rational choice theories are so modified, they resemble more the modern social bonding or social learning theories than the classical deterrence or pure rational choice models. Therefore, positive research findings on these modified versions are more appropriately viewed as validating these other theories from which the more powerful explanatory variables are taken, rather than validating deterrence or rational choice theories alone.

The main proposition in routine activities theory is that the rate of criminal victimization is increased when there is one or more persons likely to commit a crime, a vulnerable target or victim is present, and formal or informal guardians to prevent the motivated offender are absent. Research has not tested full models of the theory, and the major variables are usually measured indirectly. Its empirical validity has not yet been firmly established, but most of the research done so far reports findings consistent with the theory.

Notes

1. For Beccaria's writings, see Beccaria (1963; 1972) and Monachesi (1973). For Bentham's writings, see Bentham (1948) and Geis (1973). For general discussions of the classical criminology of both, see Vold (1958), Vold and Bernard (1986), and Wright (1993b).

2. Piers Beirne (1991) argues that Beccaria's main purpose was neither legal reform nor a rational explanation of crime. Rather, it was to introduce a deterministic "science of man" which ran contrary to the assumptions of free-will, volitional acts. Therefore, his theory was just as positivistic as subsequent theories.

3. See, for instance, Jensen, (1969), Waldo and Chiricos (1972), Anderson et al. (1977), Jensen et al. (1978), Tittle (1980), Paternoster et al. (1983), Klepper and Nagin (1989), Nagin and Paternoster (1994), Miller and Iovanni (1994).

4. For general and specific rational choice models, many of which are basically expansions on deterrence theory, see Cornish and Clarke (1986), Piliavin et al. (1986), Klepper and Nagin (1989), Paternoster, (1989a; 1989b), Williams and Hawkins (1989), Grasmick and Bursik (1990). For general critiques of rational choice theory, see Gibbs (1989) and Akers (1990).

5. Since routine activities theory stresses the ecological distribution of victims, crime opportunities, and motivated offenders, it could well be classified with social disorganization as an ecological theory of crime (see Chapter 7). It is not rational choice or deterrence theory. However, the concept of guardianship includes formal actions by police to deter crime and incorporates elements of the deterrence doctrine. Also, it makes the assumption that motivated offenders choose to commit a crime after assessing the presence of guardians and the vulnerability of crime targets. Therefore, it is often interpreted as a rational choice theory. For these reasons, a discussion of it is included in this chapter.

CHAPTER 3

BIOLOGICAL AND PSYCHOLOGICAL THEORIES

Introduction

Social structural and social psychological theories, to be introduced and evaluated in later chapters, either ignore or specifically exclude biological or psychological factors in crime. This is not because such theories assume that biological and psychological factors play no part in human behavior or that individuals are all the same. They focus solely on the social factors in crime with the assumption that biological and personality variations among individuals are more or less within the normal range. Little or no criminal behavior is considered to be directly caused by abnormal physiology or abnormal psychology.

Traditional biological theories, on the other hand, take the opposite approach by focusing on anatomical, physiological, or genetic abnormalities within the individual which separate law-breakers into a distinctly different category of persons from the law-abiding majority. In turn, such theories ignore or downplay the effect of social environmental factors in crime. Recent biological theorizing, which emphasizes biological variations within the normal range, has begun to include the interplay of biological, social, and psychological variables in crime and delinquency.

Psychoanalytic and personality theories recognize the effects of an individual's experiences, especially in early childhood, on one's emotional adjustment and the formation of personality traits and types. But such factors are not viewed as the cause of criminal behavior. Criminal behavior results from abnormal emotional adjustment or personality traits residing within the individual.

Lombroso and Early Biological Theories

The classical school of criminology retained a virtual monopoly on the study of crime until the latter part of the nineteenth century. By the 1870s, the classical theory, which upheld the belief that persons rationally calculate pleasure and pain during the exercise of free will to commit or refrain from crime, began to give way to biological "positivism." This new theory proposed that crime is not a rationally reasoned behavior which will occur unless prevented by the proper threat of punishment, but rather is the result of inborn abnormalities. An individual's physical traits index a bodily constitution with an associated mental and psychological makeup that causes one to violate the rules of modern society. Rational decisions, the theory argues, have nothing to do with it. Although environmental conditions and situations can provoke or restrain criminal behavior, they do not cause the commission of a crime. While some normal persons may on occasion succumb to temptations and pressures to commit a crime, the real criminal is born with criminal traits and will always be at odds with civilized society. The early biological criminologists viewed criminals as a distinct set of people who were biologically inferior to law-abiding citizens or inherently defective in some way.

While society is certainly justified in punishing criminals for its own protection, the certainty or severity of punishment will have no effect on natural-born criminals, since their crimes are caused by an innate biological makeup which no law can affect. While the classical school of criminology was humanistic and focused on the crime itself, biological positivism was scientific and concentrated on the individual criminal (see Wolfgang, 1972; Vold and Bernard, 1986).

Lombroso's Theory of the Born Criminal

The most important of the early biological theories, the one from which nearly all other biological theories stem, was first introduced in 1876 by Cesare Lombroso in *The Criminal Man*. Lombroso revised and enlarged this original publication through five editions and published separate volumes on the causes and remedies of crime and of the female criminal (Lombroso, 1912; Wolfgang, 1972). Lombroso observed the physical characteristics (head, body, arms, and skin) of Italian prisoners and compared them to Italian soldiers. From these comparisons he concluded that criminals were physically different from law-abiding citizens and that these differences demonstrated the biological causes of criminal behavior.

Lombroso believed that certain physical features identified the convict in prison as a "born criminal." The born criminal comes into the world with a bodily constitution that causes him to violate the laws of modern society. The born criminal is an "atavism," Lombroso theorized, a throwback to an earlier stage of human evolution. He has the physical makeup, mental capabilities, and instincts of primitive man. The born criminal, therefore, is unsuited for life in civilized society and, unless specifically prevented, will inevitably violate its social and legal rules. Lombroso maintained that this born criminal can be identified by the possession of certain visible "stigmata"—for example, an asymmetry of the face or head, large monkey-like ears, large lips, receding chin, twisted nose, excessive cheek bones, long arms, excessive skin wrinkles, and extra fingers or toes. The male with five or more of these physical anomalies is marked as a born criminal. Female criminals are also born criminals, but they may be identified with as few as three anomalies.

In addition to the born criminal, Lombroso recognized two other types, the "insane criminal" and the "criminaloid." The insane criminal, with whom Lombroso included the idiot, imbecile, epileptic, and psychotic, is mentally unfit for society. These criminals are no more capable than born criminals of controlling their criminal tendency, but they do not possess the criminal stigmata of the evolutionary throwback. Criminaloids are motivated by passion or have an emotional makeup that compels them, under the right circumstances, to commit crime. Of these types, the born criminal is the true criminal type, the most seriously incorrigible and dangerous to society.

Lombroso originally viewed the great majority of criminals as born criminals, but later reduced the proportion to one-third as he added more social, economic, and political conditions as factors in crime. Nevertheless, the concept of the born criminal remained the centerpiece of Lombrosian theory. This basic concept of innate criminality became the dominant perspective on crime and triggered an onslaught of biological theorizing about crime. Any theory that refers to inherited traits, physical abnormalities, the biological inferiority of certain races and categories of people, body type, feeblemindedness, biochemical imbalances, and biological defects and malfunctions that cause individuals to commit crime, can be traced back to Lombroso's theory (see Vold and Bernard, 1986).

The Criminal as Biologically Inferior

Charles Goring, an English prison medical officer, published in 1913 *The English Convict*, a report of findings from a laborious study that took years to complete. Goring employed the most sophisticated physical measurements and statistical techniques of the day. Comparing prison inmates with university undergraduates, soldiers, professors, and hospital patients, his study found no statistically significant differences between behavior and 37 physical traits that included head sizes, color of eyes, and facial features. As a result, he concluded that Lombroso was wrong: there was no such thing as a physical criminal type. His findings provided no support at all for Lombroso's theory that criminals are clearly differentiated from law-abiding citizens by physical appearance and measurable stigmata.

Goring's study came to be viewed by many scholars as the definitive refutation of Lombrosian theory. In truth, although Goring rejected Lombroso's particular theory of the criminal as an evolutionary atavism, he accepted the Lombrosian notion that criminals are born with criminal traits. His own theory dismissed the effects of social factors on crime and proposed that criminals are inherently inferior to law-abiding citizens.

Of all of the measurements he took, Goring found statistically significant differences (even while controlling for social class and age) between prisoners and civilians on two characteristics—body stature and weight. The prisoners in his study were shorter and thinner than the civilians. They were also judged (by the researcher's impression rather than by IQ tests) to be of lower intelligence. Goring took these findings as evidence that criminals suffer innately from both a "defective physique" and "defective intelligence." He later added inherent "moral defectiveness" to include recidivists who did not appear to be physically or mentally defective. In one way or another, he concluded, all offenders have a general inherited inferiority to law-abiding citizens (Driver, 1972; Wilson and Herrnstein, 1985; Vold and Bernard, 1986).

Subsequently, American anthropologist E. A. Hooten in *Crime and the Man* (1939) attacked Goring's methods and conclusions. Hooten conducted an elaborate study of 17,000 subjects in several states. The study included meticulous measurements of the physical characteristics of inmates in prisons, reformatories, county jails, and other correctional facilities. These were compared with measurements of the same characteristics in college students, hospital patients, mental patients, firemen, and policemen. This comparison of prisoners with civilians was made within one elaborate typology of racial and nationality groups and within another typology of criminal offenses.

Although he included "sociological gleanings" concerning prisoners, Hooten concluded that sociological factors were not important, because criminals are basically "organically inferior."

> [T]he real basis of the whole body of sociological, metric, and morphological deviations of criminals from civilians is the organic inferiority of the former. . . . [W]hatever the crime may be, it ordinarily arises from a deteriorated organism. . . . You may say that this is tantamount to a declaration that the primary cause of crime is biological inferiority—and that is exactly what I mean. . . . Certainly the penitentiaries of our

society are built upon the shifting sands and quaking bogs of inferior human organisms. (Hooten, 1939)

Just as Hooten found Goring's techniques deficient, Hooten's work was itself criticized on several grounds. The differences he discovered between prisoners and non-prisoners were actually quite small. Furthermore, he did not take into account the fact that his civilian sample included a large proportion of firemen and policemen who had been selected for their jobs based on their size and physical qualities. In addition, there was more variation among the prisoners than there was between the prisoners and civilians. The prisoners may have been involved in many types of crime in the past, but only their most recent crime was recorded to identify the physical characteristics of types of offenders. Hooten began with the assumption of the biological inferiority of criminals and only interpreted the differences between prisoners and civilians (e.g., foreheads, nasal bridges, jaws, eye colors, eyebrows, tattoos, and ears) as the confirmation of that inferiority. No differences in measurements were interpreted as an indication of the superiority of the inmates, and similarities between the two groups were ignored altogether. Hooten's conclusion that criminals were biologically inferior to law-abiding citizens was clearly a case of the circular reasoning of tautology (Vold, 1958:62-63); that is, it was foreordained by the assumption with which he began. There was no possible way to falsify his theory, which was true because he assumed it to be true.

The Lombrosian notion of criminal inferiority promoted by Goring and Hooten is also found in theories of feeblemindedness, inherited criminal traits, endocrine imbalances, and body types, along with many similar explanations that flourished in the late nineteenth and early twentieth centuries (see Vold and Bernard, 1985; Shoemaker, 1990). Social and non-biological factors were occasionally recognized by these early biological theorists, but environmental factors were seen as incidental when compared to the certain destiny of the physical criminal type. In all these theories the central proposition was that criminals, at least the most serious and dangerous ones, were born by nature rather than made or nurtured. Criminals did not simply behave differently from ordinary people, it was proposed, they were inherently different with an inferior or defective biology that predetermined their criminal behavior (Rafter, 1992).

Recognizing the Inadequacies of Early Biological Theories

This singleminded biological determinism was later criticized by sociologists for ignoring or giving insufficient attention to social, economic, and environmental factors. The critics were very successful in pointing out the methodological flaws in the biological research, the tautological reasoning, and the fact that the empirical evidence did not really support the theories. By the 1950s, biological theories in criminology had been thoroughly discredited. Criminology and delinquency textbooks continued to discuss Lombroso and other biological theorists for their historical interest, but the authors were highly critical of biological theory. Journal articles proposing or testing the biological explanations of crime became virtually nonexistent. Biological theory had by that time been regarded by criminologists as unfounded and inconsequential.

To some extent, the dismissal of biological theories was based on the disciplinary predilections of sociologists, the strongest critics of biological theory. Sociological approaches to crime were always treated more favorably in America and, by mid-century, sociologists dominated criminological theory and research. This sociological preeminence in American criminology persists today, although it is not as pervasive as it once was (Akers, 1992a).

C. Ray Jeffery (1979; 1980) and other modern proponents of biological theories of crime claim that even in recent times these theories are not only totally ignored, but are treated as a taboo subject and systematically suppressed by closed-minded, sociologically oriented criminologists (see Holzman, 1979; Gordon, 1980; Taylor, 1984). This claim, however, seems to be highly questionable (Karmen, 1980). Publications on biological theories in criminology have actually flourished in the past two decades and continue to find a prominent place in scholarly journals (see the extensive literature in Fishbein, 1990).

Though sociologists and other sociologically-minded criminologists usually dismiss biological variables from their theories and remain the staunchest critics of biological theories, they are also vehement critics of each other's sociological theories. Much of the objection to biological theory is based on its controversial implications for policy. If biological factors are innate or genetic, the theory proposes, one can only change them through medical or surgical procedures to modify brain or biochemical functions. If the biological factors cannot be changed, then the only alternative for society is the long-term isolation and incarceration of criminals or selective breeding to prevent the biologically defective from reproducing (Rafter, 1992).

The major reason for the rejection of these earlier biological theories has in reality very little to do with disciplinary or policy issues. It is simply because the theories were found to be untestable, illogical, or wrong. They seldom withstood empirical tests and often espoused simplistic, racist and sexist notions that easily crumbled under closer scrutiny. The earlier biological theories were rejected primarily because of the:

[S]orry history of this perspective in the last hundred years [with its] extravagant claims, meager empirical evidence, naivete, gross inadequacy, and stated or implied concepts of racial and ethnic inferiority. . . . (Dinitz, 1977:31)

Even the strongest supporters of modern biological theories of crime and delinquency recognize that the discrediting of Lombrosian positivism was "due to the serious methodological flaws of these early studies and the weakness of their efforts to integrate their findings with sociological theory and data" (Mednick and Shoham, 1979:ix).

In genetic research on criminal behavior much of the early research was based on methodologically questionable twin studies or, even worse, ideologically tainted studies from Nazi Germany. (Mednick, 1987)

"[B]iological criminology" was eventually discredited because its findings were largely unscientific, simplistic, and unicausal. Biological factors were globally rejected due to the inability of theorists to posit a rational explanation for the development of criminal behavior. (Fishbein, 1990)

In light of this recognized "sorry history" of the biological explanations for crime, is it any wonder that the modern resurgence of biological theories of crime and delinquency over the past two decades has been met with strong skepticism? Some of these modern proponents have not offered any new theories, but have simply resurrected many of the older biological explanations of crime, relied on the same old, flawed studies, and presented little evidence that could be any more convincing.[1]

XYY: The Super-Male Criminal

One theory that has been advanced since the 1960s to explain the behavior of violent male criminals is the proposal of a chromosomal abnormality, in which such males have an XYY, instead of the normal XY, male chromosomal pattern. The extra Y chromosome, so goes the hypothesis, turns these criminals into "super-males." This extra dose of maleness supposedly creates such a strong compulsion that the XYY carrier is at extreme risk of committing violent crime. The finding in some studies that the proportion of XYY males in prison populations (from 1 to 3%) is higher than in the general male population (less than 1%) is accepted as irrefutable evidence that this chromosomal abnormality is a significant cause of criminal behavior (Taylor, 1984).

If the XYY syndrome plays any role in criminal causation, it would seem to be a very minute one. It can offer no explanation for female crime and would at best apply to a tiny portion of incarcerated offenders, let alone an even tinier portion of male offenders in general. Its scope is extremely limited, to say the least. More importantly, there is little empirical evidence to support the XYY theory. Males with the XYY chromosomal abnormality found in prison populations are *less* likely than other prisoners to be incarcerated for violent offenses. In fact, the percentage of institutionalized males who have the Klinefelter syndrome (an extra female chromosome of XXY) equals or exceeds the percentage with the extra male chromosome. Only a small proportion of XYY males commit crimes of any kind, and there is simply no evidence that the XYY syndrome is a specific cause of any criminal behavior. Even major contemporary proponents of biological explanations of crime dismiss the XYY theory as scientifically invalid (National Institute of Mental Health, 1970; Fox, 1971; Witkin, 1977; Mednick et al., 1982; 1987).

Modern Biological Theories of Crime and Delinquency

Current biological theorists, for the most part, reject the kind of simplistic biological determinism characteristic of the theories of Lombroso, Goring, Hooten, and the XYY syndrome. More recent biological explanations have been founded on newer discoveries and technical advances in genetics, brain functioning, neurology, and biochemistry. Because of this, biological explanations of crime have come to occupy a new place of respectability in criminology. Though they must still contend with methodological problems and questionable empirical validity, they are taken more seriously today than at any time in the latter part of this century. The emphasis in biological theory has shifted from speculation over physical stigmata and constitutional makeup of the born criminal to careful studies of the genes, brain, central and autonomic nervous systems, nutrition, hormonal (male and female) balances, metabolism, physiological arousal levels, and biological processes in learning.[2]

Most of the modern theorists claim that they have no desire to dredge up old, meaningless debate over nature versus nurture or to resurrect the Lombrosian theory of the born criminal (Gove and Carpenter, 1982). Rather, they have taken a new course with the assumption that behavior, whether conforming or deviant, results from the interaction of the biological make-up of the human organism with the physical and social environment. Therefore, no specific criminal behavior is inherited or physiologically preordained, nor is there is any single gene that produces criminal acts. Behavioral potentials and susceptibilities, they propose, can be triggered by biological factors. These potentialities have different probabilities of actual occurrence, depending upon the environments the individual confronts over a period of time. Few biological factors in crime are viewed today as fixed and immutable.

Rather, they interact with and may be affected by the physical and social environment.[3]

> As a rule, what is inherited is not a behavior; rather it is the way in which an individual responds to the environment. It provides an orientation, predisposition, or tendency to behave in a certain fashion. . . . Findings of biological involvement in antisocial behavior have, in a few studies, disclosed measurable abnormalities, but in a number of studies, measurements do not reach pathologic levels. In other words . . . the biological values do not necessarily exceed normal limits and would not alarm a practicing physician." (Fishbein, 1990:42 and 54)

Although he gives primacy to biological causes (especially brain functioning) and is skeptical over the importance of social factors, C. Ray Jeffery (1977; 1979) proposes that criminal behavior results from the interaction of biology, behavior, and the environment.

IQ, Mental Functioning, and Delinquency

The theory that delinquents are inherently feebleminded or suffer disproportionately from "learning disabilities" has little empirical support (Murray, 1976). Childhood intelligence does not predict adolescent delinquency very well. Parental discipline, family cohesion, religious upbringing, and a child's exposure to delinquent peers are more effective predictors (Glueck and Glueck, 1959; McCord and McCord, 1959).

Nevertheless, research has consistently found a weak to moderate negative correlation between IQ (intelligence quotient) and delinquent behavior, which does not diminish when class, race, and other factors are controlled (Gordon, 1987). The higher the IQ score, the lower the probability that the adolescent will commit delinquent acts. Gordon (1987), noting the frequency with which this IQ-delinquency relationship has been found in research literature, addresses the consistently lower average IQ score among black youth compared to white youth. He attributes the differences in black and white delinquency rates to differences in black and white IQ scores. Hirschi and Hindelang (1977) show that the relationship between delinquency and IQ scores, while not very strong, is at least as strong as that between delinquency and social class.

The extent to which IQ scores reflect only native, organically determined intelligence is disputed. Hirschi and Hindelang (1977) argue that the relationship between IQ and delinquency is an indirect one, in which low intelligence negatively affects school performance and adjustment, which in turn increases the probability of delinquency. Gordon (1987) believes that IQ tests accurately tap an underlying "g" factor of innate intelligence, which measures of school achievement simply reflect.

Racial differences in intelligence is a highly controversial and unsettled issue, and the evidence of significant differences in average delinquent behavior between black and white youth is inconsistent (see Chapter 8). The notion of an IQ effect on delinquency is often rejected because it has racist and undemocratic policy implications. However, it is difficult to dismiss entirely the evidence of correlation (albeit one of low magnitude) between IQ scores and delinquency, which does not disappear when many other factors are controlled (Gordon, 1987). The question is, what theory does this correlation support? Too often, it has been concluded that the correlations demonstrate the impact of biological factors—a conclusion which holds true only if one begins with the assumption that intelligence is biologically innate and has a direct effect on delinquency. If one starts with the assumption that IQ is at least partly the result of socialization and educational training, or that it has an indirect impact on delinquency through school achievement or the learning of delinquency, then the connection supports non-biological theories.

Terrie Moffitt and associates (Moffitt et al., 1994) have proposed a neuropsychological model of male delinquency (arguing that it does not apply to female delinquency) that goes beyond IQ to incorporate other aspects of mental functioning, such as verbal ability, visual-motor integration, and mental flexibility. Such factors are proposed as predictors only of early onset "life-course-persistent" antisocial behavior-delinquencies that begin by age 13 and continue into later life stages. They are not proposed as factors in "adolescence-limited" delinquency—onset or acceleration of delinquency after age 13 that does not persist into adulthood (Moffitt, 1993). The researchers report some support for the model for self-reported and official delinquency. But the delinquency at ages 15 and 18 are consistently related only to verbal ability and memory at age 13. None of the neuropsychological measures at age 13 were strong predictors of later delinquency.

Testosterone and Criminal Aggressiveness

Several researchers have pointed to a connection between testosterone (male hormone) levels and anti-social and aggressive behavior (Booth and Osgood, 1993). Since testosterone is a male hormone, one would expect the theory and research to be concentrated on the role that high levels of testosterone play in propensities toward male aggression and violence. However, the relationship between testosterone and a variety of other adolescent and adult behavior, such as sexual behavior, substance use, smoking, and nonviolent crime, has also been studied.

Research has found statistically significant relationships, but, except for the unsurprising finding that testosterone level is associated with increased sexual activity (Udry, 1988), the relationships appear to be weak. No one has yet proposed a general theory of crime based on testosterone. Nevertheless, the fact that the effects of testosterone level has been tested on so many different types of deviance would indicate that researchers are hypothesizing that higher levels of testosterone create a general propensity to violate social and legal norms.

Booth and Osgood (1993) have presented a theory of adult male deviance that relies on the indirect effects of testosterone levels, mediated by the degree of social integration and prior adolescent delinquency. They were able to test this theory in part with a sample of Vietnam War veterans, measuring testosterone levels in blood specimens. Self-reported adult deviance (e.g., fighting, police arrests, and passing bad checks) and previous adolescent delinquency were also obtained from the veterans. Controlling for age and race, the researchers found a relationship between testosterone and adult deviance, but one which was reduced by introducing measures of social integration and, even more so, by measures of prior delinquency.

Booth and Osgood conclude that "we have firm evidence that there is a relationship between testosterone level and adult deviance. This relationship is strong enough to be of substantive interest, but it is not so strong that testosterone would qualify as the major determinant of adult deviance" (Booth and Osgood, 1993). This seems to be a modest conclusion, but it overstates the relationship found in their research. In fact, the initial relationship between testosterone levels is extremely weak (explaining close to zero percent of the variance in adult deviance), and the relationship disappears when social integration and prior delinquency are taken into account.

Mednick's Theory of Inherited Criminal Tendencies

Of all the various biological explanations of crime, the best known and most systematically stated and tested is the biosocial theory of Sarnoff Mednick and his associates (Mednick and Christiansen, 1977; Mednick and Shoham, 1979; Mednick et al., 1981; Mednick et al., 1987; Mednick et al., 1984; Brennan et al., 1995). Mednick's theory proposes that some genetic factor(s) is passed along from parent to offspring. Criminal or delinquent behavior is not directly inherited, the theory explains, nor does the genetic factor directly cause the behavior; rather, one inherits a greater susceptibility to succumb to criminogenic environments or to adapt to normal environments in a deviant way.

Mednick has hypothesized that the susceptible individual inherits an autonomic nervous system (ANS) that is slower to be aroused or to react to stimuli. Those who inherit slow arousal potential learn to control aggressive or anti-social behavior slowly or not at all. Thus, they stand at greater risk of becoming law violators (Mednick, 1977).

[ANS responsiveness] may play a role in the social learning of law-abiding behavior. . . . Briefly stated, this theory suggests that faster ANS recovery (or half recovery) should be associated with greater reinforcement and increased learning of the inhibition of antisocial tendencies. Slow ANS recovery, on the other hand should be associated with poor learning of the inhibition of antisocial responses. (Brennan et al., 1995:84-85)

Hans J. Eysenck has also proposed a similar biosocial "arousal" theory, in which the inherent differences in individuals' levels of arousal affect their conditioning by the social environment. Those with low arousability are less likely to learn prosocial behavior and more likely to learn criminal and deviant behavior patterns (Eysenck and Gudjonsson, 1989).

Mednick and colleagues' first study, conducted in Copenhagen, Denmark, linked the criminality of biological fathers with the subsequent criminal behavior of their sons who had been adopted out and raised by adoptive parents. They found the highest rates of officially recorded criminal offenses among those sons whose biological and adoptive fathers both had criminal records, and the lowest rates when neither had criminal records. Those sons whose biological fathers had criminal records, but whose adoptive fathers did not, were more likely to be registered as criminals than those whose adoptive fathers, but not their biological fathers, had criminal records (Hutchings and Mednick, 1977c).

Later, the same type of study was conducted on a larger sample of adopted sons from all parts of Denmark. Mednick interpreted the findings from this larger study as a replication and independent confirmation of the findings from the Copenhagen study. The larger study included the criminal background of both parents, biological and adoptive, and related that to the adoptees' criminal convictions. Again, Mednick reports verification of the theory. He found that those with only criminal biological parents were more likely than those with only criminal adoptive parents to have been convicted of offenses. The highest rate of convictions were found among persons whose biological and adoptive parents both had been convicted of crimes (Mednick et al., 1984).

These Danish studies are the most famous and most frequently cited in support of the heritability of criminal propensities. However, Gottfredson and Hirschi (1990:47-63) have pointed to some serious flaws in this research, which has since raised doubts as to how much it actually validates the theory of inherited criminal potential. Here are six points to consider:

(1) The differences between the criminality effects of biological and adoptive fathers found in the Copenhagen study, while in the expected

direction, were not statistically significant. Therefore, while not dis-confirming the theory, such findings cannot be taken as evidence in favor of the theory.

(2) The larger Denmark study shifted from fathers' criminality ex-clusively to the criminal record of the parents (either the mother, father, or both). Since different measures of the independent variable were used, the second study really did not replicate the first study as Mednick claims.

(3) When considered separately in the second study, the effect of biological mothers' criminality was stronger than the effects of fathers' criminality. The finding that criminality may be more maternally than paternally inherited seems uncharacteristic in light of the fact that men are far more criminally inclined than women. If crime is inherited, why would it be inherited from the gender with a significantly lower rate of criminal behavior?

(4) Mednick incorporated all of the same subjects from Copenhagen into the larger sample from Denmark. This is inappropriate in a repli-cation study, since it contaminates the independence of replicated find-ings.

(5) The effects of the criminality of biological parents found in the Denmark study, while statistically significant because of the larger sam-ple size, were actually less than the effects found in the Copenhagen study. The percentage difference in the criminality of adoptive sons with or without criminality in biological parents was very small, even though it was somewhat more than the differences between those with or without criminality in adoptive parents.

(6) When Gottfredson and Hirschi subsequently removed the Copen-hagen sample (to eliminate the sample contamination) and analyzed data only from the larger Denmark sample, they found *no* significant relationship between the criminality of sons and biological parents.

Gottfredson and Hirschi (1990) also show that Swedish and Ameri-can adoption research purporting to duplicate Mednick's findings has in fact found very small, insignificant differences in the criminality of offspring that could be attributed to inherited traits. They estimate that the correlation between biological fathers' and sons' criminality is about $r=.03$ and conclude that "the magnitude of the 'genetic effect' as determined by adoption studies is near zero" (Gottfredson and Hirschi, 1990:60).

Another approach to testing biosocial theory is to study the behavior of twins. A central concept in twin research is known as "concordance." Concordance is a quantitative measure of the degree to which the ob-served behavior or attribute of one twin (or sibling) matches that of the other. Most studies of identical and fraternal twins, both those raised in the same family and those separated by adoption, have found higher concordance between the criminal and non-criminal behavior of identical twins than between fraternal twins. But these studies have not been successful in showing how much of this concordance is based solely on biological as opposed to social similarities (Hutchings and Mednick, 1977a; 1977b).

Based on findings from a mailed questionnaire study of twins, Rowe (1984; 1986) concluded that individual differences in self-reported delinquency were more the result of genetic factors than common or specific environmental factors. However, by adjusting for mutual sibling influence, he later reduced the estimates of the effect of heritability on delinquency from about two-thirds of the differences in delinquent behavior to about one-third (Rowe and Gulley, 1992). Also, in a later analysis of the same data into which he included specific measures of family variables, Rowe concluded that delinquency is best explained by the combined effects of heredity and family environment. Similarly, Carey (1992) found in a study of Danish identical and fraternal twins that when the imitation and other peer effects of sibling interaction are taken into account, the amount of variance attributed to genetic similarity is considerably reduced.

> The traditional models suggest a strong heritability: the genotype contributes to between 57 percent and 71 percent of the variance in [delinquency] liability. The model that permits peer influence suggests more modest estimates of heritability, in one case actually approaching 0.0. (Carey, 1992:21)

In the twin studies, the biological and social variables are seldom measured directly.[4] In the studies of adoptees, similarly biological variables are indirectly measured by the degree of behavioral similarities between biological parent(s) and offspring when the biological parent(s) does not raise the child. Social variables are assumed to be operative when similarities are found in the behavior of adoptive parents and adoptees. Concordance in the behavior of twins reared apart is attributed to biological factors on the assumption that their social environments differ. Children reared together are assumed to have had similar social environments.

Empirical Validity of Biological Theories of Criminal Behavior

As shown above, modern biological explanations of crime have far surpassed the early biological theories of Lombroso, Goring, Hooten, and others. This is partly the result of greater theoretical sophistication, less reliance on immutable biological defects or destiny, and greater attention to interaction with social and psychological variables. It is also partly the result of more sophisticated methodology in biological studies and an expanded knowledge of neurological, hormonal, and other bodily systems.

Nevertheless, such research has not yet established the empirical validity of biological theories. Tests of the theories continue to have problems with methodology, sampling, and measurement (Fishbein, 1990). Walters and White (1989) came to a similar conclusion based on their own extensive review of research on the heritability of criminal behavior. They considered studies using four basic approaches: family studies, twin studies, adoption studies, and gene-environment interaction studies. Their review found that biological research on crime suffers from several methodological deficiencies, including the measurement of criminality, sample size, sampling bias, statistical procedures, and generalizability. Walters and White believed that genetic factors are correlated with some measures of criminal behavior, but they warned that:

> [T]he large number of methodological flaws and limitations in the research should make one cautious in drawing any causal inferences at this point in time. Our review leads us to the inevitable conclusion that current genetic research on crime has been poorly designed, ambiguously reported, and exceedingly inadequate in addressing the relevant issues. (Walters and White, 1989:478)

Walters (1992) followed this up with a statistical "meta-analysis," i.e., the re-calculation of different measures of effect reported from different studies into a standard measure of effect that can be compared across studies. He found that the correlations reported from different studies were often statistically significant and usually in the expected direction. But the average overall effect of heredity on crime found in these studies was weak. The more recently and rigorously studies are conducted, the more likely they are to find the weaker effects of genetic factors on crime than did the older and more poorly designed studies. The strongest methodology, used in adoption studies, produces findings less favorable to the hypothesis of a genetic effect in crime than the weaker methodology in family and twin studies.

Thus far, newer biological explanations have garnered mixed and generally weak empirical support. Biological theories that posit crime-specific genetic or physiological defects have not been, and are not likely to be, accepted as sound explanations in criminology. The greater the extent to which a biological theory proposes to relate normal physiological and sensory processes to social and environmental variables in explaining criminal behavior, the more likely it will be empirically supported and accepted in criminology.

Rowe and Osgood (1984) argue that the operation of genetic factors between an individual's delinquent behavior and the delinquency of his or her friends can be integrated into current sociological theories of delinquency. Their stance is not that delinquency is the direct or inevitable outcome of genetic differences. Rather, they propose that "causal sequences leading to delinquency are traceable to individual differences in genes, so any social causation entails either individual differences in reactions to social processes or differential social reactions to already differing individuals" (Rowe and Osgood, 1984:526).

There is little to disagree with in the assertion that biology interacts with the environment. The real question involves the nature of that interaction and the extent to which crime is influenced by biology or environment. If a theory proposes that biological defects or abnormalities are the direct cause of all or most criminal behavior, it is not likely to be supported by empirical evidence. It is also less likely to be supported if it contends that individual biological factors better explain the full range of crime and delinquency in general than do social or social-psychological factors.

Psychoanalytic Theory

Psychoanalytic theory shares with biological theory the search for causes of crime within the makeup of the individual. Rather than seek for the causes in biological processes or anomalies, it attempts to look deep into the mind of the individual. According to Kate Friedlander (1947), classical Freudian psychoanalytic explanations of delinquency focus on abnormalities or disturbances in the individual's emotional development from early childhood. The id is the unconscious seat of irrational, antisocial, and instinctual impulses which must be controlled and shaped for social adaptation to life in society. This is done through the development of the ego, or the conscious and rational part of the mind, and through the superego, or the conscience and moralizing part of the mind. Normally, a child's emotional maturation goes through developmental stages, each of which is rooted in sexuality: an oral phase as an infant, an anal phase up to about age three, a phallic phase up to about age five, a latency phase up to the time of puberty, then finally a mature genital phase of development as an adult.

The id is uncontrolled, until the development of the ego gains control over the instincts at about age three. At the beginning of the phallic stage, the child wants to possess the parent of the opposite sex and perceives the same-sex parent as a rival for the affection of the other parent. These feelings are repressed, and an Oedipus complex (the unconscious love of the mother and hatred/fear of the father by the boy) or an Electra complex (the love of the father and hatred/fear of the mother by the girl) develops. The superego evolves by identifying with the same-sex parent and internalizing parental control; hence, the child gives up the desire to possess the opposite-sex parent. Any abnormal development during these stages, or any fixation at an infantile or childhood stage, leads to antisocial behavior by adolescence as the individual struggles with the unconscious guilt and pathology of this arrested development.

The basic premise of the psychoanalytic approach to crime is that delinquent or criminal behavior is in itself unimportant. It is only a symptom of the psychic conflict between the id, ego, and superego, arising from abnormal maturation or control of instincts, a poor early relationship with the mother or father, fixation at a stage of emotional development, and/or repressed sexuality or guilt. The most critical fixation is at the Oedipus/Electra stage. The adolescent is not consciously aware of these conflicts, because they all trace back to early childhood, the conscious memories of which are blocked by "infantile amnesia." Repressed guilt and conflict continue to be the "true" causes of delinquency, although other more visible factors may seem to be operating.

Other Freudian or neo-Freudian explanations of crime and delinquency emphasize the underdevelopment or disrupted development of the superego, due to the absence of parents or the presence of cruel, unloving parents. Some theorists stress that not only are the criminal acts themselves expressions of unresolved guilt, but criminals unconsciously seek to be caught and punished to expatiate this repressed guilt. Whatever the specific mechanism, psychoanalytic explanations rely heavily on irrational and unconscious motivations as the basic forces behind crime. In psychoanalytical theory, all criminal behavior is explained as expressions or symptoms of one or more underlying mental illnesses, emotional disorders, or psychic disturbances. Not only law violations but also various other types of deviant behavior, such as drug and alcohol abuse, are seen as dysfunctional attempts to deal with repressed guilt, feelings of hopelessness or helplessness, pent up aggression, or other unresolved unconscious and emotional turmoil. Both adolescent delinquency and adult crime are believed to stem essentially from these irrational impulses or compulsions. Early childhood events are often seen as crucial, while current or anticipated environmental and social events are seen as irrelevant or important only as triggering events for the dysfunctional behavior.[5]

The treatment and policy implications of psychanalytic theory are direct and obvious. Criminal and delinquent offenders should be treated not as evil but as sick persons who are not basically responsible for their actions in any rational or controllable sense. Therefore, punishment of offenders will be ineffective and will only provoke more guilt and unhealthy psychological reactions.

Delinquents and criminals, the theory contends, need treatment for underlying emotional disturbances. Cure that problem, and the problem of crime will be remedied. Any attempt to deal only with the symptom, the behavior, or the pent-up emotions of the offender will only result in the substitution of another deviant symptom to express itself. The criminal must undergo psychoanalytic treatment to help him or her uncover the hidden, repressed causes of the behavior, which can then be dealt with effectively by the ego and superego. Since the real causes of the behavior lie hidden in the unconscious, the objective is to reveal to the person's conscious mind the deep-seated unconscious motivations that are driving his or her deviant behavior. Once these are brought out into the open, they can be handled more rationally and resolved in a healthy way. Intensive, individual, in-depth therapeutic sessions are the ideal course to take, although other less intensive treatment is possible.

The empirical validity of psychoanalytic explanations of crime, upon which these treatment policies rest, is difficult to assess. The language used is often strongly deterministic, claiming unequivocal empirical support for a psychiatric explanation of individual cases as the outcome of mental disorder. Flora Schreiber (1984) conducted interviews with Joseph Kallinger, a shoemaker who, along with his teenage son, committed a series of burglaries and robberies and three murders. Schreiber reaches firm cause-and-effect conclusions about the connection between the elder Kallinger's criminal behavior and what she diagnoses as his psychosis caused by the psychological and physical abuse of him as a child by his adoptive parents. She concentrates especially on the time when Joseph was four years old and his parents told him that the hernia operation he had was really done to remove the demon from his penis. According to Schreiber, this and other statements made to the young boy about his penis produced "psychological castration" in Joseph. This was the primary cause of Kallinger's psychosis, which in his adult life "drives him to kill."

> Joseph Kallinger would never have become a killer without his psychosis. With it he had no other course. . . . [M]urder was the *inevitable* outcome of Kallinger's psychosis. . . . [H]e had become psychotic before he committed a single crime. . . . [T]he crimes sprang directly from the psychosis: from the delusional system and the hallucinations the psychosis had spawned. . . . One can, however, establish a cause and effect relationship between Joe Kallinger's murders and the psychological abuse of him as a child. (Kallinger, 1984:17, 390, 394)

Psychiatric studies rely heavily on clinical and case studies such as this, producing widely varying estimates of the proportions of offenders who have some diagnosable mental disorder or psychiatric problem.

Such studies concentrate on individual cases or on small samples of the most serious offenders. Unfortunately, there are very few comparisons with samples of the general population or other offenders (Pallone and Hennessey, 1992).

Moreover, there may be no way to test psychoanalytic theory directly, because the motivations are deeply hidden in the unconscious, unknown even to the offender. Therefore, it is only the interpretation of the therapist that determines when the independent variables of unconscious urges and impulses are present. Psychoanalytic interpretations, therefore, tend to be after the fact, tautological, and untestable (Shoham and Seis, 1993). Typically, the "psychopathic deviation" assumed to be the cause of criminal behavior is determined by clinical judgment, in which " 'habitual criminality' itself is a principal criterion for such a diagnosis." This procedure produces "a tautology of impressive proportions" (Pallone and Hennessy, 1992:56 and 165). Various techniques of clinical measures, such as "projective" tests, are sometimes used to add to clinical judgment. But "both the paucity of studies and the instability of the interpretations preclude any valid generalizations based on projective test data" (Pallone and Hennessy, 1992:168).

Personality Theory

Personality theories share with the psychoanalytic approach the assumption that offending behavior is important only as a symptom of an underlying problem within the individual. The implications for policy and practice based on individualized therapy are also similar. Treatment, not punishment, is needed, preferably intensive individual counseling. These policy and practice implications have been widely adopted in the criminal and juvenile justice system. Virtually every residential and non-residential delinquency and crime prevention, correctional, and treatment program in the United States includes some form of individual counseling guided by the psychological theories of emotional maladjustment.

In personality theory, the problem lies not in unconscious motivation, but in the content of the person's personality. The basic proposition here is that delinquents and criminals have abnormal, inadequate, or specifically criminal personalities or personality traits that differentiate them from law-abiding people.

One version of personality theory explains criminal and delinquent behavior as an expression of such deviant personality traits as impulsiveness, aggressiveness, sensation-seeking, rebelliousness, hostility, and so on. Another version claims that criminal and delinquent offenders differ from law-abiding persons in basic personality type. Conformity reflects normal personality. Serious criminal violations spring from an aberrant personality, variously labelled a psychopathic, antisocial, or sociopathic personality. These are vague concepts, but the psychopath is usually defined as a self-centered person who has not been properly socialized into pro-social attitudes and values, who has developed no sense of right and wrong, who has no empathy with others, and who is incapable of feeling remorse or guilt for misconduct or harm to others.

Personality theories have been empirically tested with more rigorous methodology than psychoanalytic theories. The most common technique is to measure personality traits with a written personality inventory and compare mean responses on the inventory from adjudicated delinquents with mean responses from non-delinquents. The most commonly used personality tests are the Minnesota Multiphasic Personality Inventory (MMPI) and the California Psychological Inventory (CPI). The CPI is intended to measure variations in personality traits, such as dominance, tolerance, and sociability. The MMPI uses several scales to measure "abnormal" personality traits, such as depression, hysteria, paranoia, psychopathology, introversion/extroversion, and compulsiveness (Hathaway and Meehl, 1951).

The MMPI was originally designed by Starke Hathaway (1939) for the purpose of detecting deviant personality patterns in mentally ill adults. Using it to predict delinquency is based on the assumption that delinquency is symptomatic of mental illness similar to adult patterns of maladaptive behavior (Hathaway and Monachesi, 1953). Research has found that institutionalized delinquents score higher on the scales of asocial, amoral, and psychopathic behavior, while non-delinquents tend to be more introverted. However, attempts at predicting future delinquency from MMPI measures have only been partially successful. The strongest predictive scale from the MMPI, the "F Scale," does not measure any personality trait at all. Rather, it records any inconsistent or careless responses to the questions on the MMPI or any poor reading ability in completing the questionnaire (Hathaway and Monachesi, 1963).

Other research findings on the causative effects of personality traits on criminal and delinquent behavior are inconsistent. A review of such studies at mid-century concluded that only a minority of them found significant differences in personality between delinquents and non-delinquents (Schuessler and Cressey, 1950). However, a subsequent review reported that a majority of the more carefully conducted studies found significant differences (Waldo and Dinitz, 1967), and studies continue to find correlations of personality traits with self-report and other measures of delinquency and crime (Caspi et al., 1994). Other current analyses, on the other hand, have reported mixed findings in the research on personality and criminal behavior (see Sutherland, Cressey, and Luckenbill, 1992).

Personality theories and research testing also have problems with tautology. The concept of the psychopathic personality, for instance, is so broad that it could apply to virtually anyone who violates the law. For this reason, there have been widely different estimates of the proportion of offenders who are psychopaths, from 10 percent to 80 percent, depending on who applies the definition. Moreover, some of the diagnostic measures used to classify persons as psychopathic are simply indicators of a prior history of deviant or criminal behavior, such as frequent arrests, abuse of others, and fighting.

Similar problems of tautological relationships are found in the studies using personality inventories. In the MMPI, the main scale that differentiates delinquents from non-delinquents also measures psychopathic tendencies. But this same scale includes items about "trouble with the law," the very thing it is supposed to explain. Furthermore, the items on this scale and the socialization scale of the CPI were originally developed by creating various questions to which delinquents would respond differently than non-delinquents. When the same items are later submitted to groups of delinquents and non-delinquents, different responses will automatically be expected. The research using personality inventories and other methods of measuring personality characteristics have not been able to produce findings to support personality variables as major causes of criminal and delinquent behavior (Vold and Bernard, 1986; Shoemaker, 1990; Pallone and Hennessy, 1992; Sutherland, Cressey, and Luckenbill, 1992).

Summary

Early biological positivism proposed that criminal behavior is directly determined by the person's biological makeup. This basic concept of innate criminality, of the criminal as a distinctly different type of person from law-abiding citizens, was proposed in theories of the born criminal, which listed physical abnormalities, biological inferiority, body type, biochemical imbalances, and biological defects as the primary causes of crime. This kind of biological theory has largely been discredited. Current biological theorizing tends to move beyond the simplistic determinism of early theories. The older biological theories have given way to theories relating crime and delinquency to measurable variations in inherited characteristics, brain functioning, central and autonomic nervous systems, nutrition, hormonal balances, metabolism, physiological arousal levels, biological processes in learning, and similar variables.

Modern biological theories propose the interaction of these factors with the social environment. However, they do not support the view that specific biological defects produce specific criminal behavior or that a single gene produces criminal acts. Biological factors are not regarded as fixed and immutable or as having any greater power over behavior than social or psychological variables. Rather, their effects are viewed as indirect and mediated by other factors.

The newer biological explanations of crime have found greater acceptance in criminology, but they have been criticized for their dependence on research with serious methodological problems that produce questionable empirical validity. Research has provided some evidence in favor of the newer biological theories of criminal behavior, but problems with methodology, sampling, and measurement have resulted in mixed and generally weak empirical support.

Psychoanalytic and personality theories also concentrate on the causes of crime arising from within the individual, but the causes are not seen as inherited or biologically predetermined. The causes are dysfunctional, abnormal emotional adjustment or deviant personality traits formed in early socialization and childhood development. The policy implications of these theories are widely adopted in correctional treatment programs. Empirical tests of these theories have been hampered by tautological propositions and measures of key concepts. Personality theories are more testable than psychoanalytic theories, but empirical research has produced mixed results.

Notes

1. See, for instance, the biological theorizing in Wilson and Herrnstein (1985) or Taylor (1984).
2. See the papers in Mednick et al. (1987) and the review of various biological studies in Shah and Roth (1974), Vold and Bernard (1986), Walters and White (1989), and Fishbein (1990).
3. See Mednick and Christiansen (1977), Mednick and Shoham (1979), Jeffery (1977; 1979), Mednick et al. (1981), Mednick et al. (1987), Eysenck and Gudjonsson (1989), Fishbein (1990), and Brennan et al. (1995).
4. Some studies do directly measure these variables. See Mednick et al. (1981) and Rowe (1986). Also, social variables are seldom directly measured. See Rowe (1986).
5. See Lindner (1944), Aichhorn (1963), Halleck (1967), and the reviews of psychoanalytic theory in Hakeem (1957-58), Vold and Bernard (1986), Shoemaker (1990), Holman and Quinn (1992), Pallone and Hennessy (1992), and Shoham and Seis (1993).

CHAPTER 4

SOCIAL LEARNING THEORY

Introduction

The designation of "social learning theory" has been used to refer to virtually any social behavioristic approach in social science, principally that of Albert Bandura and other psychologists (1977; Bandura and Walters, 1963; Rotter, 1954). As a general perspective emphasizing "reciprocal interaction between cognitive, behavioral and environmental determinants" (Bandura, 1977:vii), variants of social learning can be found in a number of areas in psychology and sociology (see White et al., 1991). Gerald Patterson and others have applied learning principles to delinquent and deviant behavior (Patterson et al., 1975; 1992; Patterson and Chamberlain, 1994; Patterson, 1995; Jessor and Jessor, 1977).

In the field of criminology, however, social learning theory refers primarily to the theory of crime and deviance developed by Ronald L. Akers. Akers' social learning theory was originally proposed in collaboration with Robert L. Burgess (Burgess and Akers, 1966b) as a behavioristic reformulation of Edwin H. Sutherland's differential association theory of crime. It is a general theory that has been applied to a wide range of deviant and criminal behavior. It is one of the most frequently tested theories in criminology (Stitt and Giacopassi, 1992).

Sutherland's Differential Association Theory

The late Edwin H. Sutherland is widely recognized as the most important criminologist of the twentieth century. Sutherland is known for pioneering sociological studies of professional theft (Sutherland, 1937) and white-collar crime (1940; 1949). He is best known for formulating a general sociological theory of crime and delinquency—the "differential association" theory.[1]

Sutherland was the author of America's leading criminology textbook. It was only in the pages of this text that he fully stated his theory.

The first edition of his *Criminology*, published in 1924, made no mention of the theory; the second edition in 1934 (retitled *Principles of Criminology*) contained only some preliminary ideas. The first full statement of differential association theory appeared in the textbook's third edition (1939:4-8).

This 1939 version of the theory proposed that "the specific causal process in the development of systematic criminal behavior" is "differential association" with those who commit crime or those who are law-abiding. Sutherland presented differential association primarily as a processual theory of how individuals come to commit crimes. His theory also had a structural dimension which included statements proposing that conflict and social disorganization are the underlying causes of crime, because they determine the patterns of differential association.

The final version of the theory was included in the 1947 edition of Sutherland's criminology textbook. In this edition, Sutherland dropped the concepts of conflict and disorganization from the statement of his theory. He retained them separately in comments about "differential social organization," the term that he suggested should be used in place of social disorganization. He perceived differential social organization as the cause of differences in group or societal crime rates, which is consistent with differential association as the explanation of differences in individual behavior. Today we would interpret differential social organization as a macro-level or structural theory, and differential association as a compatible micro-level or processual theory. Sutherland gave only brief attention to differential social organization, however, and concentrated his efforts on fully explicating differential association. The theory as he finally stated it (Sutherland, 1947:6-7) is as follows:

1. Criminal behavior is learned.

2. Criminal behavior is learned in interaction with other persons in a process of communication.

3. The principal part of the learning of criminal behavior occurs within intimate personal groups.

4. When criminal behavior is learned, the learning includes (a) techniques of committing the crime, which are sometimes very complicated, sometimes very simple, and (b) the specific direction of motives, drives, rationalizations, and attitudes.

5. The specific direction of motives and drives is learned from definitions of the legal codes as favorable or unfavorable.

6. A person becomes delinquent because of an excess of definitions favorable to violation of law over definitions unfavorable to violation of law.

7. Differential associations may vary in frequency, duration, priority, and intensity.

8. The process of learning criminal behavior by association with criminal and anti-criminal patterns involves all of the mechanisms that are involved in any other learning.

9. Although criminal behavior is an expression of general needs and values, it is not explained by those general needs and values, because noncriminal behavior is an expression of the same needs and values.

The first proposition is that criminal behavior is learned, and the terms "learned" and "learning" are included in other statements. Criminal behavior is learned in a process of symbolic interaction with others, mainly in primary or intimate groups. Although all nine statements constitute the theory, it is the sixth statement that Sutherland identified as *the* "principle of differential association." This is the principle that a person commits criminal acts because he or she has learned "definitions" (rationalizations and attitudes) favorable to violation of law in "excess" of the definitions unfavorable to violation of law.

It is not a simple theory of association with "bad companions," nor does it speak of association with particular kinds of people. Rather, it is directed at learning criminal behavior in communication with criminal and non-criminal "patterns" and "definitions." The theory explains criminal behavior by the exposure to others' definitions which are favorable to criminal behavior, balanced against contact with conforming definitions. Although one expects that law-violating definitions are typically communicated by those who have violated the law, it is possible to learn law-abiding definitions from them, just as one can be exposed to deviant definitions from law-abiding people (Cressey, 1960:49). The seventh principle in the theory makes it clear that the process is not a simple matter of either criminal or non-criminal association, but one that varies according to what are called the "modalities" of association. That is, if persons are exposed first (priority), more frequently, for a longer time (duration), and with greater intensity (importance) to law-violating definitions than to law-abiding definitions, then they are more likely to deviate from the law.

After Sutherland's death, Donald R. Cressey revised *Principles of Criminology* from the fifth through the tenth editions. Cressey became the major proponent of differential association, clarifying it and applying it to a number of different areas in criminology (see Akers and Matsueda, 1989). However, in all of the revisions of the text, Cressey purposely left the original nine statements of differential association theory unchanged from the way Sutherland had them in 1947. After Cressey's death, David F. Luckenbill revised the text for its eleventh edition (Sutherland, Cressey, and Luckenbill, 1992), and he too has changed nothing from the 1947 statement.

Both Cressey and Luckenbill were well aware of and discussed revisions and modifications of the theory made by others, but they preserved Sutherland's original statement. Others, however, have proposed modification of differential association theory. For instance, Daniel Glaser (1956) suggested that the process of differential association might be clarified by reference to the concept of "differential identification." In differential identification the "person pursues criminal behavior to the extent that he identifies with real or imaginary persons from whose perspective his criminal behavior seems acceptable" (Glaser, 1956:440). These persons may be close friends or more distant reference groups. Other modifications have been suggested (see De-Fleur and Quinney, 1966), but the most thorough and most tested revision of Sutherland's theory is found in Akers' social learning theory.

Akers' Social Learning Theory

Development of the Theory

Sutherland asserted in the eighth statement of his theory that all the mechanisms of learning are involved in criminal behavior. However, beyond a brief comment that more is involved than direct imitation (Tarde, 1912), he did not explain what the mechanisms of learning are. These learning mechanisms were specified by Burgess and Akers (1966b) in their "differential association-reinforcement" theory of criminal behavior. Burgess and Akers produced a full reformulation that retained the principles of differential association, combining them with, and restating them in terms of, the learning principles of operant and respondent conditioning that had been developed by behavioral psychologists.[2] Akers has subsequently developed the differential association-reinforcement theory, most often labeling it "social learning" and applying it to criminal, delinquent, and deviant behavior in general (see Akers, 1973; 1977; 1985). He has modified the theory, devised specific measures of its key concepts, and tested its central propositions.

Social learning theory is not competitive with differential association theory. Instead, it is a broader theory that retains all the differential association processes in Sutherland's theory (albeit clarified and somewhat modified) and integrates it with differential reinforcement and other principles of behavioral acquisition, continuation, and cessation (Akers, 1985:41). Thus, research findings supportive of differential association also support the integrated theory. But social learning theory explains criminal and delinquent behavior more thoroughly than does the original differential association theory (see, for instance, Akers et al., 1979; Warr and Stafford, 1991).

Burgess and Akers (1966b) explicitly identified the learning mechanisms as those found in modern behavioral theory. They retained the
concepts of differential association and definitions from Sutherland's
theory, but conceptualized them in more behavioral terms and added
concepts from behavioral learning theory. These concepts include differential reinforcement, whereby "operant" behavior (the voluntary actions of the individual) is conditioned or shaped by rewards and
punishments. They also contain classical or "respondent" conditioning
(the conditioning of involuntary reflex behavior); discriminative stimuli (the environmental and internal stimuli that provides cues or signals
for behavior), schedules of reinforcement (the rate and ratio in which
rewards and punishments follow behavioral responses), and other principles of behavior modification.

Akers followed up his early work with Burgess with a fuller, more
detailed presentation of the concepts and propositions of the theory in
successive editions of *Deviant Behavior: A Social Learning Approach*
(Akers, 1973: 1977; 1985). In this book, Akers shows how social learning
theory relates to other theories of crime and deviance and gives a social
learning explanation of drug and alcohol behavior, sexual deviance,
white-collar crime, professional crime, organized crime, violent crime,
suicide, and mental illness. Akers also retains Sutherland's and
Cressey's concern with social structure and relates the social learning
process to variations in the group rates of crime and deviance.

Social learning theory retains a strong element of the symbolic interactionism found in the concepts of differential association and definitions from Sutherland's theory (Akers, 1985:39-70). Symbolic
interactionism is the theory that social interaction is mainly the exchange of meaning and symbols; individuals have the cognitive capacity
to imagine themselves in the role of others and incorporate this into
their conceptions of themselves (Ritzer, 1992). This, and the explicit
inclusion of such concepts as imitation, anticipated reinforcement, and
self-reinforcement, makes social learning "soft behaviorism" (Akers,
1985:65). As a result, the theory is closer to cognitive learning theories,
such as Albert Bandura's (1973; 1977; 1986; Bandura and Walters,
1963), than to the radical or orthodox operant behaviorism of B. F.
Skinner (1953; 1959) with which Burgess and Akers began.

The Central Concepts and Propositions
of Social Learning Theory

Social learning theory offers an explanation of crime and deviance
which embraces variables that operate both to motivate and control
criminal behavior, both to promote and undermine conformity. (See
the discussion of questions of criminal motivations and inhibitors in

Chapter 5.) The probability of criminal or conforming behavior occurring is a function of the balance of these influences on behavior.

> [T]he principal behavioral effects come from interaction in or under the influence of those groups with which one is in differential association and which control sources and patterns of reinforcement, provide normative definitions, and expose one to behavioral models. . . .
>
> Deviant behavior can be expected to the extent that it has been differentially reinforced over alternative behavior (conforming or other deviant behavior) and is defined as desirable or justified when the individual is in a situation discriminative for the behavior. (Akers, 1985:57-58)

While referring to all aspects of the learning process, Akers' development of the theory has focused on four major concepts: *differential association, definitions, differential reinforcement,* and *imitation* (Akers et al., 1979; Akers, 1985; Akers and Cochran, 1985; Akers, 1992a).

Differential Association

Differential association refers to the process whereby one is exposed to normative definitions favorable or unfavorable to illegal or law-abiding behavior. Differential association has both behavioral *interactional* and *normative* dimensions. The interactional dimension is the direct association and interaction with others who engage in certain kinds of behavior, as well as the indirect association and identification with more distant reference groups. The normative dimension is the different patterns of norms and values to which an individual is exposed through this association.

The groups with which one is in differential association provide the major social contexts in which all the mechanisms of social learning operate. They not only expose one to definitions, they also present them with models to imitate and with differential reinforcement (source, schedule, value, and amount) for criminal or conforming behavior. The most important of these groups are the primary ones of family and friends, though they may also be secondary and reference groups. Neighbors, churches, school teachers, physicians, the law and authority figures, and other individuals and groups in the community (as well as mass media and other more remote sources of attitudes and models) have varying degrees of effect on the individual's propensity to commit criminal and delinquent behavior. Those associations which occur first (priority), last longer (duration), occur more frequently (frequency), and involve others with whom one has the more important or closer relationships (intensity) will have the greater effect.

Definitions

Definitions are one's own attitudes or meanings that one attaches to given behavior. That is, they are orientations, rationalizations, definitions of the situation, and other evaluative and moral attitudes that define the commission of an act as right or wrong, good or bad, desirable or undesirable, justified or unjustified.

In social learning theory, these definitions are both *general* and *specific*. General beliefs include religious, moral, and other conventional values and norms that are favorable to conforming behavior and unfavorable to committing any deviant or criminal acts. Specific definitions orient the person to particular acts or series of acts. Thus, one may believe that it is morally wrong to steal and that laws against theft should be obeyed, but at the same time one may see little wrong with smoking marijuana and rationalize that it is all right to violate laws against drug possession.

The greater the extent to which one holds attitudes that disapprove of certain acts, the less one is likely to engage in them. Conventional beliefs are *negative* toward criminal behavior. Conversely, the more one's own attitudes approve of a behavior, the greater the chances are that one will do it. Approving definitions favorable to the commission of criminal or deviant behavior are basically *positive* or *neutralizing*. Positive definitions are beliefs or attitudes which make the behavior morally desirable or wholly permissible. Neutralizing definitions favor the commission of crime by justifying or excusing it. They view the act as something that is probably undesirable but, given the situation, is nonetheless all right, justified, excusable, necessary, or not really bad to do. The concept of neutralizing definitions in social learning theory incorporates the notions of verbalizations, rationalizations, techniques of neutralizations, accounts, and disclaimers (Cressey, 1953; Sykes and Matza, 1957; Lyman and Scott, 1970; Hewitt and Stokes, 1975). (See the discussion of neutralizations in Chapter 5.) Neutralizing attitudes include such beliefs as, "Everybody has a racket," "I can't help myself, I was born this way," "I am not at fault," "I am not responsible," "I was drunk and didn't know what I was doing," "I just blew my top," "They can afford it," "He deserved it," and other excuses and justification for committing deviant acts and victimizing others. These definitions favorable and unfavorable to criminal and delinquent behavior are developed through imitation and differential reinforcement. Cognitively, they provide a mind-set that makes one more willing to commit the act when the opportunity occurs. Behaviorally, they affect the commission of deviant or criminal behavior by acting as internal discriminative stimuli. Discriminative stimuli operate as cues or signals to the individual as to what responses are appropriate or expected in a given situation.

Some of the definitions favorable to deviance are so intensely held that they almost "require" one to violate the law. For instance, the radical ideologies of revolutionary groups provide strong motivation for terrorist acts, just as the fervent moral stance of some anti-abortion groups justifies in their minds the need to engage in civil disobedience. For the most part, however, definitions favorable to crime and delinquency do not "require" or strongly motivate action in this sense. Rather, they are conventional beliefs so weakly held that they provide no restraint or are positive or neutralizing attitudes that facilitate law violation in the right set of circumstances.

Differential Reinforcement

Differential reinforcement refers to the balance of anticipated or actual rewards and punishments that follow or are consequences of behavior. Whether individuals will refrain from or commit a crime at any given time (and whether they will continue or desist from doing so in the future) depends on the past, present, and anticipated future rewards and punishments for their actions.

The probability that an act will be committed or repeated is increased by rewarding outcomes or reactions to it, e.g., obtaining approval, money, food, or pleasant feelings—positive reinforcement. The likelihood that an action will be taken is also enhanced when it allows the person to avoid or escape aversive or unpleasant events—negative reinforcement. Punishment may also be direct (positive), in which painful or unpleasant consequences are attached to a behavior; or indirect (negative), in which a reward or pleasant consequence is removed. Just as there are modalities of association, there are modalities of reinforcement—amount, frequency, and probability. The greater the value or amount of reinforcement for the person's behavior, the more frequently it is reinforced, and the higher the probability that it will be reinforced (as balanced against alternative behavior), the greater the likelihood that it will occur and be repeated. The reinforcement process does not operate in the social environment in a simple either/or fashion. Rather, it operates according to a "matching function" in which the occurrence of, and changes in, each of several different behaviors correlate with the probability and amount of, and changes in, the balance of reward and punishment attached to each behavior (Hamblin, 1979; Conger and Simons, 1995).

Reinforcers and punishers can be non-social; for example, the direct physical effects of drugs and alcohol. However, whether or not these effects are experienced positively or negatively is contingent upon previously learned expectations. Through social reinforcement, one learns to interpret the effects as pleasurable and enjoyable or as frightening and unpleasant. Individuals can learn without contact, directly or indirectly, with social reinforcers and punishers. There may be a physiological basis for the tendency of some individuals (such as those prone to sensation-seeking) more than others to find certain forms of deviant behavior intrinsically rewarding (Wood et al., 1995). However, the theory proposes that most of the learning in criminal and deviant behavior is the result of social exchange in which the words, responses, presence, and behavior of other persons directly reinforce behavior, provide the setting for reinforcement (discriminative stimuli), or serve as the conduit through which other social rewards and punishers are delivered or made available.

The concept of social reinforcement (and punishment) goes beyond the direct reactions of others present while an act is committed. It also includes the whole range of actual and anticipated, tangible and intangible rewards valued in society or subgroups. Social rewards can be highly symbolic. Their reinforcing effects can come from their fulfilling ideological, religious, political, or other goals. Even those rewards which we consider to be very tangible, such as money and material possessions, gain their reinforcing value from the prestige and approval value they have in society. Non-social reinforcement, therefore, is more narrowly confined to unconditioned physiological and physical stimuli. In *self-reinforcement* the individual exercises self-control, reinforcing or punishing one's own behavior by taking the role of others, even when alone.

Imitation
Imitation refers to the engagement in behavior after the observation of similar behavior in others. Whether or not the behavior modeled by others will be imitated is affected by the characteristics of the models, the behavior observed, and the observed consequences of the behavior (Bandura, 1977). The observation of salient models in primary groups and in the media affects both pro-social and deviant behavior (Donnerstein and Linz, 1995). It is more important in the initial acquisition and performance of novel behavior than in the maintenance or cessation of behavioral patterns once established, but it continues to have some effect in maintaining behavior.

The Social Learning Process: Sequence and Feedback Effects

These social learning variables are all part of an underlying process that is operative in each individual's learning history and in the immediate situation in which an opportunity for a crime occurs. Akers stresses that social learning is a complex process with reciprocal and feedback effects. The reciprocal effects are not seen as equal, however. Akers hypothesizes a typical temporal sequence or process by which persons come to the point of violating the law or engaging in other deviant acts.

This process is one in which the balance of learned definitions, imitation of criminal or deviant models, and the anticipated balance of reinforcement produces the initial delinquent or deviant act. The facilitative effects of these variables continue in the repetition of acts,

although imitation becomes less important than it was in the first commission of the act. After initiation, the actual social and non-social
reinforcers and punishers affect whether or not the acts will be repeated
and at what level of frequency. Not only the behavior itself, but also the
definitions are affected by the consequences of the initial act. Whether
a deviant act will be committed in a situation that presents the opportunity depends on the learning history of the individual and the set of
reinforcement contingencies in that situation.

> The actual social sanctions and other effects of engaging in the be-
> havior may be perceived differently, but to the extent that they are more
> rewarding than alternative behavior, then the deviant behavior will be
> repeated under similar circumstances. Progression into more frequent
> or sustained patterns of deviant behavior is promoted [to the extent]
> that reinforcement, exposure to deviant models, and definitions are not
> offset by negative formal and informal sanctions and definitions. (Akers,
> 1985:60; see also Akers, 1992a:87)

The theory does not hypothesize that definitions favorable to law
violation only precede and are unaffected by the initiation of criminal
acts. Acts in violation of the law can occur in the absence of any thought
given to right and wrong. Furthermore, definitions may be applied by
the individual retroactively to excuse or justify an act already committed. To the extent that such excuses successfully mitigate others' negative sanctions or one's self-punishment, however, they become cues for
the repetition of deviant acts. At that point they precede the future
commission of the acts.

Differential association with conforming and non-conforming others typically precedes the individual's committing the acts. Families are
included in the differential association process, and it is obvious that
association, reinforcement of conforming or deviant behavior, deviant
or conforming modeling, and exposure to definitions favorable or unfavorable to deviance occurs within the family prior to the onset of
delinquency. On the other hand, it can never be true that the onset of
delinquency initiates interaction in the family (except in the unlikely
case of the late-stage adoption of a child who is already delinquent who
is drawn to and chosen by deviant parents). This is also hypothesized
as the typical process within peer groups. While one may be attracted
to deviant peer groups prior to becoming involved in delinquency, associations with peers and others are most often formed initially around
attractions, friendships, and circumstances, such as neighborhood
proximity, that have little to do directly with co-involvement in some
deviant behavior. However, after the associations have been established
and the reinforcing or punishing consequences of the deviant behavior
are experienced, both the continuation of old and the seeking of new

associations (over which one has any choice) will themselves be affected. One may choose further interaction with others based, in part, on whether they too are involved in similar deviant or criminal behavior. But the theory proposes that the sequence of events, in which deviant associations precede the onset of delinquent behavior, will occur more frequently than the sequence of events in which the onset of delinquency precedes the beginning of deviant associations.

Social Structure and Social Learning

Social learning theory has a broad scope in that it purports to be a general processual explanation of all criminal and delinquent behavior. Its scope, however, does not include a general explanation of laws, criminal justice, or the structural aspects of society that have an impact on crime. The theory is capable, however, of explaining how the social structure shapes individual behavior.

Sutherland (1947) and Cressey (1960) emphasized that the differential association process in individual criminality must be consistent with and related to differential social organization as an explanation of the structural distribution of crime rates. Akers (1973; 1985; 1989; 1992a) has reiterated this theme and shown the connection between social structure and the behavior of individuals.

The society and community, as well as class, race, gender, religion, and other structures in society, provide the general learning contexts for individuals. The family, peer groups, schools, churches, and other groups provide the more immediate contexts that promote or discourage the criminal or conforming behavior of the individual. Differences in the societal or group rates of criminal behavior are a function of the extent to which cultural traditions, norms, and social control systems provide socialization, learning environments, and immediate situations conducive to conformity or deviance.

Where individuals are situated in the social structure is indicated by age, sex, race, class, and other characteristics. These characteristics relate to the groups of which persons are likely to be members, with whom they interact, and how others around them are apt to respond to their behavior. These variables affect which behavioral models and normative patterns to which persons are exposed and the arrangements of reinforcement contingencies for conforming or law-violating behavior. This general model, in which social structure is hypothesized to have an effect on the individual's behavior through its effect on the social learning process, is diagrammed in Figure 6.1.

Figure 6.1

Social Structure and Social Learning				
Social Structure →		**Social Learning**	Criminal Behavior / Conforming Behavior	
Society Age Family Community Sex Peers Race School Class Others		Differential Association Differential Reinforcement Definitions Imitation Other Learning Variables	Individual Behavior	

(Adapted from Akers, 1992:14)

Akers argues that not only class, age, and other indicators of social location, but also the structural conditions identified in other theories (e.g., social disorganization, anomie, or conflict) can have an impact on one's exposure to criminal associations, models, definitions, and reinforcement. Social learning is hypothesized as the behavioral process by which the variables specified in macro-level theories induce or retard criminal actions in individuals. It is possible, therefore, to integrate these structural theories with social learning, though this has not yet been accomplished (see Chapter 11).

Empirical Validity of Social Learning Theory

Critiques and Research on Social Learning Variables

The social learning principles of association, imitation, definitions, reinforcement, and others (often in combination with guidelines from other theories) have become the basis for group counseling and self-help programs, positive peer counseling programs, gang interventions, family and school programs, teenage drug, alcohol, and delinquency prevention programs, and other private and public programs for delinquents and adult offenders in institutions and in the community. There is a broad range of behavior modification programs operating in correctional, treatment, and community facilities for juveniles and adults that follow learning principles. (See Bandura, 1969; Stumphauzer, 1986; Bynum and Thompson, 1992; Akers, 1992a; Lundman, 1993). These programs have had some successes, but, as is true for other theories, the validity of social learning theory can be judged only indirectly by its practical applications. It needs to be evaluated by the criteria of testability and empirical evidence.

The testability of the basic behavioral learning principles incorporated in social learning theory has been challenged because they may be tautological. The way in which the principle of reinforcement is often stated by behavioral psychologists makes the proposition true by definition. That is, they define reinforcement by stating that it occurs when behavior has been strengthened, that is, its rate of commission has been increased. If reinforcement is defined this way, then the statement "If behavior is reinforced, it will be strengthened" is tautological. If reinforcement means that behavior has been strengthened, then the hypothesis states simply, "If behavior is reinforced, it is reinforced." If the behavior is not strengthened, then by definition it has not been reinforced; therefore, no instance of behavior that is not being strengthened can be used to falsify the hypothesis.

Another criticism of social learning has to do with the temporal sequence of differential peer association and delinquency. Some have argued that youths become delinquent first then seek out other delinquent youths. Rather than delinquent associations causing delinquency, delinquency causes delinquent associations. If there is a relationship between one's own delinquency and one's association with delinquent peers, then it is simply a case of "birds of a feather flocking together" rather than a bird joining a flock and changing its feathers. Differential peer associations with delinquent friends is almost always a consequence rather than a cause of one's own behavior. Association with delinquent peers takes place only or mainly after peers have already independently established patterns of delinquent involvement. No deviance-relevant learning takes place in peer groups. From this point of view, any association with delinquent youths has no direct effect on an adolescent's delinquent behavior. Therefore, association with delinquent friends has an effect on neither the onset nor acceleration, the continuation nor cessation, of delinquent behavior (Hirschi, 1969; Gottfredson and Hirschi, 1990; Sampson and Laub, 1993).

These criticisms, however, may be off the mark. Burgess and Akers (1966a) identified this tautology problem and offered one solution to it. They separated the definitions of reinforcement and other behavioral concepts from non-tautological, testable propositions in social learning theory and proposed criteria for falsifying those propositions. Others as well have proposed somewhat different solutions (Liska, 1969; Chadwick-Jones, 1976). Moreover, the variables in the process of reinforcement are always measured separately (and hence non-tautologically) from measures of crime and deviance in research on social learning theory. The theory would be falsified if it is typically the case that positive social approval or other rewards for delinquency (that are not offset by punishment) more often reduce than increase its recurrence. Also, as shown above, feedback effects are built into the reinforcement concept with both prior and anticipated reward/punishment influencing present behavior.

Furthermore, the reciprocal relationship between one's own conduct and one's definitions and association with friends is clearly recognized in social learning theory. Therefore, the fact that delinquent behavior may precede the association with delinquent peers does not contradict this theory. "Social learning admits that birds of a feather do flock together, but it also admits that if the birds are humans, they also will influence one another's behavior, in both conforming and deviant directions" (Akers, 1991:210). It would contradict the theory if research demonstrated that the onset of delinquency always or most often predates interaction with peers who have engaged in delinquent acts and/or have adhered to delinquency-favorable definitions. It would not support the theory if the research evidence showed that whatever level of delinquent behavioral involvement preceded association with delinquent peers stayed the same or decreased rather than increased after the association. Research has not yet found this to be the case. Instead, the findings from several studies favor the process proposed by social learning theory, which recognizes both direct and reciprocal effects. That is, a youngster associates differentially with peers who are deviant or tolerant of deviance, learns definitions favorable to delinquent behavior, is exposed to deviant models that reinforce delinquency, then initiates or increases involvement in that behavior, which then is expected to influence further associations and definitions (Jessor et al., 1973; Krohn, 1974; Kandel, 1978; Andrews and Kandel, 1979; Krohn et al., 1985; Sellers and Winfree, 1990; Empey and Stafford, 1991; Elliott and Menard, 1991; Kandel and Davies, 1991; Warr, 1993b; Esbensen and Huizinga, 1993; Thornberry et al., 1994; Menard and Elliott, 1994; Akers and Lee, 1996).

Kandel and Davies (1991:442) note that "although assortive pairing plays a role in similarity among friends observed at a single point in time, longitudinal research that we and others have carried out clearly documents the etiological importance of peers in the initiation and persistence of substance use." Warr (1993b) also refers to the considerable amount of research evidence showing that peer associations precede the development of deviant patterns (or increase the frequency and seriousness of deviant behavior once it has begun) more often than involvement in deviant behavior precedes associations with deviant peers. The reverse sequence also occurs and Warr proposes that the process is ". . . a more complex, sequential, reciprocal process: Adolescents are commonly introduced to delinquency by their friends and subsequently become more selective in their choices of friends. The 'feathering' and 'flocking' . . . are not mutually exclusive and may instead be part of a unified process" (Warr, 1993b:39). This is, of course, completely consistent with the sequential and feedback effects in the social learning process spelled out above. Menard and Elliott (1990;

1994) also support the process as predicted by social learning theory. Reciprocal effects were found in their research, but:

> [I]n the typical sequence of initiation of delinquent bonding and illegal behavior, delinquent bonding (again, more specifically, association with delinquent friends) usually precedes illegal behavior for those individuals for whom one can ascertain the temporal order. . . . [S]imilarly . . . weakening of belief typically preceded the initiation of illegal behavior. (Menard and Elliott, 1994:174)
>
> Hirschi's hypothesis that illegal behavior influences Delinquent Bonding more than the reverse consistently fails to receive empirical support in the analysis. This finding, as well as the consistency with which the first hypothesis is confirmed, reinforces the conclusion [that] . . . Delinquent Bonding has a direct positive influence on illegal behavior. (Menard and Elliott, 1994:185)

Another criticism of the theory is that the strong relationship between self-reported delinquency and peer associations is entirely due to the fact that associations are often measured by the individual's report of the delinquency of his or her peers; they are the same thing measured twice. One is measuring the same underlying delinquent tendency, whether youngsters are asked about the delinquency of their friends or about their own delinquency. But research shows that the two are not the same and that the respondent's reports of friends' behavior is not simply a reflection of one's own delinquent behavior (Menard and Elliott, 1990; 1991; Agnew, 1991b; Warr, 1993b; Thornberry et al., 1994).

Almost all research conducted on social learning theory has found strong relationships in the theoretically expected direction between social learning variables and criminal, delinquent, and deviant behavior. When social learning theory is tested against other theories using the same data collected from the same samples, it is usually found to account for more variance in the dependent variables or have greater support than the theories with which it is being compared (for instance, see Akers and Cochran, 1985; Matsueda and Heimer, 1987; White et al., 1986; Kandel and Davies, 1991; McGee, 1992; Benda, 1994; Burton et al. 1994).

There is abundant evidence to show the significant impact on criminal and deviant behavior of differential association in primary groups such as family and peers. The role of the family is usually as a conventional socializer against delinquency and crime. It provides anti-criminal definitions, conforming models, and the reinforcement of conformity through parental discipline; it promotes the development of self-control. But deviant behavior may be the outcome of internal family interaction (McCord, 1991b). It is directly affected by deviant parental models, ineffective and erratic parental supervision and discipline in the use of positive and negative sanctions, and the endorsement of values and attitudes favorable to deviance. Patterson has shown that the operation of social learning mechanisms in parent-child interaction is a strong predictor of conforming/deviant behavior (Patterson, 1975; 1992; 1995; Snyder and Patterson, 1995). In some cases, parents directly train their children to commit deviant behavior (Adler and Adler, 1978). And in general, parental deviance and criminality is predictive of the children's future delinquency and crime (McCord, 1991a). Moreover, youngsters with delinquent siblings in the family are more likely to be delinquent, even when parental and other family characteristics are taken into account (Rowe and Gulley, 1992; Lauritsen, 1993).

Delinquent tendencies learned in the family may be exacerbated by differential peer association (Simons et al., 1994; Lauritsen, 1993). Other than one's own prior deviant behavior, the best single predictor of the onset, continuance, or desistance of crime and delinquency is differential association with conforming or law-violating peers (Loeber and Dishion, 1987; Loeber and Stouthamer-Loeber, 1987). More frequent, longer-term, and closer association with peers who do not support deviant behavior is strongly correlated with conformity, while greater association with peers who commit and approve of delinquency is predictive of one's own delinquent behavior. It is in peer groups that the first availability and opportunity for delinquent acts are typically provided. Virtually every study that includes a peer association variable finds it to be significantly and usually most strongly related to delinquency, alcohol and drug use and abuse, adult crime, and other forms of deviant behavior. There is a sizable body of research literature that shows the importance of differential associations and definitions in explaining crime and delinquency.[3]

Many studies using direct measures of one or more of the social learning variables of differential association, imitation, definitions, and differential reinforcement find that the theory's hypotheses are upheld (Winfree and Griffiths, 1983; Elliott et al., 1985; Dembo et al., 1986; White et al., 1986; Sellers and Winfree, 1990; McGee, 1992; Winfree et al., 1993; 1994).[4] Research on expanded deterrence models (see Chapter 2), showing the strong effects of moral evaluations and actual or anticipated informal social sanctions on an individual's commission of crime or delinquency, also provides support for social learning theory (Grasmick and Green, 1980; Paternoster et al., 1983; Lanza-Kaduce, 1988; Stafford and Warr, 1993).[5]

Akers' Research on Social Learning Theory

In addition to the consistently positive findings by other researchers, support for the theory comes from research conducted by

Akers and his associates in which all of the key social learning variables are measured. These include tests of social learning theory by itself and tests that directly compare its empirical validity with other theories. The first of these, conducted with Marvin D. Krohn, Lonn Lanza-Kaduce, and Marcia J. Radosevich, was a self-report questionnaire survey of adolescent substance abuse involving 3000 students in grades 7 through 12 in eight communities in three midwestern states (Akers et al., 1979; Krohn et al., 1982; Krohn et al., 1984; Lanza-Kaduce et al., 1984; Akers and Cochran, 1985). The second, conducted with Marvin Krohn, Ronald Lauer, James Massey, William Skinner, and Sherilyn Spear, was a five-year longitudinal study of smoking among 2000 students in junior and senior high school in one midwest community (Lauer et al., 1982; Krohn et al., 1985; Spear and Akers, 1988; Akers, 1992a; Akers and Lee, 1996). The third project, conducted with Anthony La Greca, John Cochran, and Christine Sellers, was a four-year longitudinal study of conforming and deviant drinking among elderly populations (1400 respondents) in four communities in Florida and New Jersey (Akers et al., 1989; Akers and La Greca, 1991; Akers, 1992a). The fourth and fifth studies were the master's and doctoral research of Scot Boeringer, conducted under Akers' supervision, on rape and sexual coercion among samples of 200 and 500 college males (Boeringer et al., 1991; Boeringer, 1992; Boeringer and Akers, 1993). The dependent variables in these studies ranged from minor deviance to serious criminal behavior.

The findings in each of these studies demonstrated that the social learning variables of differential association, differential reinforcement, imitation, and definitions, singly and in combination, are strongly related to the various forms of deviant, delinquent, and criminal behavior studied. The social learning model produced high levels of explained variance, much more than other theoretical models with which it was compared.

The combined effects of the social learning variables on adolescent alcohol and drug use and abuse are very strong. High amounts (from 31% to 68%) of the variance in these variables are accounted for by the social learning variables. Social bonding models account for about 15% and anomie models account for less than 5% of the variance.

Similarly, adolescent cigarette smoking is highly correlated with the social learning variables. These variables also predict quite well the maintenance of smoking over a three-year period. They fare less well, however, when predicting which of the initially abstinent youngsters will begin smoking in that same period. The social learning variables do a slightly better job of predicting the onset of smoking over a five-year period. The sequencing and reciprocal effects of social learning variables and smoking behavior over the five-year period are as predicted by the theory. The onset, frequency, and quantity of elderly drinking is highly correlated with social learning, and the theory also successfully accounts for problem drinking among the elderly.

The social learning variables of association, reinforcement, definitions, and imitation explain the self-perceived likelihood of using force to gain sexual contact or committing rape by college men (55% explained variance). They also account for the actual use of drugs or alcohol, nonphysical coercion, and physical force by males to obtain sex (20% explained variance). Social bonding, self-control, and relative deprivation (strain) models account for less than 10% of the variance in these variables.

The research by Akers and others has also included some evidence on the hypothesized relationship between social structure and social learning. This research has found that the correlations of adolescent drug use and smoking, elderly alcohol abuse, and rape to socio-demographic variables of age, sex, race, and class are reduced toward zero when the social learning variables are taken into account. Also, differences in levels of marijuana and alcohol use among adolescents in four types of communities (farm, rural-nonfarm, suburban, and urban), and the differences in overall levels of drinking behavior among the elderly in four types of communities, are mediated by the social learning process. These findings show results that are predicted by social learning theory. However, at this time, there has not been enough research to confirm the relationship between social learning and the social structure expected by the theory.

Summary

Akers' social learning theory combines Sutherland's original differential association theory of criminal behavior with general behavioral learning principles. The theory proposes that criminal and delinquent behavior is acquired, repeated, and changed by the same process as conforming behavior. While referring to all parts of the learning process, Akers's social learning theory in criminology has focused on the four major concepts of differential association, definitions, differential reinforcement, and imitation. That process will more likely produce behavior that violates social and legal norms than conforming behavior when persons differentially associate with those who expose them to deviant patterns, when the deviant behavior is differentially reinforced over conforming behavior, when individuals are more exposed to deviant than conforming models, and when their own definitions favorably dispose them to commit deviant acts.

This social learning explanation of crime and delinquency has been strongly supported by the research evidence. Research conducted over many years, including that by Akers and associates, has consistently found that social learning is empirically supported as an explanation of individual differences in delinquent and criminal behavior. The hypothesis that social learning processes mediate the effects of socio-demographic and community variables on behavior has been infrequently studied, but the evidence so far suggests that it will also be upheld.

Notes

1. For detailed accounts of Sutherland's career and the way in which he developed this theory, see Cohen et al. (1956), Gaylord and Galliher (1988), and Sutherland (1973).

2. For classic statements of behavioristic "operant conditioning" principles of learning, see Skinner (1953; 1959). See also the full statement of behavioral learning theory in Burgess and Akers (1966a). Prior to the full revision of differential association by Burgess and Akers, C. Ray Jeffery (1965) proposed to replace all of Sutherland's theory with a single statement of operant conditioning, essentially rejecting the theory. Burgess and Akers criticized Jeffery for doing this and retained all the major features of Sutherland's theory in their revision.

3. A partial list of the studies would include Cressey (1953), Short (1957; 1958; 1960), Voss (1964), Matthews (1968), Jensen (1972), Krohn (1974), Burkett and Jensen (1975), Minor (1980), Matsueda (1982), Patterson and Dishion (1985), LaGrange and White (1985), Fagan and Wexler (1987), Matsueda and Heimer (1987), Rowe and Gulley (1992), Lauritsen (1993), Warr and Stafford (1991), Warr (1993a; 1993b; 1996), Agnew (1994), Dabney (1995). The theory is also supported by cross-cultural research, for instance, Kandel and Adler (1982), Junger-Tas (1992), Bruinsma (1992), and Zhang and Messner (1995). See also the other references cited in this section, because they usually include measures of differential association and definitions as well.

4. See also Conger (1976), Marcos et al. (1986), Orcutt (1987), Matsueda and Heimer (1987), Burkett and Warren (1987), White et al. (1987), Winfree et al. (1989), Loeber et al. (1991), Agnew (1991a), Warr and Stafford (1991), Inciardi et al. (1993), Elliott (1994), Conger and Simons (1995), Simons et al. (1994), and Wood et al. (1995).

5. See also Anderson et al. (1977), Meier and Johnson (1977), Jensen et al. (1978), Tittle (1980), and Paternoster (1989).

CHAPTER 5

SOCIAL BONDING AND CONTROL THEORIES

Introduction

Some proponents insist that control theory is entirely different from all other theories of crime, because it poses an entirely different question. Rather than trying to determine why some people deviate from social and legal norms, it asks: Why does anyone conform? Why don't we all violate the rules?

> In control theories, [this] question has never been adequately answered. The question remains, why *do* men obey the rules of society? Deviance is taken for granted; conformity must be explained. (Hirschi, 1969:10)

The answer offered by control theory is that we conform because social controls prevent us from committing crimes. Whenever these controls break down or weaken, deviance is likely to result (Reiss, 1951). Control theory argues that people are motivated to conform by social controls but need no special motivation to violate the law. That comes naturally in the absence of controls. This "natural motivation" assumption does not necessarily refer to in-born tendencies to crime. Rather, it refers to the assumption that there is no individual variation in motivations to commit crime; the impetus toward crime is uniform or evenly distributed across society (Agnew, 1993). Because of this uniform motivation to crime, we will all push up against the rules of society and break through them unless we are controlled. Thus, control theorists assert that their objective is not to explain crime; they assume everyone would violate the law if they could just get away with it. Instead, they set out to explain why we do *not* commit crime. For instance, Travis Hirschi, the leading control theorist today, states:

> The question "Why do they do it?" is simply not the question the theory is designed to answer. The question is "Why don't *we* do it?" There is

much evidence that we would if we dared. (Hirschi, 1969:34; emphasis added)

Later statements by Hirschi and Michael Gottfredson draw a sharp contrast between control theory and all other theories of criminal behavior, which they refer to as "positivistic." They describe the question of positivistic theories as not what prevents crime, but what factors positively motivate people to commit crimes. In their view, positivistic theories assume that everyone will conform in the absence of that motivation; whereas in contrast, control theories assume that crime will occur unless prevented by strong social and personal controls (Gottfredson and Hirschi, 1990).

It is true that all versions of control theory tend to focus more on social relationships that curb crime than on those that promote crime. However, different control theories vary considerably in the extent that they limit or exclude the study of the positive motivations behind crime. Not all control theorists simply assume that everyone is equally motivated to deviate, nor do all confine themselves only to the problem of identifying influences toward conformity. Some control theorists have specifically incorporated the crime-motivating factors of personality, social environment, or situation into their own theories (Reckless, 1967; Briar and Piliavin, 1965).

F. Ivan Nye (1958) argues for a multi-causal model which treats most crime as a result of the failure of social controls, but allows for the fact that "such 'positive' factors [personality or a delinquent subculture] sometimes combine with delinquent behavior as the product" (Nye, 1958:5). Hirschi himself rejects the assumption of an inherent impulse to delinquency. He proposes that the "natural motivation" assumption in control theory must be modified to recognize the fact that there are some inducements to delinquency, such as the approval of delinquent peers, that must be considered in addition to the inhibitors of delinquency (Hirschi, 1969). The assumption that everyone is naturally motivated to commit deviant acts is not crucial to any version of control theory. In fact, some control theories deliberately include factors which induce crime.

Consequently, there is really not much difference between control theory and other theories in the type of questions about crime that each tries to answer. Whatever their other differences, all theories of crime, including control theory, ultimately ask the same question of why some do and some do not commit crime. Like other theories, control theories propose to explain crime and delinquency, but they do not try to explain conformity, altruism, meritorious achievement, or pro-social contributions to the welfare of society.

Statements and tests of control theories have the same dependent variables (crime, delinquency, and deviance) as other theories. Empirical tests of control theories measure these variables in exactly the same way (with official and self-report data) as do tests of other theories. If the concept and measurement of the dependent variable is essentially the same, what difference does it make whether one claims that the essential question involves committing a crime or that it involves refraining from a crime? In research on control and other theories, criminal or delinquent behavior is defined as the commission of some act(s) in violation of the law; conformity is defined as the absence of those acts.

Conformity and crime are two sides of the same coin. It makes no meaningful difference which of the two a theory claims to explain, because to account for one accounts for the other. Theories vary in the extent to which they emphasize one side of the coin, whether it be the motivation of crime or the restraints on crime. It would be fair to contrast the stress on motivations to crime in some theories with the stress on inhibitors of crime in control theory (Agnew, 1993). But the difference is a matter of degree, not a qualitative difference. For this reason, it is difficult to divide explanations of crime into two mutually exclusive categories based on whether they try to explain either conformity or crime.

Early Control Theories

Reiss' and Nye's Theories of Internal and External Controls

The sociological concept of social control includes both socialization, in which a person acquires self-control, and the control over the person's behavior through the external application of social sanctions, rewards for conformity, and punishments for deviance. Albert J. Reiss (1951) provided one of the earliest applications of this concept to criminology by attributing the cause of delinquency to the failure of "personal" and "social" controls. Personal controls are internalized, while social controls operate through the external application of legal and informal social sanctions.

Nye (1958) later expanded on this and identified three main categories of social control that prevent delinquency:

(1) Direct control, by which punishment is imposed or threatened for misconduct and compliance is rewarded by parents.

(2) Indirect control, by which a youth refrains from delinquency because his or her delinquent act might cause pain and disappointment for parents or others with whom one has close relationships.

(3) Internal control, by which a youth's conscience or sense of guilt prevents him or her from engaging in delinquent acts.

Nye recognized that direct controls could be exercised through formal or legal sanctions, but he emphasized informal, indirect controls in the family. He also argued that the more adolescents' needs for affection, recognition, security, and new experiences are met within the family, the less they will turn to meeting those needs in unacceptable ways outside the family. It would seem, however, that Nye did not mean this to be a separate category of control. Rather, the insufficient satisfaction of youngsters' needs within the family, coupled with the fuller satisfaction of their needs outside the family, appears to be one of the factors that positively motivates them to commit delinquency. Therefore, this is one type of motivation toward delinquent behavior that must be counteracted by direct and indirect controls if delinquency is to be prevented.

In his research on self-reported delinquency, Nye (1958) found delinquent behavior to be related to various aspects of family relationships, such as broken homes, marital adjustment, employed mothers, family disintegration, the lack of parental discipline, parent-child value disagreements, and rejection. However, many of the associations were weak. Not all of them could be used to verify the theory, because Nye did not always clearly delineate how a particular aspect of family relationships included in his study was connected to the concepts in his control theory. For some of the family correlates of delinquency in his research, such as the social class of the family, he made no connection at all.

Reckless' Containment Theory

At about the same time Nye was formulating his control theory, Walter Reckless (Reckless et al., 1956; Reckless, 1961; 1967) proposed the "containment" theory of delinquency and crime. His containment theory was built on the same concept of internal and external control, which Reckless termed "inner" and "outer" containment. Reckless went beyond this, however, to include factors that motivate youth to commit delinquent acts; i.e., "pushes" and "pulls" toward delinquency. The basic proposition in containment theory is that these inner and outer pushes and pulls will produce delinquent behavior unless they are counteracted by inner and outer containment. When the motivations to deviance are strong and containment is weak, crime and delinquency are to be expected.

A young individual can be pushed toward delinquency by inner psychological impulses and drives (e.g., discontent, hostility, or aggressiveness). In addition, there are two types of environmental, delinquency-inducing factors: "pushes," the conditions which pressure the youth toward delinquency (e.g., poverty, deprivation, or blocked opportunities); and "pulls," the positive inducements toward delinquency (e.g., bad companions, gangs, or delinquent subcultures). Outer containment includes parental and school supervision and discipline, strong group cohesion, and a consistent moral front. Inner containment consists primarily of a strong conscience or a "good self-concept."

Apparently, either one or both types of containment can do the job. An adolescent with weak inner control facing a strong motivation to commit delinquent acts can still be controlled by a strong outer containment. If the outer containment is weak, however, control must come from the inner containment provided by a good self-concept. Reckless believed that the self-concept of the youth as either essentially a "good" kid with a strong conscience or a "bad" kid with weak self-control is the product of socialization in the family. The self-concept is essentially formed by age 12.

This self-concept, which renders one more or less vulnerable to the pushes and pulls of a deviant environment, is the key aspect of Reckless' containment theory. It has been used to explain the fact that only some youth in a high-delinquency area are delinquent. The assumption is that all youth in these areas face similar pushes and pulls toward delinquency and similar weak external controls in family and neighborhood. According to containment theory, the good kid has developed an "insulated" self-concept with which to withstand the influences that lead other peers into delinquency. Such peers who become delinquent in the adolescent years have failed to develop this insulated self-concept. They have "vulnerable" or bad self-concepts, by which they succumb to the pushes and pulls of delinquency within the neighborhood.

This self-concept hypothesis is the only part of the containment theory that has been systematically tested. Reckless and his associates conducted research on boys' self-concepts in high-delinquency areas (Reckless et al., 1956; 1957; Scarpitti et al., 1960; Dinitz et al., 1962). They found that boys with good self-concepts at age 12 were less likely to be arrested or to exhibit delinquent behavior by age 16. They interpreted these findings as confirming containment theory. But the findings related only to the hypothesis that outer pushes and pulls pressuring youngsters toward delinquency can be controlled by inner containment. The research did not touch on the other components of the theory—outer pressures versus outer containment, inner pressures versus inner containment, or inner pressures versus outer containment.

Moreover, this research on self-concept in a high-delinquency area has been severely criticized for a number of shortcomings (Tangri and Schwartz, 1967; Jensen, 1970). Reckless and associates provided no measures of the outer pushes and pulls toward delinquency. They simply assumed that, since the neighborhood areas had a high rate of juvenile arrests, the motivations toward delinquency had to be strong in the area. The measures of self-concept included many items that could have been easily interpreted as simply asking about current delinquent status and behavior. For example, teachers were asked to select a number of their sixth-grade male students whom they considered to be "good boys" and those they considered to be "bad boys." The students were then asked whether or not they had gotten into trouble with the police, at school, or at home, then were questioned about their conforming or deviant behaviors. It was on the basis of answers to these and other questions that the researchers categorized the boys as having good, "insulated," or bad, "vulnerable," self-concepts. Some of their measures of self-concept, therefore, were not really separated from their measures of delinquency and deviance. Reckless' findings, therefore, are partly tautological; they only show that delinquent behavior is related to delinquent behavior. Jensen (1973), however, devised non-tautological measures of inner containment (e.g. self-esteem and self-control) and found moderate relationships with delinquency even when peer delinquency and family variables were controlled.

Sykes and Matza: Techniques of Neutralization and Drift

Gresham Sykes and David Matza proposed a theory in 1957 that explained delinquent behavior as the result of adolescents using "techniques of neutralization." These techniques are justifications and excuses for committing delinquent acts, which are essentially inappropriate extensions of commonly accepted rationalizations found in the general culture. Believing in these neutralizing definitions does not mean that delinquents totally reject the values of conventional society, or that they have a set of values that directly contradicts general cultural values. It is simply that they have a set of "subterranean values" that circumvent, and rationalize deviations from, conventional values (Matza and Sykes, 1961). In stating their theory, Sykes and Matza left no doubt that they considered techniques of neutralization to be types of "definitions favorable" to crime and delinquency, as referred to in Sutherland's differential association theory.[1] Nevertheless, Sykes and Matza's theory is viewed by many criminologists as a type of control theory.

This interpretation of Sykes and Matza came about principally because Matza (1964) later incorporated neutralization ideas into his "drift" theory of delinquency. Drift theory proposes that the techniques of neutralization are ways in which adolescents can get "episodic release" from conventional moral restraints. It is this periodic evasion of conventional morality which allows the adolescent to drift into and out of delinquency. If conventional beliefs are seen as controlling deviance, then neutralizing those beliefs represents a weakening of social control. It is probably for this reason that, although Matza (1964) made few references to internal or external controls, his drift theory and by extension his and Sykes' theory of the techniques of neutralization have usually been classified as control theory. Neutralization is not viewed as a form of definition favorable to delinquency as originally stated by Sykes and Matza, but as a weakening of inner containment (Ball, 1968) or as a breaking of the bonds to society (Minor, 1980; 1981).

Adherence to neutralizing attitudes has been found to be moderately related to delinquent and criminal behavior, but this seems to be simply because such attitudes favorably dispose individuals to violate the law rather than function to release them from the restraints of conventional or moral beliefs (Hindelang, 1970; 1973; Austin, 1977; Minor, 1980; Hollinger, 1991). In his original statement of social bonding theory, Hirschi (1969) rejected the concept of neutralization as the delinquent's way of breaking away from strongly held conventional beliefs. Instead, he proposed that endorsement of the techniques of neutralization simply indicate that conventional beliefs are weakly held by delinquents in the first place. In those cases, there are no prior conventional beliefs to be neutralized.

Hirschi's Social Bonding Theory

All of the earlier control theories were superseded by the version proposed by Travis Hirschi (1969), who remains today the major control theorist. His control theory is usually referred to as social bonding theory. Over the past two decades, the earlier control theories have been discussed in textbooks and journal articles mainly as a background for presenting or testing Hirschi's social bonding theory. Research reports on neutralization in deviance (Hollinger, 1991) still continue, and references to earlier control theories are made in reports on direct parental controls and delinquency (Wells and Rankin, 1988). However, Hirschi's theory has become what most criminologists today refer to as control theory. It has come to occupy a central place in criminological theory. Indeed, it is the most frequently discussed and tested of all theories in criminology (Stitt and Giacopassi, 1992).

This position is well-deserved. The full statement of the theory was published in Hirschi's *Causes of Delinquency* (1969). In spite of its title, his book presented an internally consistent, logically coherent, and parsimonious theory that is applicable to any type of criminal or deviant behavior, not only delinquency. Hirschi formulated a control theory that brought together elements from all previous control theories and offered new ways to account for delinquent behavior. He not only laid out the assumptions, concepts, and propositions in a lucid fashion, he provided clear empirical measures for each major concept. Then he reported systematic tests of the theory based on data from his own major study of self-reported delinquency, using a sample of the general adolescent population in Contra Costa County, California. His combination of theory construction, conceptualization, operationalization, and empirical testing was virtually unique in criminology at that time and stands as a model today.

The Central Concepts and Propositions of Social Bonding Theory

Hirschi's theory begins with the general proposition that "delinquent acts result when an individual's bond to society is weak or broken" (1969:16). There are four principal "elements" that make up this bond—attachment, commitment, involvement, and beliefs. The stronger these elements of social bonding with parents, adults, school teachers, and peers, the more the individual's behavior will be controlled in the direction of conformity. The weaker they are, the more likely it is that the individual will violate the law. These four elements are viewed by Hirschi as highly intercorrelated; the weakening of one will probably be accompanied by the weakening of another.

Attachment to Others

Attachment to others is the extent to which we have close affectional ties to others, admire them, and identify with them so that we care about their expectations. The more insensitive we are to others' opinions, the less we are constrained by the norms which we share with them; therefore, the more likely we are to violate these norms.

To Hirschi, concepts such as self-control, internalization of norms, internal control, indirect control, personal control, and conscience are too subjective. They cannot be observed and measured. He contends that self-control was most often used by earlier control theorists in a tautological way; that is, they simply assumed that internal controls were weak when people committed criminal or delinquent behavior. Hirschi argues that attachment is a better concept than self-control, because it avoids the tautology problem and because all the concepts of internal self-control can be subsumed under the concept of attachment. "The essence of internalization of norms, conscience, or superego thus lies in the attachment of the individual to others" (Hirschi, 1969:18).

Hirschi emphasizes that attachment to parents and parental supervision are important in controlling delinquency and maintaining conformity. But he also stresses that attachment to peers can control delinquent tendencies. Although he often uses the phrase "attachment to conventional others," Hirschi maintains that it really does not matter to whom one is attached. It is the fact of attachment to other people, not the character of the people to whom one is attached, that determines adherence to or violation of conventional rules.

[H]olding delinquency (or worthiness) of friends truly constant at any level, the more one respects or admires one's friends, the less likely one is to commit delinquent acts. We honor those we admire not by imitation, but by adherence to conventional standards. (Hirschi, 1969:152)

Therefore, according to social bonding theory, even for the juvenile attached to peers or friends who are delinquent, the stronger the attachment to those friends, the less likely he or she will tend to be delinquent. The delinquent tends to have "cold and brittle" relationships with everyone, to be socially isolated, and to be less attached to either conventional or delinquent friends than the non-delinquent (Hirschi, 1969:141). Similarly, the more adolescents are attached to parents, the less likely they are to be delinquent, even if the parents are themselves criminal or deviant.

Commitment

Commitment refers to the extent to which individuals have built up an investment in conventionality or a "stake in conformity" (Toby, 1957) that would be jeopardized or lost by engaging in law violation or other forms of deviance. Investment in conventional educational and occupational endeavors builds up this commitment. The greater the commitment, the more one risks losing by non-conformity. The cost of losing one's investment in conformity prevents one from norm violation. Commitment, therefore, refers to a more or less rational element in the decision to commit crime. (See the discussion of rational choice theory in Chapter 2.)

Involvement

Involvement refers to one's engrossment in conventional activities, such as studying, spending time with the family, and participation in extra-curricular activities. One is restrained from delinquent behavior, because one is too busy, too preoccupied, or too consumed in conforming pursuits to become involved in non-conforming pursuits.

Belief

The concept of belief in social bonding theory is defined as the endorsement of general conventional values and norms, especially the belief that laws and society's rules in general are morally correct and should be obeyed. The concept does not necessarily refer to beliefs about specific laws or acts, nor does it mean that people hold deviant beliefs which "require" them to commit crime. In fact, Hirschi argues that, if deviant beliefs are present, then there is nothing to explain. What needs explaining is why people violate rules in which they already believe. Hirschi answers that their belief in the moral validity of norms and laws has been weakened. ". . . [T]he less a person believes he should obey the rules, the more likely he is to violate them" (Hirschi, 1969:26).

Measures of Social Bonding Concepts

Hirschi (1969) provided clear measures for the four principal elements of the social bond. Most research on this theory has since used Hirschi's or similar measures. A review of them will help us to understand the results of the research on social bonding theory.

An adolescent's attachment to parents is measured by close parental supervision and discipline, good communication and relationships of the adolescent with parents, and his or her affectional identification with parents (e.g., he or she would like to be the same kind of person as the parent). Academic achievement in school (as indicated by grades, test scores, and self-perception of scholastic ability) is taken as indicative of commitment, involvement, and belief, as well as attachment. Attachment to the school is directly measured by positive attitudes toward school, a concern for teachers' opinions of oneself, and an acceptance of the school's authority. Attachment to peers is measured by affectional identification with and respect for the opinions of best friends.

Adolescents' commitment to conventional lines of action refers to their desire and pursuit of conventional goals. Premature engagement in adult activities by adolescents, such as smoking, drinking, or owning a car, indicates a lack of commitment to the achievement of educational goals. Commitment to education is measured both by educational aspirations (e.g., completing more than a high school education) and achievement orientation. Commitment is also measured by occupational aspirations and expectations. Adolescent involvement in conventional activities includes working part-time, dating, sports, recreation, hobbies, doing homework, and spending time with friends.

Belief is measured by the reference to values relative to the law and the criminal justice system. This includes the extent to which an adolescent has general respect for the police and the law, believes that the law should be obeyed, adheres to the techniques of neutralization, and endorses middle-class values such as the importance of education.

Empirical Validity of Social Bonding Theory

Hirschi's own research generally showed support for the theory. He found that, except for involvement, the weaker the bonds, the higher the probability of delinquency. However, he found delinquency to be most strongly related to association with delinquent friends, a finding not anticipated by the theory. Similarly, later research has found that attachment to peers leads to conformity only when the peers are themselves conventional. Contrary to what Hirschi hypothesized, those who are strongly attached to delinquent friends are themselves more likely to be delinquent (Linden and Hackler, 1973; Conger, 1976; Elliott et al. 1985; Junger-Tas, 1992). Similarly, deviant youth have relationships with others that are no less intimate and stable than conforming youth (Krohn et al., 1988; Kandel and Davies, 1991). Jensen and Brownfield (1983) also found evidence contrary to social bonding theory's hypothesis that attachment to parents inhibits delinquency regardless of parental behavior. For example, attachment to straight parents controls drug use by adolescents, while attachment to drug-using parents does not. Parental deviance provides deviant models and undermines social control in the family (Sampson and Laub, 1993:96). On the other hand, delinquency prediction studies have consistently shown that parental discipline, child-rearing practices, and other family variables affecting the young child, all of which are important in social bonding theory, are among the best predictors of subsequent delinquency (Glueck and Glueck, 1959; McCord and McCord, 1959; Loeber and Stouthamer-Loeber, 1986).

Krohn and Massey (1980) found that the social bonding variables of beliefs, attachment, and commitment/involvement (which they combined) are moderately related to delinquent behavior but more to minor than serious delinquency (see also McIntosh et al., 1981). Agnew (1991a) found that attachment is not related and that commitment is only weakly related to minor delinquency and that social bonding variables have the expected, but weak, longitudinal effect on delinquency (Agnew, 1991b). Later, he reported findings that bonding variables are moderately related both to general and serious delinquency, but the relationships are mediated by strain and social learning variables (Agnew, 1993). Lasley (1988) found that some forms of adult crime (e.g., white-collar crime) are related to measures of social bonds. Akers and Cochran (1985) found attachment, commitment/involvement, and beliefs to be moderately related to adolescent marijuana use, but the effects of the bonding variables are much weaker than peer association and reinforcement or specific attitudes toward marijuana smoking. Attachment to both parents in an intact home is most preventive of delinquency, while children raised in single-parent families, even when they are attached to that parent, run a higher risk of delinquency (Rankin and Kern, 1994). Attachment and commitment to school is negatively related to delinquency for both black and white youth (Cernkovich and Giordano, 1992). Studies in other countries also report some support for social bonding theory (Mak, 1991; Junger-Tas, 1992)

Although Hirschi did not include religious beliefs in his original study, they are obviously representative of conventional values. Adherence to religious practices clearly indicates commitment to conventionality, involvement in conventional activities, and attachment to others. Therefore, the research findings reported by Hirschi and Stark (1969) that attachment to religion is unrelated to delinquency could be considered as evidence contrary to social bonding theory. However, a considerable amount of subsequent research has demonstrated consistently that the more adolescents have religious and moral beliefs, attachments, involvements, and commitments, the less likely they are to engage in delinquency (see Burkett and White, 1974; Stark et al., 1980; Cochran and Akers, 1989; Ross, 1994; and the review of research on this issue in Jensen and Rojek, 1992). The correlations are modest and the effects are sometimes indirect, but the findings from this research on religiosity and delinquency can be taken as supportive of social bonding theory.

On the whole, social bonding theory has received some verification from empirical research (see also Hindelang, 1973; Johnson, 1979; Wiatrowski et al., 1981; Agnew, 1985a; Cernkovich and Giordano, 1992; Rankin and Kern, 1994). However, the magnitude of the relationships between social bonding and deviant behavior has ranged from moderate to low. High correlations and levels of explained variance are seldom found in research literature on this theory. While most of the findings on delinquent behavior and the social bonds that Hirschi found in his original research favor the theory, the relationships are fairly modest and some are in the opposite direction from that expected by the theory. Nevertheless, most social bonding research since then has produced similar supportive findings.

Gottfredson and Hirschi: Self-Control Theory

Low Self-Control as the Cause of Criminal Behavior

Recently, Hirschi has moved away from his classic social bonding formulation of control theory. He has collaborated with Michael Gottfredson (Gottfredson and Hirschi, 1990) to propose a theory of crime based on one type of control only—self-control. Gottfredson and Hirschi present self-control theory as a general theory that explains all individual differences in the "propensity" to refrain from or to commit crime, including all acts of crimes and deviance, at all ages, and under all circumstances. Gottfredson and Hirschi begin with the observation that:

> [I]ndividual differences in the tendency to commit criminal acts . . . *remain reasonably stable with change in the social location of individuals and change in their knowledge of the operation of sanction systems.* This is the problem of self-control, the differential tendency of people to avoid criminal acts whatever the circumstances in which they find themselves. Since this difference among people has attracted a wide variety of names, we begin by arguing the merits of the concept of self-control. (Gottfredson and Hirschi, 1990:87; emphasis in original).

The theory states that individuals with high self-control will be "substantially less likely at all periods of life to engage in criminal acts" (Gottfredson and Hirschi, 1990:89), while those with low self-control are highly likely to commit crime. Low self-control can be counteracted by circumstances and, therefore, does not "require crime." This means that the circumstances have to be right before the lack of self-control will produce crime. Gottfredson and Hirschi do not specify whether these circumstantial factors are external controls that make up for the lack of self-control, stronger positive motivations to commit the crime, or positive motivations to refrain from crime.

The source of low self-control is ineffective or incomplete socialization, especially ineffective child rearing. Parents who are attached to their children, supervise their children closely, recognize the lack of self-control in their children, and punish deviant acts will help to socialize children into self-control. Their children generally will not become delinquent as teenagers or engage in crime as adults. The explicit disapproval of parents or others about whom one cares is the most important negative sanction. School and other social institutions contribute to socialization, but it is the family in which the most important socialization takes place. Consequently, peer groups are relatively unimportant in the development of self-control and in the commission of delinquency or crime. Once formed in childhood, the amount of self-control that a person has acquired remains relatively stable throughout life.

What Is the Relationship Between Self-Control Theory and Social Bonding Theory?

The concept of low self-control is similar to such concepts as vulnerable self-concept and internal controls in social control theories that predated Hirschi's. The concept of self-control is central to these earlier theories of crime and delinquency. However, as has been shown, there is no place for self-control as a separate element in Hirschi's (1969) social bonding version of control theory. Bonding theory rejects the self-control concept as unobservable and subsumes it under the concept of attachment. In contrast, the concept of self-control is absolutely central to Gottfredson and Hirschi's theory. Yet, the four key elements of social bonding theory (belief, attachment, commitment, and involvement) are virtually absent from Gottfredson and Hirschi's theory.

Gottfredson and Hirschi (1990) do not clarify how their self-control theory relates to Hirschi's (1969) social bonding theory or to other control theories. They offer no explanation as to why they have reversed Hirschi's position that self-control is subsumable under attachment, and why they now treat self-control as the general mechanism for the control of criminal behavior. Since Gottfredson and Hirschi refer to their formulation as a general theory, it may be assumed that not only attachment, but all four of the elements of social bonding should now be subsumed under, or taken as indicators of, the concept of self-control. It would also be reasonable to return to earlier control theory and conceptualize self-control as internal control. Hence, it would simply be another social bonding element (along with commitment, attachment, involvement, and belief) that prevents crime and promotes conformity. It may be then assumed that self-control is the key variable, and that other social bonds affect crime only indirectly through their effects on self-control.

Testability of Self-Control Theory

Low self-control not only explains crime, but also explains what Gottfredson and Hirschi call "analogous behavior." Analogous behavior includes smoking, drinking, drug use, illicit sex, and even accidents. All are seen by Gottfredson and Hirschi as alternative "manifestations of" low self-control. In testing his original social bonding theory, Hirschi considered smoking, drinking, and dating as indicators of a lack of commitment to conventionality by adolescents. At that time, lack of commitment was supposed to be a *cause* of delinquency, rather than behavior *analogous* to delinquency. Gottfredson and Hirschi stress that there is great versatility in the types of crime and analogous behavior committed by persons with low self-control, but they do not explain how measures of commitment changed from causes to analogous behavior. Self-control, according to the theory, accounts for all variations by sex, culture, age, and circumstances and "explains all crime, at all times, and, for that matter many forms of behavior that are not sanctioned by the state." (Gottfredson and Hirschi, 1990:117). This is a very large claim, which Gottfredson and Hirschi attempt to support by reviewing the known official and unofficial distribution and correlates of crime and delinquency, interpreting them as consistent with the self-control concept. They also spell out the policy implications of self-control. According to this self-control theory, official actions taken to deter or curtail crime in adulthood are not likely to have much effect. Self-control, they contend, is the result of early socialization in the family. Therefore, only preventive policies that take effect early in life and have a positive impact on families have much chance of reducing crime and delinquency. Gottfredson and Hirschi do not, however, present any new research with general or specific empirical tests of their theory.

There is a problem of tautology with self-control theory that must be resolved before research can really determine its empirical validity. The theory hypothesizes that low self-control is the cause of the propensity toward criminal behavior. The testability of this explanation is put into question, however, by the fact that Gottfredson and Hirschi do not define self-control separately from this propensity. They use "low self-control" or "high self-control" simply as labels for this differential propensity to commit or refrain from crime. They do not identify operational measures of low self-control as separate from the very tendency to commit crime that low self-control is supposed to explain. Propensity toward crime and low self-control appear to be one and the same. The hypothesis is true by definition: low self-control causes low self-control. To avoid this tautological problem, conceptual definitions or operational measures of self-control must be developed that are separate from measures of crime or propensity toward crime (Akers, 1991). Unless that step is taken, this theory will remain untestable.

Research Indirectly and Directly Testing Self-Control Theory

Other researchers have attempted to take that first step toward developing measures of self-control separately from the propensity toward crime. However, most of the research has not devised direct measures of self-control. Rather, the research assumes low self-control from the commission of certain behavior or assumes low self-control from other indicators. For example, in a study of drunk driving offenses (DUI), Keane et al. (1993) assume that offenders who reported drinking alcohol during the week prior to their drunk-driving arrests have low self-control. Not surprisingly, they report that the drinking of alcohol is related to committing DUI offenses. But this simply relates one measure of alcohol behavior with another measure of alcohol behavior. It tells us nothing about self-control which is not already assumed by the fact of the DUI charge; thus, it does not solve the tautological problem.

Others have used different indirect measures of self-control, such as the extent to which there is persistence or change in individual tendencies toward delinquency and the extent to which this can be attributed to stable/changing individual characteristics or to stable/changing life circumstances. This research has produced mixed results (Nagin and Paternoster, 1991a; Nagin and Farrington, 1992a; Nagin and Farrington, 1992b; Benson and Moore, 1992; Creechan, 1994). According to the theory, self-control is stable; therefore, persons with low self-control will have a greater, and stable, tendency to commit deviance across all social circumstances and at all stages of life after childhood. The empirical evidence, however, shows both stability and change. From analysis of data in a long-term longitudinal study, Robert Sampson and John Laub (Sampson and Laub, 1993; Laub and Sampson, 1993) found some continuity from childhood antisocial behavior to adulthood crime, but changes in criminal propensity later in life were explained by changes in the person's family, employment, and social circumstances. Although some individuals involved in adolescent deviance persist in crime in adulthood, most delinquency is "adolescence-limited" rather than "life-course persistent" (Moffitt, 1993). Most anti-social children do not become antisocial adults; most adolescent delinquents do not become adult criminals (Sampson and Laub, 1993).[2] Other researchers report that stability and change in social circumstances, rather than self-control or some other persistent individual characteristic, account for persistence and change in deviant behavior (Warr, 1996).

> Another comment concerns the relation between earlier and later delinquency. One would expect such a relationship, and indeed path analysis produces a correlation . . . . However, controlling for integration levels, the relation disappears. . . . Our research indicates that, when social conditions change, social behavior will also change. (Junger-Tas, 1192:21)
>
> Earlier involvement in minor offending (including minor forms of violence) has no significant effect on subsequent onset of serious violence. This finding, together with earlier findings that used this model to predict involvement in minor delinquency . . . does not offer much support for a causal interpretation of early aggression or delinquency leading to later serious violence; rather it suggests that the stability of aggressiveness-violence over the lifespan is due more to a stability in the nature of social relationships and social contextual factors than to some underlying individual predisposition. . . . (Elliott, 1994: 16-17)

Michael L. Benson and Elizabeth Moore (1992) provide yet another (but still indirect) way of empirically testing self-control theory. They studied offenders charged with white-collar crimes, such as embezzlement and income tax violations, and compared them to offenders charged with "common" property and drug offenses who had been convicted in federal court. Gottfredson and Hirschi (1990) contend that there is no difference between white-collar offenders and other criminal offenders. All criminal offenders commit crimes because of low self-control, commit a wide variety of offenses, and have the same propensity to engage in a number of other analogous deviant behavior. Benson and Moore (1992) found that some white-collar offenders are similar to common crime offenders, but they do not have records of committing other offenses and do not engage in deviant behavior to nearly the extent that other offenders do. In short, contrary to the theory, white-collar offenders clearly differ from other types of offenders both in versatility and deviance proneness.

Grasmick et al. (1993) provide a more direct test of the theory, using measures designed specifically to tap the different dimensions of self-control identified by Gottfredson and Hirschi (e.g., control of temper and risk-taking). Their research findings offered mixed support for the theory as an explanation of fraud and force. Burton et al. (1994) report findings on a similar measure of self-control in a study of self-reported crime. They found that self-control (along with having law-violating friends and definitions favorable to crime) was strongly related to both utilitarian and non-utilitarian crimes. Boeringer and Akers (1993) test a combined self-control/social bonding model of rape behavior and report modest support for the theory, but they measured only one dimension of self-control. Brownfield and Sorenson (1993) claim to have direct measures for self-control and report findings showing a modest relationship to delinquent behavior, but they merely used the same Contra Costa County data that Hirschi collected in the 1960s and rename some of his measures "self-control."

Low-self control theory is logically consistent, is parsimonious, and has wide scope. In a very brief time, it has generated enormous interest and attention in criminology and may supplant social bonding as the principal control theory. Thus far, the tautology issue has not been resolved, but research is moving in that direction by indirectly measuring self-control independently of measures of crime propensity. While some research reports contradict the theory, on balance the evidence gives some support for the theory. To date, however, there has not been enough research conducted to test self-control theory directly in order to come to any firm conclusions about its empirical validity.

Summary

Control theory takes motivations to commit crime and delinquency for granted and treats conformity as the real problem to be explained. In this sense, it differs from theories that concentrate on the motivations for crime, but the difference is a matter of degree and emphasis rather than irreconcilable and opposing assumptions. Ultimately, all theories of law-violating behavior address the same question of why people commit or refrain from committing crime and delinquency.

Reiss (1951) explains delinquency as resulting from the failure of "personal" and "social" controls. Nye (1958) identifies direct and indirect family controls on delinquent behavior. The basic proposition in Reckless' containment theory is that inner and outer "pushes" and "pulls" toward deviance will produce delinquent behavior, unless they are counteracted by inner and outer containment.

Sykes and Matza (1957) propose that delinquents reduce the constraints on behavior produced by their initial beliefs in the conventional norms of society by utilizing "techniques of neutralization." While there are methodological problems, findings are not consistent, and the relationships are weak, each of these theories has received some support from empirical research.

Hirschi's (1969) social bonding theory proposes four types of bonding to others: attachment, commitment, involvement, and beliefs that control the individual in the direction of conformity. Empirical research has produced moderate or weak evidence in favor of social bonding theory. In collaboration with Gottfredson, Hirschi has recently moved away from his earlier social bonding theory to propose a general self-control theory that claims to explain all crimes and deviance under all circumstances. There are unresolved problems of tautology in this theory, and not enough research has been conducted to test it directly in order to arrive at conclusions about its empirical validity.

Notes

1. See Chapter 4 on Social Learning for a discussion of how techniques of neutralization fit into differential association theory and their current status in social learning theory.

2. Sampson and Laub (1993; Laub and Sampson, 1993) have become the leading proponents of a "developmental" or "life-course" perspective in criminology (see also Moffitt, 1993; Conger and Simons, 1995). But it is unclear whether this represents a new theory or is simply a way of showing how important variables drawn from other theories operate at different life stages to explain deviant behavior. It is also unclear from which theories these variables are taken. Moffitt (1993) draws heavily from concepts in developmental psychology. Sampson and Laub use the language of "social bonds" and "informal social control," downplay the relevance of peer delinquency, and seem to take a social bonding approach to life-course changes. But their discussion of why family context is so important in the development of delinquency behavior leans very heavily on Patterson's (1982) *social learning* theory of parental modeling, reinforcement, and punishment of children's conforming and deviant behavior. Moreover, they view parental disciplinary and socialization techniques as mediating the delinquency-inducing effects of factors, such as household crowding and family disruption, that are essentially measures of social disorganization or other factors, such as parents' criminality that are measures of social learning concepts of imitation/modeling. Sampson and Laub's reference to parental discipline and supervision echoes parts of Hirschi's original formulation of social bonding theory. But there is nothing in their model or in their data that directly measures the social bonding concepts of attachment, commitment, beliefs, or involvement. They interpret their findings that abrupt "turning points" and gradual changes in a person's life, such as getting married and finding stable employment, explain why persons discontinue law violations, as inconsistent with Gottfredson and Hirschi's low self-control theory. This interpretation may be correct, but the findings are not uniquely consistent with social bonding theory.

CHAPTER 6

LABELING THEORY

Introduction

Labeling theory is so named because of its focus on the informal and formal application of stigmatizing, deviant "labels" or tags by society on some of its members. The theory treats such labels as both a dependent variable (effect) and an independent variable (cause). It views labels as the *dependent* variable when it attempts to explain why certain behavior is socially defined as wrong and certain persons are selected for stigmatization and criminalization. It views labels as the *independent* variable when it hypothesizes that discrediting labels cause continuation of the criminal or delinquent behavior.

The most often quoted statement on labeling theory is Becker's following assertion:

> [S]ocial groups create deviance by making the rules whose infraction constitutes deviance, and by applying those rules to particular people and labeling them as outsiders. From this point of view, deviance is not a quality of the act the person commits, but rather a consequence of the application by others of rules and sanctions to an "offender." The deviant is one to whom that label has successfully been applied; deviant behavior is behavior that people so label. (Becker, 1963:9; emphasis in original)

Thus, labeling theorists contend that the actual deviant behavior of those who are labeled is itself of secondary importance. The important question is, who applies the label to whom and what determines when the deviant labels will be assigned? What produces the stigmatizing label and determines the way in which it is applied, particularly by formal control agents, to different individuals and groups in society? The usual answer that labeling theorists give is that the agents of control, who function on behalf of the powerful in society, impose the labels on the less powerful. The powerful in society decide which behavior will be banned or discredited as deviant or illegal. Moreover, the designation of an individual as criminal or deviant is not directly determined by whether or not he or she has actually violated the law or committed the deviant act. Even for the same law-violating behavior, individuals from less powerful groups are more likely to be officially labelled and punished than those from more powerful groups. Branding persons with stigmatized labels, therefore, results more from who they are than from what they have done.

Law and the criminal justice system represent the interests of the middle and upper classes and dominant groups in society over those of the lower-class and minority groups. The probability that one will be arrested, convicted, and imprisoned is determined by one's race, sex, age, social class, and other social characteristics that define one's status in society and one's membership in powerful or powerless groups. This is exactly the point that conflict theorists, whom we consider in the next chapter, are trying to make about the criminal justice system.

Labeling as a Process of Symbolic Social Interaction

Labeling theory as an explanation of criminal and deviant behavior is derived from general *symbolic interactionism* theory in sociology. In symbolic interactionism, an individual's identity and self-concept, cognitive processes, values, and attitudes are seen as existing only in the context of society—acting, reacting, and changing in social interaction with others (Ritzer, 1992). From the early writings of Charles Horton Cooley (1902) and George Herbert Mead (1934) to such later theorists as Herbert Blumer (1969), symbolic interactionism has emphasized the exchange of meanings communicated in face-to-face interaction through the language, verbal utterances, and gestures and the interplay of this interaction with an individual's self-identity. Thus, this emphasis leans toward "symbolic" dimensions, the meanings of words and actions to the actors in social interactions, rather than the concrete, behavioral, and objective aspects of such interactions.

One major concept in symbolic interactionism is the "looking-glass self" (Cooley, 1902), in which our own self-concepts are reflections of others' conceptions of us. We are or become what we think others think we are. If significant others interact with someone as if he or she were a certain type of person with certain characteristics, then a sort of self-fulfilling prophecy (Merton, 1957) may be set in motion, so that the person comes to take on those same characteristics. What others think we are is communicated in part by applying labels to us; thus, our self-concept and actions can be shaped by such societal labeling. Labeling theory proposes that the labeling in this process of symbolic interaction also applies to criminal and delinquent behavior. The theory treats the application of sanctions and stigmatizing labels, with such names as "criminal," "dope fiend," "crazy person," and "delinquent," as an *independent variable* fostering criminal and deviant behavior.

This aspect of labeling theory, in which the application of socially stigmatizing labels is hypothesized to be an independent cause of criminal and delinquent behavior, is what most clearly distinguishes it from other theoretical perspectives on crime and deviance. While other theories may recognize that the enforcement of law meant to deter crime sometimes has the unintended consequence of fostering more crime, this notion is central to labeling theory.

The Label as an Independent Variable in Crime and Deviance

The basic symbolic interactionist proposition at the heart of labeling theory is that the formation of the individual's identity is a reflection of others' definition of him or her (Becker, 1963). The theory advances the thesis that individuals who are labeled or dramatically stigmatized (Goffman, 1963) as deviant are likely to take on a deviant self-identity and become more, rather than less, deviant than if they had not been so labeled. The label is attached to someone, informally or formally, in the process of reacting to and trying to prevent deviant behavior. It is intended to deter, not foster deviance. An ironic, unintended consequence of labeling, therefore, is that the person becomes what the sanctioning process meant to prevent, even if he or she did not set out that way.

Labeling theorists do not see this as only a one-way deterministic process in which identity becomes fixed. Rather, self-concept is formed and reformed in an interactive process by which the individual is self-reflexive, role-playing, and negotiating his or her self-identity. People try to manage how others view them, as well as react to what others communicate to them. Proponents of labeling theory are right to object that the theory is sometimes misinterpreted as a simplistic, one-way causative model in which a deviant label inevitably produces a deviant way of life (see Paternoster and Iovanni, 1989). These objections notwithstanding, there is a clear deterministic element in labeling theory. It is not a distortion of the theory to say that it predicts that the identity a person takes on will be *profoundly* shaped by the way in which others identify and react to him or her. It is perfectly fair to say, therefore, that labeling theory hypothesizes that the person's subsequent deviant behavior is directly and significantly affected by the labeling experience.

We can also reasonably interpret labeling theory as proposing that deviance inducement is particularly likely to occur when those who are doing the labeling are formal agents of society, empowered to enforce its social and legal norms—the police, prosecutors, courts, prisons, and governmental officials. When confronted with a label applied by those with power and authority, the individual has little power to resist or negotiate his or her identification with it. Although there is frequent reference by labeling theorists to the informal, interactive process in deviance labeling, the emphasis remains on the strong effect of being labeled by the criminal justice system, mental health system, or other formal, norm-enforcing bureaucracies.

The earliest statements of latter-day labeling theory were made in the 1930s by Frank Tannenbaum (1938). The first systematic analysis stressing the effects of the social control system on the occurrence and form of deviant behavior and crime was formed by Edwin M. Lemert (1951; 1967). However, it was the publication of Howard S. Becker's book *Outsiders* in 1963 and his edited volume of articles in *The Other Side* in 1964 (as well as his editorship of the journal *Social Problems*) that brought this perspective to prominent attention and placed it at the center of theories of crime and deviance. (See Ben-Yehuda et al., 1989.)

The importance given to labeling as a cause of continuing deviance is very clear in the statements of labeling theory proponents:

> The first dramatization of the "evil" which separates the child out of his group . . . plays a greater role in making the criminal than perhaps any other experience. . . . He now lives in a different world. He has been *tagged*. . . . The person *becomes the thing he is described as being*. (Tannenbaum, 1938:21; emphasis added)

> One of the *most crucial steps in the process of building a stable pattern of deviant behavior* is likely to be the experience of being *caught and publicly labeled as a deviant*. Whether a person takes this step or not *depends not so much on what he does as on what other people do* . . . being caught and branded as a deviant has important consequences for one's further social participation and self-image. (Becker, 1963:31; emphasis added)

> Treating a person as though he were generally rather than specifically deviant produces a self-fulfilling prophecy. It sets in motion several mechanisms which *conspire to shape the person in the image people have of him*. (Becker, 1963:34; emphasis added)

> The *societal reaction to the deviant*, then, is vital to an understanding of the deviance itself and *a major element in—if not a cause of—the deviant behavior*. (Schur, 1965:4; emphasis added)

> [The] concern is with social control and its consequences for deviance. This is a large turn away from older sociology which tended to rest heavily upon the idea that deviance leads to social control. I have come to believe that the reverse idea, i.e., *social control leads to deviance*, is equally tenable and the potentially richer premise for studying deviance in modern society. (Lemert, 1967:v; emphasis added)

> The most pretentious claim for our point of view is that it opens the way to subsume deviation in a theory of social change. Even more important, it gives a proper place to *social control as a dynamic factor or "cause" of deviation*. . . . (Lemert, 1967:26, emphasis added)

These statements should not be mistaken to mean that labeling theorists claim that stigmatizing labels inevitably lead an individual to become more deviant. Indeed, Becker went to great lengths to make the point that the outcome was the result of an interaction process that could lead in other directions. Societal reaction to some deviance may actually prevent an individual from engaging in further deviant behavior. Applying a stigmatizing label and sanctions may sometimes have the intended consequence of deterring norm or law violation rather than the unintended consequence of fostering further violations.

Nevertheless, the core position taken in the quotations above from labeling theorists is unmistakable. The theory claims that labeling persons as deviant and applying social sanctions to them in the form of punishment or corrective treatment increases or "amplifies," rather than decreases, deviance (Wilkins, 1964). The central point of the labeling perspective, then, is that the disgrace suffered by people who are labeled as delinquent or criminal more often encourages than discourages future deviant behavior. The stigmatization of deviants puts them at high risk of behaving according to the label, playing out the role of a deviant, and developing deviant self-concepts as irrevocably deviant. In labeling theory, this deviant role and self-concept provide the principal link between the stigmatizing labels and future deviant behavior.

Prior to public labeling, according to labeling theory, deviants' violations of the law are believed to be unorganized, inconsistent, and infrequent. A very important, if not the most crucial, event that leads them toward more stable and frequent patterns of offending in a deviant or criminal "career" is the reaction of the larger society through agents of formal control, as well as the reaction of informal social audiences. For this reason, the labeling perspective is often referred to as the "societal reaction" perspective (Gove, 1980). Without this societal reaction, the deviance would most likely remain sporadic and unorganized. With the societal reaction, the deviance is likely to stabilize into a deviant career.

This commission of continuing deviance in a more coherent, organized fashion is one form of _secondary deviance_ created by the societal reaction and by stigmatizing labels. The concept of secondary deviance "refers to a special class of socially defined responses which people make to problems created by the societal reaction to their deviance" (Lemert, 1967:40-41). Thus, secondary deviance is produced when deviants engage in additional deviant behavior, which they would not have otherwise done had they not been labeled as deviants.

The creation of secondary deviance can be caused not only by labeling individuals but by banning whole categories of behavior. For example, a boy labeled as delinquent may take on a more delinquent self-identity, join a delinquent gang, develop secondary deviant patterns to avoid future detection and sanction, become even tougher, and engage in a wider range of delinquent activities. Legally prohibiting gambling, drug use, and prostitution sets up conditions for a criminal black market to supply the demand for these products and services that otherwise would not have existed.

Becker (1973), Schur (1979), and Lemert (1974) later disavowed any intent to propose a theory of criminal and deviant behavior. They argued that this perspective was really meant to offer only "sensitizing" concepts, rather than a specific explanation of deviance or crime as such. More recently, Paternoster and Iovanni (1989) have contended that critics of labeling theory misunderstand it and that the theory asserts no more than a minimal, highly variable effect of stigmatizing labels on secondary deviance. But in fact, the theory does claim more than minor effects of the label, as the quotations above clearly show. From its very beginning, the theory has maintained that persons take on deviant identities and play deviant roles because they are strongly influenced, if not overtly coerced, into doing so by the application of stigmatizing labels to them.[1]

The theory that societal labeling frequently leads to further deviance was quickly adopted by sociologists, criminologists, and practitioners. It became almost an unquestioned assumption that the established social control system was a problem that made crime worse, rather than a solution to crime. One outcome of this assumption was the "diversion" movement, which gained tremendous momentum in the 1970s. Diversion programs were instituted to keep apprehended offenders, especially juveniles, away from or in minimal contact with the formal system.

Federal legislation mandated a nationwide "deinstitutionalization" of juveniles to remove status offenders, such as runaways, truants, curfew violators, and incorrigibles from the system entirely. Even juveniles charged with felonies and misdemeanors could not be held in adult jails, except for a brief time (under six hours) in non-secure booking areas. The populations of close-custody reform and training schools were reduced. Local programs were set up to divert apprehended youths away from the juvenile court and institutions into community-based programs of informal probation and community services. These actions were taken partly on the grounds of lowering costs, but they were also based explicitly on labeling theory. The assumption was made that diverting people from the system would avoid the stigma and deviance-enhancing effects of official labeling (Rojek, 1982; Siegel and Senna, 1991; Bynum and Thompson, 1992; Jensen and Rojek, 1992; Lundman, 1993). Some labeling theorists even argued for a policy of "radical non-intervention," by which it was deemed better for the community just to tolerate the behavior of many minor offenders rather than risk making them more serious deviants by formally labeling them (Schur, 1973).

Empirical Evidence on Labeling Theory

Although labeling theory gained widespread acceptance by both academics and practitioners, there were some who were highly critical of labeling theory from the start. The earliest critiques of labeling (Gibbs, 1966; Bordua, 1967; Akers, 1968) objected to the theory's disregard for the actual behavior of the deviant and the image of the deviant being coerced by the labeling process into a deviant identity and role. Even powerless people do not necessarily acquiesce to the application of a deviant label, allowing it to immediately define their self-identities. They fight back, reject, deny, and otherwise negotiate their identities (Rogers and Buffalo, 1974). Moreover, the label does not create the behavior in the first place. Other factors produce the initiation into deviance and can be expected to continue to have a major impact on the continuation of deviance, the maintenance of a deviant self-concept, and the stabilization of a deviant career. People often commit acts that violate the law or social norms for reasons that have nothing to do with labels that others apply to them. Labeling theory essentially ignores the continuing influence of these other variables after the deviant has been apprehended and labeled.

This inattention to other causes of behavior stems from labeling theory's focus on the power of official labellers to single out offenders against whom they invoke the labels, and on the relative powerlessness of those being labeled to resist. Labeling theory pays little attention to the actual behavior of the person who is so labeled. The assumption is that what a person has actually done or not done is unimportant, or at least not as important as who the person is, in determining whether or not they will be labeled as deviant.

Akers (1968) argued that this assumption is incorrect. The labeling process is not arbitrary and unrelated to the behavior of those detected and labeled. Sometimes, errors are made, labels are falsely applied, and criteria extraneous to the deviant behavior are involved in tagging persons with deviant labels. But society does not identify, tag, and sanction individuals as deviant in a vacuum. The police do not arrest routinely without any probable cause and courts do not stigmatize with the label of criminal until they legally determine that criminal acts have been committed. People are labeled as delinquent, criminal, homosexual, mentally ill, drug addicts, child molesters, and so on largely on the basis of overt acts they have committed or are believed to have committed. Therefore, the deviant behavior itself is prior to and forms the basis for the stigmatizing label. The behavior creates the label more than the

label creates the behavior, and subsequent deviant behavior continues
the label more than the label continues the behavior. Bordua (1967)
also took labeling theory to task for not recognizing that the label more
reflects than causes the deviant behavior. He criticized labeling theory
for assuming that a deviant person is an "essentially empty organism"
and for presenting a picture of "all societal response and no deviant
stimulus" (Bordua, 1967:53).

Labeling theory has been criticized for a number of other shortcomings.[2] The most serious shortcoming of all is that empirical research
has failed to give much support to its central proposition. According
to labeling theory, primary deviance is widespread, sporadic, unstable,
and probably not very serious. Only some of those who commit such
acts get detected and labeled. Those who do, especially if the labeling
is done by official criminal justice agencies, have an increased chance
of developing a deviant self-identity or self-concept. This self-concept,
in turn, increases the likelihood that the labeled person will commit
additional deviant acts and develop a stabilized career of secondary
deviance. Conversely, if the detection and labeling can be avoided, then
the deviant is not likely to develop a stabilized or serious criminal career.
There are few findings from research on the official processing of offenders that fit this model.

This lack of empirical confirmation does not mean that labels and
sanctions never have the unintended consequence of making future
deviance more probable. It only means that this infrequently happens
exclusively because of the label. Among those with the same level of
primary deviance, the ones who escape detection and labeling are just
as likely as those who are caught to repeat offenses and develop deviant
careers. As noted in Chapter 2, official sanctions have weak deterrent
effect on criminal or deviant behavior. Nonetheless, the probability that
offenders will desist is as high as, or higher than, the probability that
they will persist in their deviant activities following official labeling.
The deviance-enhancing effects of labeling does not occur as frequently
as labeling theorists would propose.

This conclusion is supported by studies of the official processing of
delinquents and criminals, the hospitalization of mental patients, the
labeling of school children by teachers, the labeling of sexual behavior,
and the labeling of other forms of crime and deviance. Although some
research does report the deviance-enhancing effects of labels (Farrington, 1977; Palamara et al., 1986; Hagan and Palloni, 1990), the
effects are not strong. The preponderance of research finds no or very
weak evidence of labeling effects. The more carefully the research keeps
other factors constant, the less likely it is to find evidence that labeling
has a significant independent effect on criminal or deviant behavior.
The soundest conclusion is that official sanctions by themselves have

neither a strong deterrent nor a substantial labeling effect. When prior offenses, personal propensities, social characteristics, and other non-labeling correlates of deviant behavior are held constant, official stigmatizing labels make little difference in either the continuation or cessation of deviant behavior, self-concept, or a deviant career.[3]

Developments and Modifications in Labeling Theory

Some proponents of labeling theory dismiss the disconfirming empirical findings, because they believe that the theory has been misstated to such an extent that "the bulk of these studies do not constitute a valid test of labeling theory" (Paternoster and Iovanni, 1989:384). However, Paternoster and Iovanni (1989) do not offer new data. They review the same body of research and reach much the same conclusion as earlier reviews that official sanctions such as court appearances and incarceration have little effect on future behavior. Nonetheless, they claim that the models tested in this research are "extreme" interpretations of labeling theory. They suggest a less extreme, more complex model that hypothesizes modest labeling effects conditional on other factors. When judged against this revised model, the findings from previous research are "inconsistent with labeling theory but not entirely contradictory" (Paternoster and Iovanni, 1989:384). Paternoster and Iovanni suggest that, when other factors in the complex model are properly taken into account, labeling theory will be supported by empirical evidence.

As yet, such support has not materialized. In fact, later research by Paternoster himself produced evidence contrary to the theory. When Smith and Paternoster (1990) tested a more complex "deviance-amplification model" of labeling theory on juvenile court cases, they found that appearance in juvenile court was related to the occurrence of future delinquency (recidivism). However, their data show that this relationship results from the fact that it is the juvenile with higher risk of recidivism in the first place who is more likely to be referred to juvenile court and thereby given the delinquency label. Juveniles who avoid the official delinquency label by being diverted from the court are lower-risk youth, those less likely to recidivate anyway. It is not the labeling that has the effect; the labeling is itself a function of the past and probable future behavior of the juveniles. The authors concluded that the "apparent labeling effect of court referral [on future delinquency] can instead be attributed to a selection artifact" (Smith and Paternoster, 1990: 1128). The design and results of this study conform to most of the past research on labeling effects. Few of those studies have tested extreme models. Instead, the studies have merely searched for any significant or substantial labeling effects, while controlling for other factors. Usually such effects have not been found.

Some labeling theorists have accepted much of the criticism of the theory as valid and have recognized that extensive revision of labeling theory is needed to render it more empirically viable. Some of these revisions have abandoned the hypothesis of labeling as deviance-causing and have instead re-emphasized the need to identify how the labeling process itself takes place (Goode, 1975; Hawkins and Tiedeman, 1975). Others have moved toward placing the labeling process into the larger context of power and social conflict (Grimes and Turk, 1977).

The more recent efforts to revise labeling theory have followed this lead. They view labeling as important only insofar as its effects are contingent upon the broader context of social structure. Stigmatizing labels are viewed as an indirect cause of deviant behavior, so that the theoretical task now is to specify the other variables through which labeling has any effect. The most notable of these efforts in criminology is by John Braithwaite (1989) in *Crime, Shame, and Integration.*[4]

The key concept in Braithwaite's theory is "reintegrative shaming." Through this concept he set out to answer the question, when is a criminal label likely to have the effect of producing a criminal self-concept and future criminal behavior, and when is it likely to have the opposite effect of preventing crime? *Shaming* is defined by Braithwaite as social disapproval, which has the "intention or effect of invoking remorse in the person being shamed and/or condemnation by others who become aware of the shaming" (1989:100). This would seem at first to be just another term for stigmatization. However, Braithwaite reserves the term stigmatization for *disintegrative shaming,* which involves no attempt to reconcile the shamed offender with the community. It is with this type of disintegrative shaming that the effect predicted in past labeling theory is to be expected, namely provoking additional crime.

Reintegrative shaming, on the other hand, is that which is "followed by efforts to reintegrate the offender back into the community of law-abiding or respectable citizens through words or gestures of forgiveness or ceremonies to decertify the offender as deviant" (Braithwaite, 1989:100-101). The social disapproval of shaming works to control crime when it is embedded in relationships which are "overwhelmingly characterized by social approval" (Braithwaite, 1989:68). Thus, applying a criminal label under these conditions will not have a crime-enhancing effect. Reintegrative shaming tends to produce lower crime rates, while stigmatization fosters high crime rates, though only in an indirect way. To specify the indirect effects of labeling, Braithwaite draws upon other theories, most notably social learning, anomie/strain, and social bonding. For instance, in his model, stigmatization renders participation in criminal groups (differential association) and taking advantage of illegitimate opportunities (strain) more attractive, which then increases the likelihood of repeating criminal behavior. (It should be noted that some of these indirect ways in which deviant labels can affect the stabilization of deviance were recognized by Becker in 1963.)

Braithwaite lays out 13 "facts a theory of crime ought to fit" (e.g., crime is disproportionately committed by young minority males, by unmarried people, by people with low educational aspirations, by those with criminal associates, in large cities, and so on) and maintains that his model fits them. He also provides a detailed examination of the process of reintegrative shaming and suggests ways to test the theory. Thus far, however, only one test of the theory has been reported, a study by Makkai and Braithwaite of changes in compliance with regulations of nursing homes in Australia. The findings from that test are supportive of the theory, in that the interaction of the inspectors' reintegrative ideology with disapproval of violations had an impact on future compliance by nursing home operators. More direct tests of the theory as an explanation of other types of white-collar crime and of other forms of criminal and deviant behavior await future research (Makkai and Braithwaite, 1994).

The Past and Future of Labeling Theory

At the center of labeling theory is the hypothesis that a stigmatizing label by itself, once applied, is very likely to cause further deviance (if it has already occurred) or creates the deviance (if the label is falsely applied to someone who has not actually committed deviant acts). Indeed, this hypothesis is unique to labeling theory. Other theories recognize that social control techniques which result in publicly identifying and stigmatizing individuals can have unintended consequences. But it is only labeling theory that gives deviant social labels a central etiological role in the commission of future deviant or criminal behavior and the development of a deviant career.

In the 1960s, labeling theory captured the imagination of social science researchers, theorists, and practitioners alike. Its emphasis on the ironic twists in the self-fulfilling prophecy of deviant labels and its focus on the responsibility of the criminal justice system for the very criminal behavior it professes to deter resonated well within the academic and political climate of the time. The theory continued as a major but far less dominant theory in the 1970s. By the late 1970s, however, labeling theory was in decline and being criticized from several quarters. Many of its proponents moved on to other perspectives. After the mid-1970s, Becker himself essentially gave no further attention to the theory. Indeed, he claimed that he had been only "minimally" involved in the study of deviance and that he had never intended to create a labeling theory at all (see Ben-Yehuda et al., 1989).

There can be little doubt that the negative labeling, which occurs in the process of attempting to sanction and control deviance, does *on occasion* backfire and harden deviant tendencies, making matters worse with more rather than less crime. This kernel of truth has sustained labeling theory. Nevertheless, it is a truth that does little to distinguish labeling. If that is all there is to it, it adds very little to our knowledge. Labeling theory gained wide acceptance, partly because it was believed to have identified deviance enhancement as a frequently occurring outcome of social control efforts, offering a strong radical critique of the established system. But when the empirical research evidence failed to support the theory and it lost its radical luster, its influence waned. It no longer generates the interest, enthusiasm, research, and acceptance it once did as a dominant paradigm two or three decades ago.

The theory continues to receive attention, however, and efforts persist to revise and perhaps integrate it with other theories of crime and deviance. Labeling theory still retains some recognition and holds some promise of continuing to influence research and public policy (see, for example, Smith and Paternoster, 1990; Triplett and Jarjoura, 1994). The underlying symbolic interaction assumption that individuals' identities are shaped by social interaction and the reactions of others is a sound and empirically valid concept. It is apparent from the research, however, that reactions embodied in official labeling do not play much of a direct role in this process. This does not mean that positive and negative labeling in social interaction have no effects on self-identity or behavior. Revised labeling models, such as Braithwaite's, that incorporate these informal dimensions and the social characteristics of the community, offer greater promise for empirical support than previous labeling theory models.

Revisions and modifications that focus more on informal labeling by parents, peers, teachers, and others in the process of symbolic interaction, rather than the power-related formal labels of the criminal justice system, are also more likely to receive empirical support. Recent studies using data from the National Youth Survey (see Elliott et al., 1985) have reported findings consistent with hypotheses about the delinquency-promoting effects of informal labeling by parents and others and, indeed, report some evidence that the label sometimes precedes the onset of primary deviance (Matsueda, 1992; Triplett and Jarjoura, 1994). However, much of the support for these hypotheses comes from the fact that informal labeling modifications incorporate variables from social bonding and social learning theory, such as attachments, attitudes and beliefs, and peer associations. Moreover, modifications such as those by Matsueda (1992) allow for the person's prior deviant behavior to have a significant effect on parents' and others' application of informal labels to the person. But this is contrary to the assumption in traditional labeling theory that the deviant behavior itself is not very important in determining to whom the labels are attached. Indeed, the finding in these studies, that the informal labels applied to youths fairly accurately reflect the actual level of their delinquent involvement, supports assertions by Akers and others that the label is more of a result than a cause of the person's deviant behavior.

Summary

Labeling theory expects differential application of stigmatizing labels to persons based on social characteristics such as class and race and explains the difference as the result of control agents selective applying labels to the less powerful in society. The theory's basic proposition regarding these labels as independent variables is that those who are labeled as deviant are likely to take on a self-identity as a deviant and become more, rather than less, deviant than if they had not been so labeled. They tend to conform to the label, even if they did not set out that way. The delinquent or criminal identity is a very likely outcome of this labeling; subsequent behavior is caused by the person acting on the basis of the identity and engaging in various forms of secondary deviance.

The principal strength of labeling theory is that it calls attention to the unintended consequences of social control. Its principal weakness is that it essentially ignores primary deviance and seriously underestimates the influence that other variables have on behavior in the first place and continue to have on its future occurrence. The assumption that what a person has actually done or not done is of little importance in determining whether or not he or she will be labeled as deviant is incorrect. The behavior precedes and creates the label more than the label creates the behavior. This is the primary reason why the preponderance of research evidence shows that, when prior offenses, personal propensities, and social characteristics are held constant, official stigmatizing labels make little difference in the development of negative self-concept, a stabilized deviant career, or the continuation or cessation of deviant behavior. Labeling theory no longer generates the interest, enthusiasm, research, and acceptance it once did as a dominant paradigm in criminology and the sociology of deviance.

Recent efforts to revise labeling theory have viewed stigmatizing labels as only indirectly tied to criminal and deviant behavior. The key concept in Braithwaite's theory is "reintegrative shaming," in contrast to stigmatizing shaming. The application of criminal labels in reintegrative shaming tends to produce lower crime rates, while stigmatization fosters high crime rates. Also, recent revisions emphasize informal labeling processes, rather that criminal justice processing, in producing self-identity and secondary deviance. These modifications have sustained labeling theory, which continues to have an impact, although less than in the past, on criminological research and criminal justice policy

Notes

1. See Tannenbaum (1938), Lemert (1951; 1967), Becker (1963), Erikson (1964), Kitsuse (1964), Schur (1965; 1971; 1973; 1984), and Scheff (1966).
2. See Hirschi (1973), Hagan (1973), Taylor et al. (1973), Vold and Bernard (1989), Braithwaite (1989), Gibbons, (1994), and Curran and Renzetti, (1994).
3. See Mahoney (1974), Tittle (1975), Gove (1980; 1982), Shoemaker (1984), Thomas and Bishop (1984), Braithwaite (1989), and Smith and Paternoster (1990).
4. See also Melossi (1985), Palamara et al. (1986), Somner et al. (1988), Dotter and Roebuck (1988), Link et al. (1989), Matsueda (1992); and Triplett and Jarjoura (1994).

CHAPTER 7

SOCIAL DISORGANIZATION, ANOMIE, AND STRAIN THEORIES

Introduction

Social disorganization and anomie (also referred to as strain) theories have evolved from different theoretical and research traditions. They are included in the same chapter, however, because they have a common theme. Both propose that social order, stability, and integration are conducive to conformity, while disorder and malintegration are conducive to crime and deviance. A social system (a society, community, or subsystem within a society) is described as socially organized and integrated if there is an internal consensus on its norms and values, a strong cohesion exists among its members, and social interaction proceeds in an orderly way. Conversely, the system is described as disorganized or anomic if there is a disruption in its social cohesion or integration, a breakdown in social control, or malalignment among its elements.

Both theories propose that the less there exists solidarity, cohesion, or integration within a group, community, or society, the higher will be the rate of crime and deviance. Each attempts to explain high rates of crime and delinquency in disadvantaged lower-class and ethnic groups. At one time or another, both theories have focused specifically on delinquent or criminal gangs and subcultures.

Social Disorganization and the Urban Ecology of Crime and Delinquency

Social disorganization theory was first developed in the studies of urban crime and delinquency by sociologists at the University of Chicago and the Institute for Juvenile Research in Chicago in the 1920s and 1930s (Shaw and McKay, 1942; 1969). Since then, the theory has most often been applied to urban crime and deviance, though the concept of social disorganization has also been applied to the conditions of a family, a whole society, or some segment of society (Rose, 1954). The Chicago studies plotted out the residential location of those youths who had been referred to juvenile court from different areas of the city. These studies showed that the distribution of delinquents around the city fits a systematic pattern. The rates of delinquency in the lower-class neighborhoods were highest near the inner city and decreased outwardly toward the more affluent areas. The inner city neighborhoods maintained high rates of delinquency over decades, even though the racial and ethnic makeup of the population in those areas underwent substantial change. The same pattern of declining rates of delinquency as the distance from the inner city neighborhood increased was found within each racial or ethnic group (Shaw and McKay, 1942; 1969).

These findings were explained by reference to a theory of urban ecology which viewed the city as analogous to the natural ecological communities of plants and animals (Park et al., 1928). The residential, commercial, and industrial pattern of urban settlement was described as developing an ecological pattern of concentric zones that spread from the center toward the outermost edge of the city. Directly adjacent to the city's commercial and business core of the city was a "zone in transition," which was changing from residential to commercial. It was in this area that the highest rates of delinquency were found.

This transition zone was characterized by physical decay, poor housing, incomplete and broken families, high rates of illegitimate births, and an unstable, heterogeneous population. The residents were at the bottom end of the socio-economic scale with low income, education, and occupations. In addition to high rates of delinquency, this area had high official rates of adult crime, drug addiction, alcoholism, prostitution, and mental illness. All these forms of deviance and lawlessness were interpreted as the outcome of social disorganization within this urban area. The Chicago sociologists emphasized that residents in this area were not biologically or psychologically abnormal. Rather, their crime and deviance were simply the normal responses of normal people to abnormal social conditions. Under these conditions, criminal and delinquent traditions developed and were culturally transmitted from one generation to the next. Industrialization, urbanization, and other social changes in modern society were seen by the Chicago sociologists as causing social disorganization by undermining the social control of traditional social order and values.

These sociologists were also concerned with the implications of their theory and research for delinquency prevention. They developed the

Chicago Area Projects in several of the lower-class, high-delinquency neighborhoods. These efforts were met with mixed success, though delinquency rates were in fact reduced in some neighborhoods. The objective of the Chicago Area Projects was to counter disorganization with social organization and informal social control geared toward conventional values and activities. Neighborhood organization was fostered by the development of local groups and clubs run by law-abiding adults in the community. Delinquent gangs were identified and social workers were assigned to make contact with them and try to involve them in alternatives to delinquent behavior. Recreational and athletic teams and other non-delinquent activities were organized for the youths in the area (see Lundman, 1993).

Research on Social Disorganization

Since the pioneering studies of Shaw and McKay, a great deal of research has been done on the ecology of urban crime and delinquency. Studies and research data on urban crime remain an important part of criminological research. While some studies have been patterned closely after the social disorganization approach of the early Chicago studies, others only indirectly relate to it.[1]

It is difficult to judge the extent to which the original Chicago research and subsequent research has verified social disorganization as an explanation of crime. A trend in the migration of both white and black middle-class residents, as well as industry and business, out of the large cities into suburban communities has resulted in even more deprivation, decay, and other conditions of social disorganization within the urban centers. This trend has left a population of the "truly disadvantaged" (Wilson, 1987) or an "under class" with high rates of unemployment, welfare support, illegitimate births, single-parent families, drug use and abuse, and violence. Research continues to find that arrests, convictions, incarcerations and other measures of official rates of crime and delinquency are alarmingly high among the residents in these neighborhoods.

To what degree the relationship between inner-city residence and crime is the result of social disorganization remains uncertain. Often the research does not carefully measure social disorganization. The very fact that crime and deviance are high within an area is itself sometimes used, tautologically, as an empirical indicator that the area is socially disorganized (see Bursik's 1988 review of this issue). Furthermore, even in those areas characterized as the most disorganized, only a minority of youths and even smaller minority of adults are involved in crime. There is also the question of how much concentration of official crime rates in these areas results from higher rates of criminal behavior among its residents or from race and class disparities in police practices (Warner and Pierce, 1993).

Moreover, exactly what physical, economic, population, or family conditions constitute social disorganization? Is it true that physical, economic, and population characteristics are objective indicators of disorganization, or does the term simply reflect a value judgment about lower-class lifestyle and living conditions? By the 1940s, the term "differential social organization" (Sutherland, 1947) had been introduced to emphasize that these urban neighborhoods may not be so much *dis*organized as simply *organized around* different values and concerns. Edwin Sutherland's (1947) education and part of his academic career was at the University of Chicago, and he acknowledged the influence of the Chicago sociologists (Sutherland, 1973). His theory of "differential association" complements differential social organization by explaining crime as behavior learned through an exposure to different conforming and criminal patterns (see Chapter 4 on social learning theory).

In recent years, social disorganization has received renewed theoretical attention through the work of Robert Bursik, Robert Sampson, and others who have re-analyzed the theory, related it to current theories, and addressed some of the criticisms of this theory (Sampson, 1995). Bursik (1988) points out that Shaw and McKay were not trying to propose that urban ecology, economic conditions of urban neighborhoods, and rapid social changes are the direct causes of crime and delinquency. Rather, he argues, they were proposing that social disorganization undermines or hinders informal social controls within the community and neighborhood, thus allowing high rates of crime to occur. Therefore, the absence or breakdown of social control is a key component behind the concept of social disorganization which, Bursik contends, ties it to modern social control theory (see Chapter 5). Bursik also links the assumptions of the ecological distribution of crime opportunities in routine activities theory to the social disorganization approach.

Sampson and Groves (1989) have pointed to the same problem identified by Bursik: social disorganization theory does not propose that such factors as social class and the racial composition of a community are direct causes of crime and delinquency. Yet, these are the variables that have been used to measure social disorganization. Research has not directly measured the *components* of social disorganization itself. Therefore, Sampson and Groves (1989:775) concluded that, "while past researchers have examined Shaw and McKay's prediction concerning community change and extra-local influence on delinquency, no one has directly tested their theory of social disorganization."

Sampson and Groves (1989) proffered an empirical model of social disorganization that remedied this problem. Their model contains the usual measures of "external" factors affecting social disorganization, such as social class, residential mobility, and family disruption, but then goes beyond these variables to include the measures of three key components of the concept of social disorganization: community supervision of teenage gangs, informal friendship networks, and participation in formal organizations. Their data from British communities supported this model. They found that most of the external factors were related to social disorganization, as predicted. The links in the model were completed by showing that the measures of social disorganization were good predictors of rates of crime victimization. Though not very adequately, the model also explained the rates of criminal offenses.

More recent research has not followed the Sampson and Grove model of measuring social disorganization directly. Social disorganization continues to be measured indirectly by social conditions in different areas of the city. Warner and Pierce (1993), for instance, report strong relationships between rates of telephone calls to police (by victims of assaults, robbery, and burglary) and neighborhood poverty, racial heterogeneity, residential instability, family disruption, and high density of housing units as measures of social disorganization. Gottfredson and associates (1991) tested social disorganization theory by correlating census-block level data on disrupted families, poverty, unemployment, income, and education with individual-level self-reports of delinquent behavior of interpersonal aggression, theft and vandalism, and drug use. The independent variables accounted for individuals' delinquency, but the relationships were not strong and varied by type of delinquency and gender. Moreover, the adolescents' social bonds and peer associations mediated the effects of social disorganization on delinquency.

‿ Anomie/Strain Theory

Merton's Anomie Theory

Anomie theory provides an explanation of the concentration of crime not only in the lower-class urban areas but also in lower- class and minority groups in general, as well as the overall high crime rate in American society. This theory leans heavily on the work of Emile Durkheim, one of the founders of sociology. Durkheim (1951 [1897]) used the term *anomie* to refer to a state of normlessness or lack of social regulation in modern society as one condition that promotes higher rates of suicide. Robert Merton (1938; 1957) applied this Durkheimian approach to the condition of modern industrial societies, especially in the United States. To Merton, an integrated society maintains a balance between social structure (approved social means) and culture (approved goals). Anomie is the form that societal malintegration takes when there is a dissociation between valued cultural ends and legitimate societal means to those ends.

Merton argued that American society evinces this means-ends disjuncture in two basic ways. First, the strong cultural emphasis on success goals in America is not matched by an equally strong emphasis on socially approved means. Everyone is socialized to aspire toward high achievement and success. Competitiveness and success is glorified by public authorities, taught in the schools, glamorized in the media, and encouraged by the values that are passed along from generation to generation. Worth is judged by material and monetary success. The American dream means that anyone can make it big.

Of course, this success is supposed to be achieved by an honest effort in legitimate educational, occupational, and economic endeavors. However, Merton perceived American values to be more concerned with acquiring success, getting ahead, and getting the money at any cost, than with the right and proper way to do so. While other industrial societies may have the same problem, American society is especially prone to stress achievement of the ends over utilization of approved means. Americans, then, are more likely than members of more integrated societies to do whatever it takes to achieve success, even if it means breaking the law. Hence, we have higher crimes rates than other societies.

Second, there is a discrepancy between means and ends perpetuated by the class system in American and, to a lesser degree, other industrialized societies. The success ethic permeates all levels of the class structure and is embodied in the educational system to which persons of all social classes are exposed. The American dream promotes the ideal that equal opportunity for success is available to all. In reality, however, disadvantaged minority groups and the lower class do not have equal access to such legitimate opportunities. They are socialized to hold high aspirations, yet they are relatively blocked off from the conventional educational and occupational opportunities needed to realize those ambitions. This anomic condition produces *strain* or pressure on these groups to take advantage of whatever effective means to income and success they can find, even if these means are illegitimate or illegal.

Merton (1938) identified five "modes of adaptation" to strain. The first, "conformity," is the most common response: one simply accepts the state of affairs and continues to strive for success within the restricted conventional means available. The second type of adaptation, "innovation," is the most common deviant response: one maintains commitment to success goals but takes advantage of illegitimate means to attain them. Most crime and delinquency, especially income-producing offenses, would fit into this adaptive mode. Another deviant mode, "rebellion," rejects the system altogether, both means and ends, and replaces it with a new one, such as a violent overthrow of the system. Yet another, "retreatism," refers to an escapist response: one becomes a societal dropout, giving up on both the goals and the effort to achieve them. Merton placed alcoholics, drug addicts, vagrants, and the severely mentally ill in this mode. Finally, there is "ritualism," in which one gives up the struggle to get ahead and concentrates on retaining what little has been gained, by adhering rigidly and zealously to the norms.

Innovation is the most frequently adapted non-conformist mode among members of the lower class. The high rate of crime in the lower class, therefore, is explained by its location in a society which subjects it to high levels of anomie-induced strain. This strain is produced by the disjuncture between society's dream of equality and success for all and the actual inequality in the distribution of opportunities to realize that dream. This inequity is most severe for members of the lower class, the disadvantaged, and minority groups. Relatively deprived of legitimate means, while still imbued with the American dream, they respond by resorting to illegitimate means.

Cohen: Status Deprivation and the Delinquent Subculture

Albert K. Cohen (1955) followed Merton by emphasizing the structural sources of strain that leads to deviant adaptations by the lower class. But Cohen applied it specifically to the delinquent subculture found among lower-class adolescent males. He recognized that the delinquent subculture has an effect on and plays a role in influencing individual lower-class boys to become involved in delinquent behavior. But he denied any interest in the explanation of variations in individual behavior. Instead, he wanted to explain, not why the delinquent subculture was maintained over a period of time, but why it existed in the first place.

Cohen's version of anomie theory is in basic agreement with Merton's theory, because both perceive blocked goals as producing deviance-inducing strain. However, rather than the inability to gain material success, in Cohen's view, it is the inability to gain status and acceptance in conventional society that produces the strain. Status in conventional society is achieved by meeting society's standards of dress, behavior, scholastic abilities, and so on. The most pervasive of these standards, according to Cohen, are those of the middle class. Adolescents are most likely to be confronted by the middle-class criteria of respectability and acceptance in the public schools. Middle-class expectations are imposed by teachers and administrators on students from all class backgrounds. Such standards as good manners, appropriate demeanor, non-aggressive attitudes and behavior, attention to grades, studying, and active participation in school activities are among the ways that students gain status and approval.

Middle-class adolescents, supported by middle-class parents, are best able to meet these standards. They achieve recognition and gain status by measuring up to these standards, not only in the eyes of adults but to a large extent in the eyes of their peers. However, lower-class youths, especially boys, cannot always meet these standards. They do not have the verbal and social skills to measure up to the yardstick of middle-class values. As a result, their "status deprivation" produces "status frustration."

According to Cohen, the delinquent subculture is a "reaction formation" to this frustration. The criteria for acceptability found in this subculture can be met by lower-class boys, who gain status in delinquent gangs by adhering to "malicious" and "negativistic" values in opposition to conventional standards. If non-aggression is acceptable in the middle class, then a reputation for aggressive toughness is the way to gain status in the delinquent subculture. If polite classroom behavior and making good grades will gain greater standing in the eyes of the teachers, then classroom disruption and disdain for academic achievement will gain greater standing in the delinquent subculture.

Cohen argued that Merton's image of deviants turning to illegitimate means because of the deprivation of legitimate means is too rationalistic to apply to the "non-utilitarian" delinquent subculture. For example, most of the property offenses committed by delinquent youths are really not intended to produce income or gain material success by illegal means. Rather, they are non-utilitarian responses to status frustration that also meet with the approval of delinquent peers.

Cloward and Ohlin: Differential Opportunity and Delinquent Subcultures

Shortly after Cohen's theory was published, Richard Cloward and Lloyd Ohlin (Cloward 1961; 1959) proposed a "differential opportunity" theory of delinquency. Their theory drew from the anomie theory of Merton and Cohen's subcultural theory on the one hand, and from Shaw and McKay's social disorganization and Sutherland's differential association theories on the other. Although the general propositions of their theory have subsequently been applied to a whole range of delinquent and criminal behavior, Cloward and Ohlin developed it specifically to account for types of, and participation in, delinquent subcultures.

In Cloward and Ohlin's view, Merton's anomie theory incorrectly assumed that lower-class persons, who are denied access to legitimate opportunities, automatically have access to illegitimate opportunities. They interpreted Sutherland, as well as Shaw and McKay, as focusing on the cultural transmission of delinquent values in lower-class urban areas and implicitly demonstrating the importance of the availability of illegitimate opportunities. Their theory combines anomie, differential association, and social disorganization by proposing that deviant adaptations are explained by location in both the legitimate and illegitimate opportunity structures.

Motivation and the aspiration to succeed by themselves do not account for either conforming or deviant behavior, argue Cloward and Ohlin. The individual must be in deviant or conforming "learning environments" which allow one to learn and perform the requisite skills and abilities. Just because legitimate opportunities are blocked does not necessarily mean that illegitimate opportunities are freely available. Some illegitimate roles may be available, while others may not be at all. Just as there is unequal access to role models and opportunities to fulfill conforming roles, there is unequal access to illegitimate roles and opportunities.

Among adolescent boys, it is clear that deprivation of legitimate means produces a strain toward delinquent activities, but what kind of delinquent patterns they will become involved in depends on what illegitimate opportunities are available to them in their community. Boys from racial and ethnic minorities, especially those in the lower-class neighborhoods of large urban centers, are most likely to be deprived of legitimate educational and occupational opportunities. Therefore, high rates of delinquency are to be expected among them. But the kind of subculture or gang delinquency they adopt depends on the nature of the illegitimate opportunities available to them. These opportunities are determined by the social organization of the neighborhoods or the areas of the city where they are raised.

While Cohen posited a single delinquent subculture, Cloward and Ohlin saw several subcultures. Though they recognized that delinquent gangs carry on a variety of illegal activities, they argued that these gangs develop more or less specialized delinquent subcultures, depending on the illegitimate opportunities in their neighborhoods.

The first major type of specialized delinquent subculture, "criminal," is characterized by youth gangs organized primarily to commit income-producing offenses, such as theft, extortion, and fraud. Theirs is a more or less utilitarian choice of illegal means that corresponds with Merton's innovation adaptation. Such gangs are found in lower-class ethnic neighborhoods organized around stable adult criminal patterns and values. Organized and successful criminals reside or operate openly in these neighborhoods, providing criminal role models and opportunities as alternatives to legitimate ones.

The second major type of delinquent subculture, "conflict," is expressed in fighting gangs. Status or "rep" in these groups is gained by being tough, violent, and able to fight. They are found in the socially disorganized lower-class neighborhoods with very few illegal opportunities to replace the legal opportunities that are denied them. There are few successful or emulated adult role models, either conventional or deviant. Youths become alienated from the adult world and view most of the adults they encounter as "weak." They are unable to develop the skills, either legitimate or illegal, to achieve economic success and see no way to gain conventional or criminal status. In frustration they turn to gangs in which the only status to be gained is by fearlessness and violence.

The third major type of delinquent subculture, "retreatist," is primarily focused on the consumption of drugs and alcohol. Retreatist gang members have given up on both goals and means, whether conventional or illegal. Cloward and Ohlin did not specify the type of neighborhood in which retreatist gangs are found, but they described their members as "double failures." Double failures not only perform poorly in school and have little or no occupational prospects, they are neither good crooks nor good fighters. They escape into a different world in which the only goal is the "kick" and being "cool." While most sustain themselves by one type or another of a non-violent "hustle," status and admiration can only be gained within the gang by getting high and maintaining a drug habit.

Miller: Focal Concerns of Lower-Class Culture

Walter B. Miller (1958), following Cohen and Cloward and Ohlin, concentrated on the delinquency of lower-class male gangs (or, in Miller's terms, "street corner groups") in economically deprived neighborhoods. He also agreed with strain theorists that the commission of delinquent behavior is motivated by the attempt to gain desired ends. But rather than positing a distinct delinquent subculture(s) adapted to the availability of legitimate or illegitimate opportunities, Miller proposed that delinquent behavior is a youthful adaptation to a distinct lower-class culture. Delinquency is one way of achieving or gaining acceptance according to the expectations of this lower-class culture. Lower-class youth learn and act according to the central values or "focal concerns" of lower-class adults, but the delinquent adolescents express and carry out these values in an exaggerated way. These are *trouble* (revolving around getting away with law violations), *toughness* (showing physical power and fearlessness), *smartness* (ability to con or dupe others), *excitement* (seeking thrills, risk-taking, danger), *fatalism* (being lucky or unlucky), and *autonomy* (freedom from authority, independence). By demonstrating toughness, smartness, autonomy, and the other characteristics implied in the focal concerns, lower-class males achieve status and belonging in the street corner groups. These qualities can be demonstrated and the valued ends achieved by fighting and other forms of illegal and deviant behavior.[2]

Research on Anomie/Strain Theory

Is Crime and Delinquency Concentrated in the Lower Class and Minority Groups?

Anomie theory provides some clear policy implications. If blocked legitimate opportunities motivate persons to achieve through criminal activity, then that activity can be countered by the provision of greater access to legitimate opportunities through educational and job-training programs. If delinquent gangs form in the city because of unequal opportunity and the availability of delinquent subcultures and illegal opportunities, then the objective should be to work directly with these gangs to offer alternatives to their subculture and provide law-abiding models and opportunities.

For instance, Cloward and Ohlin's theory became the specific theoretical framework for the New York community-based delinquency prevention program known as "Mobilization for Youth" in the 1960s. This project was designed to organize the local lower-class community and enhance the ability of youths to gain legitimate success through job opportunity, education, and skill training. Youth gang workers attempted to lead gangs away from delinquent values and activities and redirect their energies into sports and positive activities. Mobilization for Youth, unfortunately undermined by political opposition, was never completed. Neither that nor similar programs that followed were able to achieve their ambitious goal of changing the social structure of communities and thereby preventing crime and delinquency. Nevertheless, equal-opportunity and job-training programs for school dropouts and lower-class youths, and community delinquency prevention programs, still continue to this day (Siegel and Senna, 1991; Bynum and Thompson, 1992).

In both theory and practice, anomie theory emphasizes the predominance of crime and delinquency among the lower-class and minority populations, the most deprived of legitimate opportunities. All varieties of this theory discussed so far have predicted an inverse relationship between social class and law-breaking, and by extension of the assumptions and logic of anomie, one is also led to expect higher rates of crime and delinquency in disadvantaged minority groups.

As we have already seen, early urban research based on official statistics found a disproportionate amount of crime and delinquency in the lower-class and minority groups. Studies of self-reported delinquent behavior that began in the 1950s, however, raised serious questions about the class distribution of delinquency (Nye, 1958; Akers, 1964).

By the 1970s, nearly all of the self-reported delinquency studies, as well as the few self-report studies of adult crime, found little differences in the levels of delinquent behavior by socio-economic status (SES) (Tittle and Villemez, 1977). Studies using official measures of crime and delinquency continued to find more offenders in the lower class than in the middle and upper classes, but even in these studies the correlations were not high (Tittle et al., 1978). The effects of class and race were stronger in longitudinal studies of official arrest histories from delinquency to adult crime (Wolfgang et al., 1972; Wolfgang et al., 1987).

Some researchers have argued that, if self-report studies would utilize more effective measures of illegal behavior, then they too would find crime and delinquency to be related to both social class and race (Hindelang et al., 1979). They contend that self-report studies only measure the more trivial offenses and do not include high-frequency offenders, whereas official measures pick up the more serious, frequent, and chronic offenders. Their conclusion, then, is that there may be little difference by class and race in low-frequency, minor offenses, but there are considerable class and race differences in the most frequent and serious offenses.

This suggests that, if self-report studies would only do a better job of measuring more frequent and serious offenses, then they too would find that delinquency is strongly related to race and class. Some self-report studies that include high-frequency and serious offenses have found them most likely to occur in the lower class, as is found in studies using official measures (Hindelang et al., 1980; Elliott and Ageton, 1980; Thornberry and Farnworth, 1982). Up to now, however, "overall . . . recent analyses concerning the strength of an SES/delinquency relationship, as revealed by officially recorded measures relative to self-report measures, show mixed results" (Tittle and Meier, 1990).

Other researchers have concluded that, while there is no relationship between class and delinquency or crime in general, there is a relationship under some conditions. Some argue that a correlation exists when social class is dichotomized and the most disadvantaged underclass is compared with every other class level. Others maintain that the relationship is stronger among blacks than whites and among males than females. It has also been suggested that the relationship will hold true for urban centers but not for suburban communities, and for lower-class youths in middle- or upper-class communities but not for those in predominantly lower-class neighborhoods. However, research evidence does not clearly support a class/crime relationship under these conditions.

It is possible that the relationship between class-related access to legitimate opportunities and the official crime rate is different for blacks and whites. Lafree et al. (1992), for example, found that the burglary, homicide, and robbery arrest rates in the United States since 1957 were related in the expected direction to indicators of economic well-being among white males but not among black males. The unemployed are expected to experience the greatest strain of blocked opportunities and are more likely to commit crime than the gainfully employed. There is mixed support for this hypothesis. It is also proposed that offenders who are apprehended and imprisoned are more likely to come from the ranks of the unemployed (Chiricos, 1991). However, there is little evidence that unemployment motivates people to commit criminal acts. Moreover, crime is as likely to affect unemployment as vice versa (Thornberry and Christenson, 1984; Cantor and Land, 1985).

Self-report studies find class and race variations in criminal and delinquent behavior, but they are not as great as the class and race differences in officially arrested, convicted, and/or imprisoned populations. This may result in part from disparities in criminal justice decisions. But it may also result from a tendency for relatively small numbers of serious, chronic offenders who commit a large number of offenses, and who are the most likely to be caught up in the criminal justice system, to come from lower-class and minority groups. (See Chapter 8.)

Other Social Structural Correlates of Crime

Correlating crime with social class as a test of anomie conforms to Messner's (1988) argument that Merton's anomie theory is a theory of social organization, not a theory of individuals' criminal motivations. Therefore, the proper test of the empirical validity of anomie theory is to determine the social structural correlates of rates of crime. Bernard (1987) also contends that anomie theory is a structural theory that makes no direct predictions about individual criminal behavior, and anomie theory cannot be verified or falsified by individual-level tests (see also Burton and Cullen, 1992; Bernard and Snipes, 1995). There have been a number of macro-level studies testing the effects on city, region, and state crime rates of such structural factors such as class, poverty, inequality, unemployment, family instability, and racial heterogeneity. Although there are inconsistent findings in these studies, some have found fairly strong effects of these structural variables on both property and violent crime rates. (For a review of these studies and a report of new research on structural correlates of crime that resolves some of the earlier inconsistencies, see Land et al., 1990).

Much of this research is not presented as a test of anomie theory, and none of it provides a direct measure of anomie as malintegration of cultural goals and societal means. In this sense, no structural version of anomie has yet received substantial empirical support. Nevertheless, it is reasonable to infer anomie from conditions of inequality (and perhaps other structural variables). Thus, the findings on structural correlates of crime can be viewed as consistent with anomie theory. They are also consistent with social disorganization theory, because the variables included in the research are very similar to those measured at the local community or neighborhood level in research on social disorganization theory.

Steven Messner and Richard Rosenfeld (1994) propose that the impact of anomie fostered by economic inequality is conditional on the strength or weakness of non-economic social institutions that provide normative restraints against achieving material success by deviant means. The ability of the family, school, religion, law, and the political system to control the use of deviant means and support the utilization of legitimate means may be undermined by malintegration of cultural ends and social means. Therefore, the rate of crimes that offer monetary rewards, such as property offenses, may not be affected by expansion or contraction of economic opportunity without concomitant changes in other social institutions. Chamlin and Cochran (1995:415) provide partial support for this hypothesis that "the effect of economic conditions on instrumental crime rates will depend on the vitality of non-economic institutions." They found that the effect of poverty (as an indicator of economic inequality) on state rates of property crime are dependent in part on levels of church membership, divorce rates, and percentage of voters participating in elections (as indicators of strength of noneconomic institutions).

Gangs and Delinquent Subcultures

There can be little doubt that gang delinquency continues to be concentrated in the lower-class, black and Hispanic neighborhoods of Los Angeles, Chicago, Detroit, New York, and other large cities. Yet, there is considerable doubt as to how closely these urban gangs fit the theoretical specifications of Cohen and of Cloward and Ohlin. (See Schrag, 1962.)

Lower-class and non-white gang boys perceive more limited legitimate and more available illegitimate opportunities than middle-class, non-gang white boys. But whether these perceptions precede or result from gang membership is not clear (Short and Strodtbeck, 1965). Moreover, neither gang members nor other delinquents sustain a distinct subculture that promotes values and norms directly contrary to conventional culture. They are more likely to agree in general with conventional values and to "neutralize" or excuse their behavior that violates those values. Such excuses themselves come from the general culture and are conceptually linked to the concept of definitions in social learning (Sykes and Matza, 1957; Matza and Sykes, 1961). (See Chapter 4.)

As yet, researchers have been unable to verify Cloward and Ohlin's three major types of delinquent subcultures located in specific kinds of neighborhood opportunity structures. Recent research shows that there is some tendency for offense specialization by delinquent groups (Warr, 1996). However, this specialization does not conform closely to the types of subcultures identified in differential opportunity theory. Delinquent gangs can be very versatile, committing a wide range of violent, criminal, and drug offenses. Though some gangs and gang members are heavily involved in drug trafficking, there do not appear to be any "retreatist" gangs as described by Cloward and Ohlin, organized around the need for drugs. Drug use is high among all gangs, but then so is fighting and theft. (See Short and Strodtbeck, 1965; Spergel, 1964; see also Empey, 1967; Huff, 1990.)

School Dropout and Delinquency

According to anomie theory, particularly Cohen's version (1955), the school is an important arena in which lower-class youths are confronted with the failure to live up to the conventional standards for status. It is there that they continually face the realities of their academic and social liabilities. The school experience, therefore, is often filled with failure and a strain toward delinquency. If this is true, then dropping out of school would reduce the strain and the motivation to commit illegal acts. Elliott and Voss (1977) found some support for this hypothesis by comparing officially detected crime (up to age 19) for high school graduates with that of youngsters who had dropped out of school. The school dropouts had fairly high rates of delinquency while in school, but they reduced their offenses considerably after dropping out. However, the dropouts still had higher rates than the school graduates. It is also unclear how much of the decline in their delinquency resulted from leaving a stressful school situation and how much stemmed from the tendency for law violations to decline after age 17 among all groups.

Thornberry et al. (1985) found that arrests among school dropouts increased the year after leaving school and remained higher than the arrest rate for high-school graduates through age 25. Controlling for social class and race does not seem to change the findings (Thornberry et al., 1985). A later study with a national sample of adolescents found that dropping out of school sometimes increases delinquent involvement and sometimes lowers it. The effects of dropping out of school depend on the reasons for doing so and other factors such as race, age, and gender. When these other variables are controlled, most of the relationships between dropping out of school and delinquent behavior become statistically non-significant (Jarjoura, 1993).

Perceived Discrepancy Between Aspirations and Expectations

The gap between the cultural ends and social means proposed by anomie theory at the structural level implies that individuals in anomic situations may perceive this discrepancy. At the social psychological level, then, anomie can be directly measured by the difference between an individual's aspirations and expectations. Aspirations refer to what one hopes to achieve in life, economically, educationally or occupationally (e.g., how much schooling one would like to complete). Expectations refer to what one believes is realistically possible to achieve (e.g., how much education one would expect to get). Anomie theory would hypothesize that the greater the discrepancy between aspirations and expectations, the higher the probability of law violation.

There is not much empirical support for this hypothesis, however. The delinquent behavior of those youths who perceive a great discrepancy between their educational or occupational aspirations and their expectations do not differ much from the delinquency of those who perceive little or no gap between their aspirations and expectations. A bigger difference in delinquent behavior is found between those who have low aspirations and those who have high aspirations, regardless of the level of their expectations (Hirschi, 1969; Liska, 1971; Elliot et al., 1985; Burton and Cullen, 1992). Strain theory receives less empirical support than either social learning or social bonding when all three theories are directly compared (Akers and Cochran, 1985; McGee, 1992; Benda, 1994; Burton et al., 1994).

Farnworth and Leiber (1989) claim that these studies do not correctly measure anomie because they concentrate on gauging the difference between *educational* aspirations and expectations and between *occupational* aspirations and expectations. They propose that a better indicator would be the "disjunction between economic goals [the desire to make lots of money] and educational expectations" (Farnworth and Leiber, 1989:265). Their research found that the discrepancy between economic goals and educational expectations was a better predictor of delinquency than economic aspirations alone or the gap between the two. Contrary to their argument, however, the best predictor in the study was educational aspirations alone, without regard to expectations.

This suggests that the low level of empirical support for anomie/strain theory is not simply a matter of using poor measures of the concepts. This is underscored by research reported in Burton et al. (1994). They used the Farnworth-Lieber measure of the gap between economic aspirations and educational aspirations and included two other measures, perceived blocked opportunities and relative deprivation, in an adult white sample. They found that the gap measure was not related to self-reported crime. The other two measures were weakly related to criminal behavior. However, when variables from social bonding (marital status and family attachment), self-control (low impulse control), and social learning (definitions and differential association) theories were added the effects of anomie/strain variables disappear.

While Merton's anomie theory is broad in the sense that it can be applied to a fairly wide range of deviance, it is primarily designed as an explanation of one phenomenon, namely, concentration of crime in the lower class. Its scope is limited principally to ordinary property crime among the lower class or relatively disadvantaged. Later variations on the anomie theme, such as Cohen's and Cloward and Ohlin's theories narrow the scope of the theory even further by focusing only on lower-class, male, subcultural delinquency. Therefore, there seem to be limitations of theoretical scope and empirical verification in anomie/strain theory. Recognition of these limitations has led to reformulations of anomie theory to render it more general and empirically valid. I have mentioned examples of conceptual and empirical modifications in structural anomie theory. But the major revisions of anomie theory have been in social psychological strain theory.

Agnew's General Strain Theory of Crime and Delinquency

The most notable of these is the revision by Robert Agnew (1985; 1992). His approach is primarily to broaden the concept of strain, beyond that produced by the discrepancy between aspirations and expectations, to encompass several sources of stress or strain. According to Agnew's theory, crime and delinquency are an adaptation to stress, whatever the source of that stress. He identifies three major types of deviance-producing strain: the failure to achieve an individual's goals, the removal of positive or desired stimuli from the individual, and the confrontation of the individual with negative stimuli.

Failure to Achieve Positively Valued Goals
Included within this are three subtypes. First is the traditional concept of strain as the disjuncture between aspirations and expectations. Agnew expands this slightly to include not only ideal or future goals but more immediate goals. He also includes failure based not only on blocked opportunities but also on individual inadequacies in abilities and skills. Second is the gap between expectations and actual achievements, which leads to anger, resentment, and disappointment. The third subtype results from a discrepancy between what one views as a fair or just outcome and the actual outcome. In this subtype, the positive consequences of an activity or relationship are not perceived as comparable to the amount of effort put into it and are viewed as unfair when compared to others' efforts.

Removal of Positively Valued Stimuli

This source of strain refers primarily to the individual's experience with the stressful life events that can befall adolescents, such as the loss of something or someone of great worth. The loss of a girlfriend or boyfriend, the death or illness of a friend or family member, suspension from school, or changing schools can all produce anomic feelings.

Confrontation With Negative Stimuli

This type refers to another set of stressful life events that involve the individual's confrontation with negative actions by others. An adolescent may have been exposed to child abuse, victimization, adverse school experiences, and other "noxious stimuli." Since adolescents cannot legally escape from family and school, legitimate ways to avoid stress from parents or teachers are blocked. This motivates the individual to react in a deviant way.

Deviant actions may be taken to deal with stress by getting around it, seeking vengeance against the perceived source of the strain, or retreating into drug use. Deviance is most likely to occur when the response to strain is *anger*. Anger results when the system or others, rather than oneself, are blamed for the adverse experiences (see also Bernard, 1990).

As in previous strain theories, Agnew's general strain theory views crime and delinquency as only one of several possible adaptations to strain. Whether a conforming or deviant mode is adopted depends on a number of internal and external constraints on the individual. These constraints, such as peer associations, beliefs, attributions of causes, and self-efficacy, affect the individual's predisposition to select a delinquent response to strain.

Agnew's theory represents a significant advancement beyond traditional strain theory. He has given more viability to strain theory, which should better facilitate its purpose to explain crime and delinquency than earlier strain theories. Its focus remains primarily on negative pressures toward deviance which, Agnew claims, clearly distinguishes it from social bonding and social learning theories. Moreover, since the various strains are experienced by individuals in any class or race, there is no need for strain theory to be tied only to class or race differences in delinquent behavior. Since strain is not confined only to the disjunctures between means and ends, a number of other measures beyond the discrepancy between aspirations and expectations can now be used. In specifying the types of strain (especially the second and third) and outlining factors that influence each adaptation, Agnew moves strain theory closer to social bonding and social learning theories, thereby incorporating a number of explanatory variables from those theories.

Agnew and White (1992) reported empirical support for general strain theory. They found that a summary measure of various sources of strain are positively related to delinquency and drug use. The effects of strain are conditioned by, but not wholly dependent on, variables taken from social learning and social control theories. However, they also found in their study that the variable with the strongest effect on delinquency and drug use is the delinquency of peers. Brezina (1996) tested the hypothesis from general strain theory that delinquency is an adaptive response that reduces the "negative affect" (anger, resentment, fear, and despair) generated by stress in the family and school. The hypothesis was supported with cross-sectional data but not with longitudinal data. General strain theory should fare better empirically than the more limited strain theories of the past, but additional research is needed before adequate assessment of its empirical validity can be made.

Summary

Anomie/strain and social disorganization theories hypothesize that social order, stability, and integration are conducive to conformity, while disorder and malintegration are conducive to crime and deviance. Anomie is the form that societal malintegration takes when there is a dissociation between valued cultural ends and legitimate societal means to those ends.

The more disorganized or anomic the group, community, or society, the higher the rate of crime and deviance. Merton proposed that anomie characterizes American society in general and is especially high in the lower classes because they are more blocked off from legitimate opportunities. High levels of anomie and social disorganization in lower-class and disadvantaged ethnic groups, therefore, are hypothesized to be the cause of the high rates of crime and delinquency in these groups. At the individual level, the strain produced by discrepancies between the educational and occupational goals toward which one aspires and the achievements actually expected are hypothesized to increase the chances that one will engage in criminal or delinquent behavior. Research provides some support for these hypotheses in regards to class and race, but the relationships are usually not strong. Other structural variables are more strongly related to crime rates. Self-perceived aspirations/expectations discrepancy seems to be only weakly related to delinquency.

Cohen, and Cloward and Ohlin, modified Merton's theory to apply anomie to lower-class delinquent gangs. Miller theorized that the delinquency of street corner groups expresses the focal concerns of lower-class culture. Research shows clearly that gang delinquency continues to be concentrated in the lower-class and minority neighborhoods of large cities. But research has not verified that urban gangs fit very well into the theoretical specifications of Cohen, Cloward and Ohlin, and other subcultural versions of anomie theory.

Messner and Rosenfeld suggest that the crime effect of economic inequality is dependent upon the strength of non-economic institutions. Agnew has proposed a modification of anomie/strain theory, primarily by broadening the concept of strain to encompass several sources of strain, failure to achieve goals, removal of positive or desired stimuli from the individual, and exposure to negative stimuli. Research offers some support for this modified strain theory, but there has not been enough done as yet to assess its empirical validity.

Notes

1. See the studies in Lander (1954), Shaw and McKay (1969), Voss and Petersen (1971), Wilson (1987), and Simcha-Fagan and Schwartz (1986). For recent reviews of theoretical issues and research on social disorganization that address and offer solutions to some of the problems inherent in the earlier theory, see Bursik (1988), Sampson and Groves (1989), and Warner and Pierce (1993). See also the introductory reviews of social disorganization theory and research in Vold and Bernard (1986), Shoemaker (1990), Holman and Quinn (1992), and Curran and Renzetti (1994).

2. Others have used the concept of subculture as a specific explanation of violence. Wolfgang and Ferracuti (1982) relate the violence of lower-class, young, and disproportionately black males to a subculture of violence. Others have attempted to explain the high rates of homicide in the South by referring to a Southern regional subculture of violence. Research casts doubt on the subculture of violence thesis of both the regional and class type (Erlanger, 1974; 1976).

CHAPTER 8

CONFLICT THEORY

Introduction

Conflict theory begins with the assumption that society is not held together by agreement and consensus on major values but rather is:

> [A] congeries of groups held together in a dynamic equilibrium of opposing group interests and efforts. The continuity of group interactions, the endless series of moves and countermoves, of checks and cross-checks . . . in an immediate and dynamically maintained equilibrium . . . provides opportunity for a continuous possibility of shifting positions, of gaining or losing status, with the consequent need to maintain an alert defense of one's positions. . . . Conflict is viewed, therefore, as one of the principal and essential social processes upon which the continuing on-going society depends. (Vold, 1958:204)

Power is the principal determinant of the outcome of this conflict. The most powerful groups control the law, so that their values are adopted as the legal standards for behavior. The members of less powerful groups, though they suffer legislative and judicial defeats, continue to act in accordance with their internal group norms, which means violating the law. Thus, conflict theory offers both an explanation of law and criminal justice and an explanation of criminal and deviant behavior. In the first part of this chapter, conflict theory is contrasted with consensus/functionalist theory as an explanation of law and criminal justice. In the second part, the theory that crime is produced by group and culture conflict is presented and evaluated.

Law is a Type of Social Control

Social control consists of a normative system with rules about the way people should and should not behave, and a system of formal and informal mechanisms used to control deviation from, and promote conformity to, these rules. Informal social control exists in the family, friendship groups, churches, neighborhoods, and other groups in the community. Formal social control includes law and the criminal justice system, in which the rules are officially promulgated and enforced by legally authorized agents.

— These two forms of social control are viewed by some theorists as inversely related. A breakdown in informal control brings about an increase in formal control, and informal controls grow out of the need to fill gaps left by the disintegration of formal control. Donald Black (1976) hypothesizes the following:

> Law is stronger where other social control is weaker. *Law varies inversely with other social control.* . . . Thus, it varies across the centuries, growing as every kind of social control dies away—not only in the family but in the village, church, work place, and neighborhood. (Black, 1976:107-109; emphasis in original)

Social control relies in large measure on socialization. Socialization is the process of teaching and learning values, norms, and customs through example and the application of positive and negative social sanctions. Conventional morality and values are acquired through socialization within the family, church, and other social institutions. An important outcome of this socialization process is the individual's internalization of societal norms and the development of self-control. To the extent that the law contains the same values and norms which individuals have learned and now adhere to, they will constrain their own behavior in conformity with the law. The fact that most members of a society, most of the time, conform to social expectations rests primarily on the strength of this self-control. However, no informal or formal social control system depends entirely on internal control. External sanctions are applied both directly and indirectly, not only in the socialization of children, but in the informal interaction and socialization that continues through adulthood in society. The giving or withholding of affection, praise or ridicule, acceptance or rejection, and other forms of social sanctions all help to maintain compliance with social norms (Akers, 1985:5-6).

Law differs from other types of social control, however, in that it relies primarily on the external application of formal negative sanctions in the form of punishment for wrongdoing. The main feature of law that differentiates it from other forms of social control in modern society is the fact that its sanctions are supported by the legitimized and authoritative coercion of the state (Akers, 1965). Law is the system of rules promulgated and enforced by the sovereign political state that exercises authority over a territory and recognizes no higher secular authority (see the definitions in Davis, 1962:41; Akers and Hawkins, 1975:5-16).

> Every normative system induces or coerces activity. The normative system we have defined as "law" uses State power to this end. (Chambliss and Seidman, 1971:10)

This definition encompasses both the substantive law on the books and the law in action.

There are two major perspectives on the enactment and enforcement of the law by the political state. The first views the law as developing out of a widespread normative *consensus* in society and reflecting the common interests of society as a whole. The second views law as the product of a *conflict* between group interests and the exercise of power in society. The law on the books and in action endorses and protects the narrow interests of those groups as they wield economic, social, and political power (Quinney, 1969; 1970; Chambliss and Seidman, 1971; 1982; Bernard, 1983). Consensus and conflict theorists agree that the law is both shaped by and has an impact on the social structure. However, they differ on their basic image of society (Sutherland, Cressey, and Luckenbill, 1992:32-42; Ritzer, 1992:230-273).

Consensus and Functionalist Theories of Law

Until the 1960s, the major sociological approach to law and social control was based on some form of *consensus* theory, which views the formal system of laws and enforcement as incorporating those norms in society on which there is the greatest normative consensus. This approach is represented principally by the writings of late nineteenth- and early twentieth-century sociologists (Sumner, 1906; Ross, 1901; Durkheim, 1964 [1893]; Weber, 1954 [1921]).

Emile Durkheim (1964 [1893]) theorized that the content and general nature of the law evolves from the type of "solidarity" that characterizes the society. His thesis was that in those less complex societies with "mechanical solidarity," whose members are integrated by their common values and beliefs, the law is especially "repressive" or punitive. In complex and diverse societies that are integrated more by functional interdependence, "organic solidarity," than by cultural sameness, the criminal law moves from harsh and brutal forms of punishment to deprivation of liberty through incarceration as the main penalty for crime. The law is aimed more toward restitution than severe punishment and geared primarily toward civil and constitutional law. Max Weber (1954 [1921]) proposed that, as the social organization of economically advanced societies become more rational, the law also becomes more rational. The rationality of law is based on adherence to the rule of law characterized by due process and fair procedure determined by established legal principles and rules ("formal rationality") rather than on the fairness of the actual outcome of the process judged according to the interests or ideology of particular individuals or groups ("substantive rationality").

While E. A. Ross (1901) and other early sociologists espoused similar views, the classic statement of consensus theory of law was given by William Graham Sumner (1906). To Sumner, the content of the law is developed primarily by the formal codification, through legislation and court rulings, of the prevailing "folkways and mores." These are unorganized, intuitive principles of right and wrong that have gradually evolved over a long period of time and to which all segments of society subscribe. While not immutable, folkways and mores are persistent and slow to change. When laws are passed, they express these underlying mores. Legislation cannot create new mores, nor does law readily change existing mores. Sumner should be interpreted to mean that legislation cannot modify the mores quickly or easily, rather than that all law flows directly from the mores or that it cannot induce any social change (Ball et al., 1962). Nevertheless, Sumner's main emphasis was on how the law is shaped by the customs of society. He dismissed attempts to alter custom through law as futile exercises in social engineering. (For a good review of Weber's, Durkheim's, and Sumner's theories of law, see Trevino, 1996.)

This type of consensus model was more dominant in the early part of this century. However, its importance has declined since the 1950s, and today no major theorist considers this to be the best model of the law. To the extent that assumptions or hypotheses about consensus theory are still given credence in current theories of law, they are most apt to be found in "mutualist" models, "the mutually reinforcing potential of laws and norms" (Schwartz 1986:65), or in some type of conflict model.

The same can be said of *functionalist* theory that "underscores the *consensual* norms and values of society, the social system's orderly state of *equilibrium*, and the law's ultimate function of social *integration*" (Trevino, 1996:333). Functionalism overlaps with, and may be considered to be a variant of, consensus theory. It views the law as functioning for the greater public welfare. By the orderly settlement of disputes, regulation of disruptive behavior and control of crime, the law serves the interests of everyone in society and not just the special interests of certain powerful groups. This should not be taken to mean that the emphasis in functionalism is only on the effectiveness of the law in controlling deviance in society. The theory also recognizes that laws serve *symbolic* functions for society and officially condemn certain behavior, whether or not they actually deter it. Although functionalist explanations of law have had more recent adherents than the traditional consensus model (Davis, 1966; Friedman, 1975), neither has many proponents today. However, functionalist and consensus notions have not been dropped entirely. They have been recast and retained in pluralistic conflict theory.

Conflict Theory of Law and Criminal Justice

Conflict theory began to challenge consensus and functional models in sociology in the 1950s (Dahrendorf, 1959). Although discussions of conflict theory often refer to Karl Marx, this approach is more directly traced back to the European sociologist Georg Simmel (1950), who viewed conflict as a fundamental social process. Its chief proponent in criminology at that time was George Vold who, in his classic *Theoretical Criminology* (1958), proposed that group conflict explains not only criminal law and justice but criminal behavior as well.

> [T]he whole political process of law making, law breaking, and law enforcement becomes a direct reflection of deep-seated and fundamental conflicts between interest groups and their more general struggles for the control of the police power of the state. Those who produce legislative majorities win control over the police power and dominate the policies that decide who is likely to be involved in violation of the law. (Vold, 1958:208-209)

Thomas Bernard has maintained Vold's statement of the theory with some extensions and expansions in his revisions of Vold's book (Vold and Bernard, 1986).[1]

In the 1960s, several criminologists, most notably Richard Quinney (1964; 1969; 1970), William Chambliss (1964: 1969), and Austin Turk (1964; 1966; 1969a) further developed the conflict approach and placed it at the forefront of criminological theory. They argued that criminological theory had for too long focused almost exclusively on explaining criminal behavior, and that theoretical attention needed to be shifted toward the explanation of criminal law. Turk (1964:1969a) maintained that the central task of criminological theory was not to untangle the causes of criminal behavior but to explain criminality, the process by which certain behavior and individuals are formally designated as criminal. Chambliss (1975:i-ii) agreed: "Instead of asking, 'Why do some people commit crimes and others do not?' we ask, 'Why are some acts defined as criminal while others are not?' " Conflict theory answers that question: both the formulation and enforcement of the law serve the interests of the more powerful groups in society.[2]

Even the early consensus theorists observed that the law on the books and the law in action often favor the interests of special groups (Ball and Simpson, 1962; Sumner, 1906:39, 55, 169). But this observation is not at the heart of consensus theory; it is central to conflict theory. Diversity and lack of uniformity, not commonality of values, is the hallmark of modern society. Conflict theory portrays society in a more or less continuing state of conflict among groups (Ritzer, 1992:262-271). Social structure is the working arrangements, coalitions, and balancing forces "in a shifting but dynamic equilibrium of opposing group interests and efforts" (Vold, 1958:204).

The values and interests of various groups conflict with one another to the degree that what is considered normal in one group may be considered deviant in another. The dominant groups can see to it that their particular definitions of normality or deviance will become enacted as law, ensconced in public policy, and protected by the operation of the criminal justice system. When the behavior of members from subordinate groups clash with the law, they are less able to resist official apprehension, prosecution, conviction, and incarceration for criminal charges. The theory is succinctly stated by Quinney:

> (Formulation of Criminal Definitions): Criminal definitions [laws] describe behavior that conflicts with the interests of the segments of society that have the power to shape public policy. (Quinney, 1970:16)
>
> (Application of Criminal Definitions): Criminal definitions are applied by the segments of society that have the power to shape the enforcement and administration of criminal law. (Quinney, 1970:18)

Class, race, sex, age, ethnicity, and other characteristics that denote social position in society determine who gets apprehended and punished. Thus, the economically and socially disadvantaged groups of lower class, minorities, youth, women, and others will be similarly disadvantaged and differentially processed through the criminal justice system.

The theory developed by Quinney, Chambliss, Turk, and others emphasized power and coercion in the formulation and administration of law, but it left some room for consensus and the protection of the interests of the less powerful by the law:

> In many cases there is no conflict whatsoever between those in power and those not. For most crimes against the person, such as murder, assault, and rape, there is consensus throughout society as to the desirability of imposing legal sanctions for persons who commit these acts. It is also true that laws are passed which reflect the interests of the general population and which are antithetical to the interests of those in power. (Chambliss, 1969:10)

Although consensus is recognized, law and criminal justice are explained primarily by reference to power and group conflict. Law is both the result of, and a weapon to be used in, group conflict (Turk, 1976). Although some groups or alliances maintain considerable power over a period of time and on many issues, no single group or interest is all-powerful. There are the social, economic, and political elites that may have overlapping interests but do not constitute a monolithic, all-powerful class that perpetually gets its way in the law, economy, and society.

Quinney (1970) and other conflict theorists rejected "pluralism," because they believed it views the political state as nothing more than a fair and neutral arena for the expression and adjudication of competing interests. This disdain for pluralism is also found in the radical, critical, and Marxist theories to which many of the conflict theorists of the 1960s came to subscribe in the 1970s (see Chapter 9). Nevertheless, their earlier statements of conflict theory are clearly pluralistic in the sense that they recognize several power centers, rather than one all-encompassing power elite, and admit that criminal law does indeed embody some common values. These are the central features of the *pluralistic conflict* model explicated by Akers (Akers and Hawkins, 1975; Akers, 1985).

Theoretical efforts, such as the "integrative conflict model" of McGarrell and Castellano (1991), have continued to develop the pluralistic conflict model of criminal law. McGarrell and Castellano propose three levels of factors that come into play in the process of crime legislation and policy making. At the highest level are the fundamental social-structural conflicts generated by heterogeneity and inequality and the symbolic cultural conflicts in public perceptions and "myths" about crime. At the mid-level are rates of victimization, fear of crime, and persistent public demands for the punishment of criminals. At the third level are the more immediate events and activities that trigger legislative action to change policy, such as media reports on crime problems, interest-group activities, reform campaigns, and political events.

Recent developments of the pluralistic conflict model continue to reject the image of the system as tightly controlled by a small, powerful elite at the top. Instead, it is characterized as a decentralized, "loosely coupled" system into which multiple elites and competing groups interject their influence, but which responds to institutional, economic, and political changes (Hagan, 1989c; Wright, 1993a; McGarrell, 1993; Walker et al., 1996).

> Policies gradually emerge through a complex process of negotiation, bargaining, and compromise. Implemented policies seldom resemble the initial proposals of particular interest groups; rather, goals and solutions are twisted, amended, watered-down, combined, and distorted, so that while most parties are appeased, few are fully satisfied. (Wright, 1993a:145)

The pluralistic conflict model applies to democratic societies in which competing interest groups attempt to uphold their values through the legislature and government. There is an underlying agreement among all groups on the legitimacy of the political system, which no group will use its power to overthrow. Within this system and process, however, the groups with the most power and resources, best organization, or greatest numbers will be the winners. Highly organized political pressure groups actively seek the protection of their values and interests by legislation and try to influence the actions of governmental officials and bureaucrats in administering the laws. Pressure groups also try to influence executive appointments and the legislative confirmation of judges to appellate and supreme courts in an effort to ensure appointments of those who share their views and special interests. These interest groups need not take any direct action to have their influence felt. Many lawmakers, judges, police officers, and government executives require virtually no direct pressure to act according to the best interests of the groups with which they identify.

A complete listing of interest groups would be an endless task, but the variety of interests can be categorized into a more limited number of groupings. For instance, one study of all registered state lobbyists in the United States categorized over 39,000 different lobbying actions into 14 distinct types of interest groups. These include single-issue pressure groups, trade groups, governmental bodies, citizen activist groups, professions, unions, manufacturing groups, and others. These various interests fit into four general clusters: industry and finance groups, resource producers and economic growth groups, single-issue groups, and governmental bodies, unions, and non-profit organizations (Brunk and Wilson, 1991).

Such competing interests, however, need not exist only in distinct, organized pressure groups with headquarters, budgets, and registered lobbyists. They can be found in large-scale social movements and in broadly defined economic, political, social, regional, religious, gender, ethnic, racial, age, and other divisions and segments of society. Of course, many of these are represented by one or more political-action groups. It should also be noted that the interests threatened or defended by criminal law may be as much symbolic as material. Laws against prostitution, drugs, and certain kinds of sexual behavior, for instance, will be staunchly defended and actively promoted by certain groups, because such laws formally endorse a moral stance against such behavior, even though these groups have no economic or political stake in the laws and know that they may be ineffective in controlling such behavior.

Although politically dominant subgroups and segments of society may be successful in imposing their interests on public policy, the law also reflects the general interests of society as a whole. Not all legislation and administration of laws stem from compromises and victories by identifiable group interests. The core of criminal law—prohibitions of and sanctions for personal violence, destruction of property, fraud, and other predatory crimes—mirrors and protects the interests of the entire society. This core outlaws offenses that are *mala in se*, wrong in themselves, and that would be abhorred by society even if not condemned by the law. On the other hand, there is likely to be more conflict and less consensus on offenses that are seen as only *mala prohibita*, wrong only because they have been prohibited by law. Laws on sexual behavior, drugs, alcohol, business activities, and other areas usually generate more conflict in the process of their passage and enforcement. Even for *mala in se* offenses, there remains considerable conflict over what the proper legal sanctions should be. All condemn murder, for instance, but not all agree on what behavior and/or circumstances constitute murder or what moral grounds justify the death penalty.

Furthermore, even some of the core criminal law, on which there is strong consensus today, may have originally been devised to serve the interests of one segment of society. For instance, while we now categorize embezzlement as a crime, at one time it was not considered a crime at all. Taking possession of entrusted property or money was then perceived as a matter of personal injury to one person who foolishly trusted another with his or her money or goods. It was not deemed as criminal theft. Legally, theft had to involve actual trespass on someone's property to steal valuables. The landed aristocracy was served by the trespass law, while the interests of the merchant class were better served by adding laws that defined the conversion of entrusted property as a crime. At that time the power of the aristocracy was in decline, while the rising class of entrepreneurs was gaining power. Hence, the ultimate change in law reflected that shifting power balance in society (Hall, 1952).

Even when the law has been subjected to direct pressure by interest groups or modified to the benefit of powerful classes or segments of society, broad public opinion may still be a factor. A powerful group or coalition of groups frequently tries to shape public sentiments, so they at least take on the appearance of consensus. At the same time, a group that champions a cause which is consistent with existing common values and public opinion has a far better chance of success in winning over a conflict with other groups. The news media play a major role in this process (Hollinger and Lanza-Kaduce, 1988; Castellano and McGarrell, 1991). Politicians and the public alike may be alerted to a problem perceived to be in need of legislation through news stories and editorials. Public opinion both shapes and, in turn, is shaped by media coverage.

This conflict approach to law and criminal justice was incorporated into labeling theory that also was developed in the 1950s and 1960s (see Chapter 6). Therefore, there is essentially no difference between conflict and labeling theory in explaining the formation and operation of social and legal norms. The two do offer different explanations of criminal and deviant behavior.

◈ Empirical Validity of Consensus and Conflict Theories of Law and Criminal Justice

Research on Legislation and Public Opinion on Crimes

There are three types of empirical studies that try to evaluate the validity of conflict and labeling theory as an explanation of criminal law and justice. The first type studies the influence of interest groups on legislation, administrative regulations, and court decisions. It may involve research on law making during early historical periods or on law and policy in more recent, contemporary times. These studies have investigated the background and nature of group conflict in the formation of laws on theft, vagrancy, prostitution, drugs, smoking, kidnapping, gun control, juvenile delinquency, computer crimes, and other areas of crime-control policy.[3]

These studies have identified specific groups involved in influencing the enactment of the law and the establishment of public policy. Some of these are well-organized pressure groups, while others are more diffuse regional, labor, business, farm, religious, professional, and other interests. Even law enforcement agencies and government bureaucracies have themselves acted as special-interest groups in the formation and enforcement of laws. The preponderance of evidence from these studies provides little support for either a pure consensus model or a model in which one elite group controls all legislation. The findings are most consistent with a pluralistic conflict model.

> What emerges [from the research] is a picture of crime-control legislation that is the product of conflict and competition among a number of interest groups that differ over time and issue. The consistent finding of conflict over values and interests, and the finding that most laws appear targeted at the urban poor raise fundamental questions about the moral functionalist position. The lack of identifiable business or capital involvement raises questions about the moral Marxist interpretation. (McGarrell and Castellano, 1991:176)

The second type of study relevant to evaluating conflict theory includes research on the consensus or dissensus in public opinion about what, and how strongly, acts are disapproved. If the laws resonate with agreed-upon public morality and values, then there ought to be some consensus in public opinion and some congruence between the legal and social definitions of wrong-doing and consequent penalties. These studies show that there is a consensus that cuts across class, age, sex, educational, racial, and regional groups on the condemnation of criminal behavior found in the core criminal law. Those acts defined by criminal law as the most serious offenses that carry the most severe penalties (e.g., murder, assault, rape, robbery, and theft) are the same ones that citizens agree are the most heinous and threatening to society. Violent personal crimes are rated as the most serious, with drug trafficking offenses not far behind and property offenses ranking somewhat lower. Offenses to public morality and order (e.g., public drunkenness or disorderly conduct) and consensual acts committed in private (e.g., prostitution) rank the lowest, with considerably more disagreement on their disapproval (Rossi et al., 1974; Wellford, 1975; Pease et al., 1975; Thomas et al., 1976; Wolfgang et al., 1985).

There is a sizable variation in the average opinion for some kinds of behavior (Miethe, 1982). Differing circumstances often mitigate the severity of sanctions advocated by certain people for different acts, even when there is a consensual agreement that they are wrong and should be defined as illegal (Lanza-Kaduce et al., 1979). The consensus found in these studies is real and not simply an artifact of the research methods. However, the findings do not support a pure consensus model of the law. Rather, they are more in line with a pluralistic conflict explanation. The acts prohibited by criminal law are the ones over which there is the most consensus and greatest moral condemnation in society. But there are many areas of the law over which there is just as much conflict and disagreement.

Research on Legal and Extra-legal Variables in the Criminal Justice System

The third type of relevant study, and the most frequently conducted, examines the exercise of discretion in applying the law against accused or suspected juvenile or adult law violators. Conflict and labeling theorists contend that criminal justice decisions (to arrest, prosecute, convict, and punish) will be biased against the less powerful in society. In their view, the criminal justice system upholds the values and interests of the middle and upper classes, protects property and business, and favors the protection of the more influential and powerful members of society. Therefore, members of less powerful groups are more likely to be arrested, prosecuted, convicted, and given more severe penalties for committing the same offenses than the members of favored groups. Specifically, the hypothesis proposes that criminal justice decisions are based more on *extra-legal variables,* such as race, class, age, and gender, than on relevant behavioral and *legal variables,* such as the defendant's charged offenses, prior criminal record, and guilt or innocence. (For tests of a different set of hypotheses regarding police-citizen contacts taken from Turk's conflict theory, see Greenleaf and Lonn Lanza-Kaduce, 1995, and Lonn Lanza-Kaduce and Greenleaf, 1994).

Paternoster and Iovanni (1989) claim that labeling and conflict theories make no strong claims in this regard. They argue that they only hypothesize that extra-legal variables play "some" role, however minor or insignificant, in formal labeling decisions. This would be a very minimal claim which, if it were the main prediction by the theory, would be very easy to support, because finding anything with more than a zero effect of extra-legal variables would count in its favor. However, labeling and conflict theories can just as easily be interpreted as making the more extreme prediction that *only* extra-legal variables determine who gets labelled as criminal. In this version, the offense behavior and other legally relevant variables play no part whatsoever in the actions by police, courts, and correctional officials. It would be very difficult to find evidence to verify this prediction, because a finding of anything more than a zero effect of the legal variables would falsify it. Neither of these extremes, however, represents the most common and reasonable interpretation of the conflict perspective on criminal justice. It is usually interpreted to predict that extra-legal variables have substantial effects on criminal justice decisions that are as strong as, or stronger than, the effects of legal variables.

This makes the theory much more testable. It is some version of this hypothesis that usually gets tested in empirical research. The preponderance of evidence from that research weighs against the hypothesis. Criminal justice decisions are more likely to be based on legally relevant, neutral, and non-biased legal factors than they are on extra-legal variables. There is little question that disproportionate numbers of some groups undergo arrest, conviction, and imprisonment. Adolescent and young adult, lower-class, and minority males are very much over-represented in arrests, prosecutions, convictions, and imprisonments. But by itself, a finding of differences by race, class, sex, or age in the criminal justice system does not support conflict theory. One cannot simply assume that the observed differences have resulted primarily from decisions biased against the less powerful. Before such a conclusion can be accepted, other questions must be answered.

The first question is, do the differences correspond to the ones hypothesized in the theory? Some in fact do. For instance, blacks and the poor are over-represented in the criminal justice system (Walker et al., 1996). But other differences contradict the hypothesis that the less powerful will be treated more harshly and be more stigmatized than the more powerful. For example, as a group, men have more power and status in society than women; yet, male offenders vastly outnumber female offenders in the criminal and juvenile justice systems. They are much more likely to be arrested, convicted, and given long prison sentences than women.

Similarly, American Indians are more disadvantaged and less powerful than black Americans who in turn are on the whole more disadvantaged that white Americans. Yet, a recent study found that black and Native American youth are more likely to receive lenient treatment in the juvenile justice system than whites, with the Indian youth more likely to receive lenient treatment than youth in either of the other two groups. "[T]he disparity in outcome for minority youths, as compared with white youths, lies with the youth themselves and with their families rather than with the decision makers and the law" (Lieber, 1994:273).

Second, and more important, is the question of the extent to which the decisions are based on these social characteristics, rather than on the behavior of the offender and the legal aspects of the case. To support the conflict/labeling hypothesis, research must demonstrate that people are treated differently based on their social status, even for the same criminal behavior and legal circumstances. That is, to support the hypothesis, the observed differences should be based primarily on something other than law-violative behavior and legally relevant variations in offense seriousness and criminal background. Even if men were less powerful than women, the theory would not be confirmed—because men are much more likely than women to be the most serious and frequent criminal offenders. Men's predominance in arrested, convicted, and incarcerated populations, then, results from their predominance in the population of offenders rather than from their gender. Thus, one must control for legal variables to determine if the extra-legal variables have an independent effect on criminal justice decisions.

It is on this point that research evidence is the most damaging to the hypothesis that decisions in the criminal justice process are predominantly based on extra-legal variables. When legal variables (e.g., seriousness of the offense, prior criminal record, and aggravating circumstances) are controlled, differences in arrests, court outcomes, and the severity of sentencing by race, class, sex, age, and ethnicity either disappear or are reduced to small, statistically insignificant levels.[4] One theorist has been so convinced by research on the primacy of legal over extra-legal variables in the criminal justice system that he calls the common assumption of racism in the system a "myth" (Wilbanks, 1987). This overstates the case, however. It may be a myth that the system is grossly discriminatory, with legal niceties always laid aside in favor of race-based or other biased decisions. Overall, research has found a relatively even-handed law enforcement, judicial, and correctional system. It is not a myth that race, class, and other extra-legal variables in some places do in fact influence decisions about adults and juveniles in the justice system.[5] As Walker et al. (1996) note, there is "contextual discrimination" in which race-based decisions occur in some parts, at some stages, and by some individuals but not by others in the criminal justice system.

However, the influence of these variables on criminal justice decisions tends not to produce large differences in typical outcomes. Even studies that have found the independent effects of extra-legal variables often report such effects as fairly small and secondary to the effects of the legal variables (for instance, see Bishop and Frazier, 1989).

In more recent research, Bishop and Frazier (1996) have found significant disparities by race that remain, even controlling for legal variables in juvenile cases. In Florida, black youth were treated more harshly in the juvenile justice system for major offenses, while white youth were treated more harshly for minor status offenses. However, Bishop and Frazier found that these differences were not based on deliberate discrimination. Rather, formally race-neutral policies, practices, and judicial philosophies that affect judges' decisions were in practice correlated with race, favorable to white youth in delinquency cases, and unfavorable to them in dependency and status offense cases.

> Intentional race discrimination does not appear to play a major role in accounting for racial disparities in processing. . . . Without question, there are some justice officials who hold and act upon racially prejudicial attitudes. . . . However, we are not inclined to conclude that the disparities we observed are largely attributable to intentional race discrimination. . . . Instead, we see much evidence of institutional racism. . . . (Bishop and Frazier, 1996:412)

In most research, the more serious the offense, the more likely it is that decisions will remain neutral on race, class, and other status characteristics of the offender. Discretionary decisions are more apt to produce such disparities in minor offenses. There appears to be some racism, sexism, and class bias in the system, but they have relatively weak effect on actual arrest, conviction, and sanctioning outcomes. On the whole, whatever effect these factors may have operate in a subtle, complex fashion, rather than in a direct, unequivocally discriminatory manner.

An illustration of this complex intertwining of variables is found in research involving race effects on the imposition of the death penalty in homicide convictions. In spite of a "history of capital punishment in the United States prior to the Furman decision [that] is marked by inequality and discrimination" (Radelet, 1981:918), research on the death penalty has not found significant disparities in capital sentencing based on the race of the offender. Indeed, when racial differences are found, convicted white murderers face double the risk of a death sentence than do black murderers. However, there *is* a pattern of prosecution and sentencing disparities based on the race of the homicide *victim*. The greater probability of a death penalty for white murderers appears to result from the fact that their victims are also likely to be white. When murder victims are white, regardless of the race of offender, the convicted murderer is more likely to be sentenced to death. This is primarily because the one who murders a white person is more likely to be indicted and prosecuted for first-degree homicide, the only conviction that carries the possibility of capital punishment. The most likely offender-victim combination to result in prosecution for first-degree murder and the death penalty is that of a black murderer and a white victim, even when all measurable legal variables are controlled (Radelet, 1981; Radelet and Pierce, 1991). Neither race of offender nor offender/victim race category is related to rate of incarceration or length of sentence for violent crimes in general; rather, the strongest predictors of sentencing are legal variables, such as seriousness of the crime committed and the offender's prior criminal record. But the race of offender/race of victim is a significant variable in sentencing for murder and sex offenses (Spohn, 1994).

A similar pattern is observed in sentencing of female murderers in Alabama from 1929 to 1985. White female murderers were twice as likely to be given life sentence as black female murderers. However, there is a noticeable difference in life sentencing among the small number (20) of cases of interracial homicides. In those cases, half of the black offenders who had murdered white victims received life sentences, while no white offender who had murdered a black victim received a life sentence. Moreover, this sentencing inequity was more prominent in the pre-civil rights era (1929-1964) than in the post-civil rights era (Hanke, 1995).

Not all racial differences can be interpreted as racially motivated. Rather they may reflect what Petersilia and Turner (1987) call "disparities" rather than "discrimination" in the system.

> Racial *discrimination* occurs if the system officials make ad hoc decisions based on race rather than on clearly defined objective standards. . . . However, racial *disparity* occurs when such standards are applied but have different results for different racial groups. (Petersilia and Turner, 1987:153; emphasis in original)

The final question that remains is, how is it that a system found by careful research to be relatively even-handed in arrest, prosecution, conviction, and sentencing can produce a prison population that is so disproportionately black, male, and poor? Research conducted at any stage of criminal justice processing reports little difference by race, class, or gender when the proper legalistic variables are controlled. Yet, as one moves from the beginning stage of arrest to the end stage of imprisonment or intermediate sanctioning, class, gender, and other disparities increase. One answer may be that relatively small differences at each decision point accumulate to the extent that larger differences seem to exist at the end of the process (Liska and Tausig, 1979; Bishop and Frazier, 1989; Horowitz and Pottieger, 1991).

Another answer may lie in the research on habitual and career criminals. These are the chronic offenders who commit multiple offenses, continue their criminal activity at a high level, fill the jails, and populate the prisons. For example, a study of an urban birth cohort found that, by age 18, 50 percent of black male youths and 28 percent of white male youths have had at least one encounter with police. Among these delinquent offenders was found a small group of chronic recidivists (6 percent) who accounted for more than half (52 percent) of police arrests. Race and social class were among those most strongly related to the seriousness and repetitiveness of their delinquency (Wolfgang et al., 1972). Although most of those with juvenile arrest records did not continue into adulthood with a criminal record, almost 80 percent of the small group of chronic juvenile offenders pursued criminal careers as adults, again with black and lower-class men over-represented among them (Wolfgang et al., 1987; see also Shannon, 1982).

These "chronic persisters" (Blumstein et al., 1985), whose behavior and lifestyle place them most at risk for official attention by the criminal justice system are disproportionately black and poor. This results in more frequent arrests, accumulating an official record on which later criminal justice sanctioning decisions are based. They may also be subjected to the policy of "selective incapacitation" (Blumstein et al., 1978; Bernard and Ritti, 1991), in which habitual offenders are singled out for longer prison terms to keep them off the streets for a longer time. The over-representation of certain groups in prison populations, then, may be the end product of a combination of their higher frequency and longer lasting criminal behavior and the greater attention they attract at an early stage from law enforcement.

The research on disparities in the criminal justice system almost exclusively examines formal decision points—arrest, indictment, conviction, and sentencing. It does not look closely at racial and neighborhood disparities in informal and unauthorized actions taken on the street. It may be that racial and class biases are found in the patterns of police patrols, citizen harassment, stop and search, stop and interrogate, use of excessive force, and other actions taken by the police in the community that do not get recorded.

It may be that it is this ongoing pattern known to the black community, along with well-publicized and sensational cases, such as the infamous beating of a black traffic offender, Rodney King, by white Los Angeles police officers, that continues to support the image of an extremely racially-biased and class-biased criminal justice system (see below). When brought to trial on criminal charges of brutality and excessive force in the beating, the white officers were acquitted by a largely white jury. But the characterization of the whole system cannot be based on such highly publicized court decisions. Nor can it be based on a single famous murder trial, such as that in which a largely black jury acquitted O. J. Simpson, a famous black athlete and movie star, of charges that he murdered his ex-wife Nicole and Ron Goldman, both of whom were white. It cannot be based on local cases, such as those in my home community of Alachua County, Florida, in which it was discovered that the black county criminal justice administrator had a prior criminal conviction for homicide and had recently violated conditions of parole by having a weapon in his home. This fact had been known to, but kept secret by, the county executive who had hired him. The criminal justice administrator was not arrested and was allowed by the local state's attorney to enter into a pre-trial diversion agreement for a period of six months without facing charges in court and without the possibility of serving prison time for the violation. At the same time, a self-employed white man with the same history and the same violation of fire arms possession was arrested, convicted, and given a severe prison sentence. Conclusions about the empirical validity of conflict and labeling theory, regarding the extent of racial or other discrimination in the system, cannot be based on anecdotes and singular cases such as these. Rather they must be based on careful observation and research findings.

Conflict Theory of Criminal Behavior

Conflict theory views the whole process of law-making, law-breaking, and law enforcement as implicated in the conflict and power differentials among social, economic, and political interest groups. Criminal behavior is a reflection of this ongoing collective conflict. This conflict explanation is best exemplified in Vold's group conflict theory (1958:203-219). It also bears a relationship to the cultural and normative conflict theories of crime by Thorsten Sellin (1938) and Edwin Sutherland (1947; 1973). Conflict theory explains crime and deviant behavior as the ordinary, learned, and normal behavior of individuals caught up in *cultural* and *group* conflict. Crime is an expression of that conflict and results when persons acting according to the norms and values of their own group violate those of another group that have been enacted into law (Sellin, 1938; Sutherland, 1947; Sutherland and Cressey, 1970).

For example, foreign immigrants may violate the laws of a new country simply by behaving according to the customs of the old country.

Even rural migrants within the same country may carry a set of conduct norms and values with them into a city, which results in a conflict with urban laws. Religious, ethnic, and other cultural minority groups may adhere to a set of behavioral standards that conflict with those of dominant conventional society.

Other crimes may result from direct group conflict. Both major and minor crimes are committed by dissident groups protesting against or trying to induce change in the established political and social order. Civil rights protestors have engaged in civil disobedience and broken the law, not because they were personally motivated to commit crime, but because they espoused the interests of a group that define the laws as instruments of an unjust system. On the other side of the coin, blacks have been lynched, churches have been bombed, and other acts of violence have been inflicted on both blacks and whites by those (including some in law enforcement) who support a system they believed to be right and just.

In the case mentioned above, a large-scale 1992 riot in the predominantly black South-Central Los Angeles area followed the not-guilty verdict for white police officers charged with criminal assault against Rodney King, a black citizen who had been stopped for speeding. Allegedly perceived as a serious threat by the officers, King was stungunned and repeatedly beaten. A subsequent review of communications tapes among the officers indicated racism, and an eyewitness video tape of the beating was publicized nationwide. The case against the officers seemed airtight. Their subsequent acquittal was met by outrage, dismay, and disbelief all across the country, but many black citizens in South-Central Los Angeles reacted with violence. They took to the streets and burned buildings, looted business establishments, and severely beat white motorists. In the ensuing melee both black and white residents were killed.

Certainly, many of the rioters were motivated simply by the opportunity to steal, a large number of them already with long criminal records. But a major motivation for many blacks, Hispanics, and others was the view that the verdict confirmed what they already believed—the whole criminal justice system is racist and serves mainly to suppress minorities. Their behavior, then, reflected long-standing racial and ethnic conflict. Similarly, many of the attacks targeted against Korean businesses was a continuation of a long-term conflict between Korean immigrants and native black residents in the area.[6]

Law violation growing out of group conflict may be a non-violent disruption or simply non-compliance with police orders to disperse, but often it goes beyond this to violence and property damage. For example, pro-life activists have damaged property and broken laws in their efforts to close down abortion clinics; on the other hand, pro-abortion activists have assaulted anti-abortion protestors. In another case, a clinic abortionist was murdered by an anti-abortion zealot. Both sides adamantly believe they are right, resulting in violence and an open defiance of the law.

If such protest reached the point of questioning the entire system, the outcome could be a violent revolution. During the Vietnam War era, for example, protests against the war and the draft often resulted in large-scale conflict with the law. Radical groups, determined to change the system, bombed buildings and committed violence in the name of their own brand of justice. In a revolution, all forms of terrorism are justified by ideology. As radical groups clash with the police, such criminal offenses as murder, sabotage, seizure of property, destruction, theft, and burglary may occur. To protect the established legal system, the police and other authorities may also violate the law (e.g., "police brutality") in the course of controlling the protests.

Such crimes are typically *political crimes* (Vold, 1958; Quinney, 1964). Political crimes are best defined as law violations motivated by the desire to influence existing public policy, the political system, or power relations (Minor, 1975). Political crime may be committed by those who oppose the existing system and want to change or destroy it. It may also be committed by officials in the government, law enforcement, or the criminal justice system in order to defend the status quo or change the system in the desired direction. The infamous crimes and obstruction of justice committed by President Nixon and his White House staff in the 1970s, commonly known as Watergate, are a clear historical example of political crime. They used the power of government and law enforcement agencies against groups and individuals who were perceived as threats to the power and authority of the established regime.[7]

Who is deemed a criminal depends on which side prevails in the conflict. If a protest or revolution is successful, the former rulers become the criminals; if not, the rebels remain the criminals. White supremacists, who previously enforced the Jim Crow laws and branded blacks who broke them as criminals, are today the ones who are more likely to be considered criminals for violating civil rights laws. The collapse of the Soviet Union and communist regimes in eastern Europe is another example. Those who were dissidents violated communist law under the old regimes, but now many of them are in power. Former rulers have been indicted and convicted of crimes or are now fugitives being sought by law enforcement under the control of the newly elected governments.

In politically or ideologically motivated crimes, offenders perceive themselves as fighters for the cause of higher loyalties and values. They publicly announce their violations and disavow the law. Conflict theorists, however, often try to explain crime even when these elements are absent and the offenders acknowledge the legitimacy of the laws they are breaking. For instance, Vold viewed delinquent gangs as groups supporting values in conflict with the dominant majority. He also analyzed organized crime as a type of business system that is in conflict with the laws of legitimate society.

Empirical Validity of Conflict Theory of Criminal Behavior

Many other illustrations of crime related to group and culture conflict could be given here, but research that explicitly tests hypotheses from conflict theory of criminal behavior is quite rare. One study found no correlation between the number of political interest groups and the crime rate, but did find some relationship between crime and the *type* of interest groups (Brunk and Wilson, 1991). The dearth of such studies means that the validity and scope of conflict theory have not been adequately tested. Despite this fact, some observations can be made on the theory's empirical applicability to crime.

Conflict theory portrays modern society as so heterogeneous that there is little value consensus among the population at large. Crisscrossing and balancing cleavages and group compromises form the basis for the organization of society today. There is some validity to this conflict image, but it remains incomplete. There is more to society than the working arrangement of a congeries of conflicting groups and interests. Society is also held together by the larger or smaller number of widely supported values, common assumptions, and images of the world. This is a chief factor in providing some continuity and unity in a diversified society. We cannot explain the criminal behavior of those who violate these broad values and norms as simply acting on behalf of some group interest in conflict with the dominant view. Of course, groups conflict and values clash in the enactment of laws, but it does not necessarily follow that most crime is simply the result of a continuation of that conflict beyond legislative battles. Nor is it true that those from groups who win a political battle will faithfully adhere to the law, while those on the losing side will typically violate the law.

Vold emphasized conflict among more or less organized interest groups. He excluded the "impulsive, irrational acts of a criminal nature that are quite unrelated to any battle between different interest groups in organized society" (Vold, 1958:219). He also warned that the "group conflict hypothesis should not be stretched too far" (Vold, 1958:219). Nevertheless, he stretched the theory to cover many types of crime, including organized crime and white-collar crime (Vold, 1958:220-261), and "a considerable amount of crime" in general (Vold 1958:219).

However, the empirical scope of conflict theory is much less than this. Conflict theory applies accurately to a narrow range of crimes, of which only politically or ideologically motivated crimes will fit the model well. The vast majority of juvenile delinquency and adult crime cannot be explained as simply behavior incidental to group and cultural conflict. Most crime is intra-group, committed by members inside a group against one another, rather than inter-group.

Partly acknowledging the limited scope of conflict theory to explain criminal behavior, other conflict theorists have typically refrained from or disavowed efforts to explain criminal behavior as the result of group or cultural conflict. Rather, they have emphasized group power and conflict in the process of making and enforcing laws, while turning to other explanations to answer the question of why people violate the law. Quinney (1970), for instance, uses power and conflict to explain the formulation and application of criminal law. But when addressing the behavior of those who violate the law, he relies on differential association, learning, self-concept, and other variables outside of conflict theory. Bernard (Vold and Bernard, 1986:286-290) proposes a "unified conflict theory of crime" to explain both criminal behavior and criminal law, which retains Vold's emphasis on "disparate and conflicting sets of values and interests." In so doing, Bernard "incorporates into the context of Vold's argument the principles of operant conditioning and social learning, as developed by Ronald Akers" (Vold and Bernard, 1986:288). (See Chapter 11.)

Summary

Law is the formal part of the overall social control system of society. It both reflects and has an impact on social, economic, political, and other institutions in society. Consensus theory explains the content and operation of the law by reference to a broad-based agreement in society on social and moral norms and the common interests of all elements of society. Conflict theory proposes that law and the criminal justice system primarily embody the interests and norms of the most powerful groups in society, rather than those of the society as a whole; and that the law will be enforced by the criminal justice system in a manner that unfairly labels and punishes the less powerful in society.

The empirical evidence on consensus and conflict theories stems from studies of the enactment of law, studies of public opinion on crime, and studies of race, class, sex, and age disparities in arrests, convictions, and penalties. The research tends to favor a pluralistic conflict model, in which there is consensus on core legal norms but conflict among competing interest groups in making and enforcing the law. Research evidence does not show that racism and sexism blatantly infests the criminal justice system. At the same time, it does not show that the system is free of bias. The preponderance of research findings, however, support the conclusion, contrary to extreme conflict theory but consistent with pluralistic conflict theory (Walker et al., 1996), that the criminal justice system makes decisions based more on legally relevant variables than on extra-legal variables.

Conflict theory explains crime as the behavior of individuals caught up in cultural and group conflict. There is very little research, however, to test this theory of criminal behavior. Politically or ideologically motivated crime would seem to fit the conflict model well. On the other hand, conflict theory does not fit juvenile delinquency nor the vast majority of crime, such as murder, theft, burglary, rape, arson, white-collar crime, and organized crime. Conflict theory has greater empirical support as an explanation of law formation than as an explanation of the operation of the criminal justice system or as an explanation of criminal behavior.

Notes

1. See the summary of Bernard's "unified conflict theory" of criminal behavior and criminal law in Chapter 11.

2. For early statements of the conflict theory of criminal law, see Chambliss (1964; 1969), Chambliss and Seidman (1971), Quinney, (1969; 1970), Turk (1966; 1969a), and Hills (1971). For later statements, see Akers and Hawkins (1975), Akers (1985), Turk (1977; 1979), Alix (1978), and Reasons and Rich (1978). For recent reviews and updating of conflict theory, see Bridges and Myers (1994).

3. See Hall (1952), Becker (1963), Chambliss (1964), Dickson (1968), Roby (1969), Platt (1969), Alix (1978), Galliher and Walker (1977), Hagan and Leon (1977), Hagan (1980), Troyer and Markle (1983), Hollinger and Lanza-Kaduce (1988), and Castellano and McGarrell (1991).

4. There is a very large body of literature on this point. See, for instance, Hagan (1973), Blumstein (1982), Marshall and Thomas (1983), Hagan (1974), Blumstein (1982), Kleck (1985), Zatz (1987), Klein et al. (1988), Corley et al. (1989), and reviews of a wide range of studies in the literature by Hagan (1974), Williams (1980), Wilbanks (1987), Tittle and Curran (1988), Paternoster and Iovanni (1989), and Walker et al. (1996). A related body of literature has to do with what effect the "demeanor" of the suspect toward the police has on the police decision to arrest. Research on this issue finds that controlling for demeanor reduces racial differences in arrests and that even when suspected criminal conduct is held constant, a hostile or disrespectful demeanor increases the chances that the suspect will be arrested (Klinger, 1996; Worden and Shepard, 1996). This finding suggests that hostility is interpreted by the police as a challenge to authority. However, since demeanor may be seen as relevant to probable cause, it is unclear whether it is a legal or extra-legal variable.

5. See the findings in Petersilia (1983), Petersilia and Turner (1987), Kempf and Austin (1986), Bridges and Crutchfield (1988), Bishop and Frazier (1989), Horowitz and Pottieger (1991), Smith and Akers (1993), and Walker et al. (1996).

6. Two of the police officers were subsequently convicted in federal court for violation of Mr. King's civil rights, though they were given short prison sentences. Neither this verdict nor the sentences were followed by disorder in the streets.

7. Crimes by public officials for personal monetary or political gain, on the other hand, are instances of occupational or white-collar crime, rather than politically motivated crime.

CHAPTER 9

MARXIST AND CRITICAL THEORIES

Marxist Theory

onflict theory, along with labeling theory, gained prominence in American sociology and criminology in the 1960s. In the 1970s, some conflict theorists in the United States began to shift toward a Marxist perspective and rejected their earlier conflict approach. By the mid-1970s, Richard Quinney (1974a; 1974b), William Chambliss (1975; Chambliss and Seidman, 1982), Anthony Platt (1977; Platt and Tagaki, 1981), Herman and Julia Schwendinger (1981; 1984), and other conflict theorists of the 1960s had repudiated their earlier adherence to conflict theory of law and criminal justice and had embraced Marxist theory or endorsed "radical" or "critical" theories that were viewed as synonymous with or closely related to Marxist theory.[1] This historical connection of Marxist theory with conflict theory presents an "interesting paradox of a Marxism reared in the womb of theoretical structures to which it was, and is, ostensibly largely opposed" (Beirne and Quinney, 1982:8).

Marxist theory has in common with conflict theory an interest in explaining both law and criminal justice but rejects the multi-group conflict image of society and endorses a power-elite model of society, in which social, economic, and political power has been concentrated into the hands of a small ruling class in "late-stage capitalism." Late-stage or advanced capitalism is the label that Marxists have given to highly industrially developed democracies (Mankoff, 1970). In Marxist theory, capitalism is a two-class system comprised of the ruling class that owns the means of production (the capitalists or the bourgeoisie) versus the proletariat, the workers or masses who have only their labor to sell. The capitalists' monopoly on the means of production allows them also to control the political state. This political power is used to manipulate the legal and criminal justice system to promote the interests of the capitalist class and to perpetuate its position of power. Repressed by this system, the masses of workers have no power whatsoever to ameliorate or modify their oppression. This situation will remain until they become organized for revolution, take power into their hands, overthrow the government, and destroy the capitalist economy. After this revolutionary period, the proletariat will establish a socialist system that will ultimately evolve into a class-free communist system, in which there will be economic and social equality, justice will prevail, the political state will wither away, and the law will be unnecessary.

A major example of Marxist theory in criminology is found in the work of Richard Quinney (1974a; 1974b; 1979; 1980). Quinney proposes that whatever conflicts exist amidst the diversity of interests in society are concentrated within the basic, underlying struggle between the proletariat and the bourgeoisie. What appears to be internal conflicts within each of these two main classes is not real. In America and other late-stage capitalist societies, we are all either members of the ruling elite or members of the oppressed masses. If we are not owners of the means of production, we are workers subject to capitalist oppression, some of whom serve as lackeys to do the bidding (willingly or unwillingly) of the ruling elite. The objective interests of the masses lie with the proletariat. Any worker who does not recognize this objective interest and subjectively identifies with the bourgeois class possesses "false class-consciousness." Quinney (1979) claims that most intellectuals and academics in American society have false class-consciousness. This includes non-Marxist, "traditional" criminologists, who provide knowledge of criminals and criminal law for use by the ruling class to manipulate the crime problem in its own interests. Even though criminologists may view themselves as objective social scientists, in reality they serve the interests of the capitalist class.

All real power and authority is exclusive to the ruling class, whose primary goals are to maintain power and continue the existing capitalist order. In pursuit of these goals, capitalists promote interests that are antithetical to those of the proletariat, trampling the rights and aspirations of the masses. This basic contradiction between the reality of oppression and the democratic ideals of freedom and equality forces the capitalist elite to face a constant "crisis of legitimacy." If the masses ever reach the point of fully recognizing their repression by the elite, they will organize, revolt, and overthrow the system. They cannot be forever kept in check by force alone. Therefore, the elite must wage a ceaseless battle to maintain a cultural and ideological "hegemony" (sovereign control) over the "ruling ideas" of society. The ruling class manipulates the mass media, the intellectual and academic community, and other sources of public opinion, so that the masses will continue to believe in the legitimacy of the system. Quinney recognizes that there may be consensus on certain laws, but this does not necessarily show that these laws reflect the common experiences and support the interests of society as a whole. Existing consensus and order are imposed from above through force and the manipulation of public opinion.

Marxist Theory of Law and Criminal Justice

The law appears to operate in the interests of the whole society, while in reality it is structured to serve only the interests of the ruling elite. The criminal justice system is used against, rather than for, the people. Under capitalism, the system of law and punishment is inherently unjust, designed not to control crime for the good of society but to subjugate the population. For instance, imprisonment is imposed less as a direct punishment for convicted offenders than as a way to siphon off surplus labor from the population. Since a cycle of growth and depression is inherent in capitalism, there will be times when there are too many workers which the economy cannot absorb. These surplus laborers are a potential threat to the capitalists, since they could mobilize and organize themselves into a revolutionary movement. Therefore, the theory explains the imprisonment of criminal offenders as simply another way to regulate the availability and cost of labor. Imprisonment rates are expected to be high during times of recession and high unemployment, which is indicative of the capitalists' efforts to remove surplus workers from society until they are needed again for production.

According to Quinney, the criminal justice system is designed not to protect society against crime but, along with other institutions of the capitalist state, to repress the people. Since this is inevitable in a capitalist system, there is no way to accomplish real reform in order to ameliorate the plight of the proletariat. The whole system must be, and inevitably will be, destroyed. The only real solution to the crime problem is to join the class struggle, overthrow the capitalist system, and establish a socialist state. Marxist ideology maintains that this can only be brought about by violent means. In this case, however, Quinney departs from the Marxist stance, arguing that the system can be overthrown nonviolently and replaced with some form of democratic socialism.

Instrumentalist and Structuralist Marxism

Quinney's and similar explanations of law and the criminal justice system (see Balkan et al., 1980) are known as *instrumental* Marxism. This theory of the political state as only and always an instrument of the capitalist class underwent strong criticism by other criminologists. Some of the critics were themselves Marxists who proposed an alternative *structuralist* model of Marxism (Balbus, 1977; Chambliss and

Seidman, 1982). Partially in response to these criticism, Quinney and other instrumental Marxists modified their position to adhere closer to this structuralist model (Beirne and Quinney, 1982). The principal difference between the two is that the structuralists view the political state as having "relative autonomy." In other words, the state is not totally under the dominion of the ruling elite, and the law is not always just an instrument for the promotion of its interests. In the short run, then, the state may be autonomous. Much of the law and the criminal justice system do not automatically mirror the interests of the capitalists. Indeed, many laws may be passed that are directly counter to capitalist interests. Even individual members of the ruling class, if discovered breaking the law, may be apprehended and punished. Moreover, the structural model does not propose that this capitalist class is an entirely monolithic group. There may be internal factions within it that clash with each other. Particular laws and policies may promote the interests of some ruling-class members yet work against the interests of others. (See Balbus, 1977; Beirne, 1979; Greenberg, 1981a; Beirne and Quinney, 1982; Chambliss and Seidman, 1982).

This distinction between instrumentalist and structuralist Marxism can be sustained only in the short run. In the long run there is no difference between instrumentalist and structuralist Marxism. Both agree that the long-term historical tendency of the legal system is to reflect and protect the interest of the capitalist class and oppress the masses (Lynch and Groves, 1986). The only difference is that structural Marxism contends that in the short run, there are conflicts beyond the clash between capitalists and the proletariat, and that other power centers exist in society with the ability to counterbalance the power elite. The greater the extent to which Marxist theory is modified to account for a multiplicity of conflicts and power groups, the closer it becomes a variation on pluralistic conflict theory. Therefore, the structuralist model represents something of a movement by some Marxist criminologists back toward conflict theory.

Empirical Adequacy of Marxist Theory of Law and Justice

Marxist theory has been criticized for stating tautological propositions and dogmatic ideology rather than stating a testable theory of law making and law enforcement. Akers (1979) argues that much of what passes for Marxist theory is really an ideological condemnation of Western democracies and a call for revolutionary action to overthrow them. But he distinguishes the political philosophy of Marxism from Marxian analysis that does offer a verifiable theory.

One example of a testable Marxist hypothesis is that, as was explained earlier, the elite will ensure that imprisonment rates are high in times of depression and low in times of economic prosperity in order to control the labor supply. This effect of unemployment on imprisonment should remain even when changes in the crime rate are taken into account. However, the historical evidence to support this hypothesis is contradictory. Imprisonment rates were high during the Great Depression of the 1930s; yet, during times of economic growth and relatively low unemployment in the 1980s and 1990s, there has been the greatest increase in prison population in American history. In the few instances where this hypothesis has been tested directly with quantitative data, the empirical evidence has not supported it. The data show some fluctuation in imprisonment rates with changes in unemployment, but the magnitude of the changes in prison populations is not enough to have much effect on the number of unemployed persons in free society (Jankovic, 1977; Greenberg, 1980). The assumption of an inverse relationship between employment and imprisonment is not unique to Marxist theory, but it is certainly one that can be derived from it.

As a whole, however, there is little in Marxist theory of law and criminal justice that is empirically testable in this way. Marxists will argue that such attempts to create testable hypotheses and judge them on the basis of quantitative data is "bourgeois positivism" and not the proper way to evaluate Marxist theory. The only way to apply Marxist theory, they contend, is to examine history. Critics respond that, when Marxist theorists use historical analysis, they tend to focus only on the failings, fallacies, and injustices in Western democracies and pay scant attention to the historical elitism, repression, and injustices in systems founded on Marxist principles (Turk, 1979; Klockars, 1979; Akers, 1979).

This does not necessarily mean that the Marxist critiques of capitalist society have no validity. There is little doubt that the historical tendency in capitalist systems leans toward greater concentrations of wealth and power. We are currently in the era that seems to concern itself primarily with promoting and protecting a global system of trade and commerce that treats labor as a fungible commodity. In the process of downsizing, large corporations eliminate jobs in countries with relatively high income for the labor force, such as the United States, and move their industrial facilities to countries where workers are more impoverished and powerless. One does not need to read beyond newspaper headlines to know that the power of unions and the living standards of middleclass and working-class populations have been severely curtailed, while the living standards of the executives and owners of manufacturing and financial corporations are maintained or elevated. Domestic policies and the foreign policies of free trade serve more the interest of multinational corporations and international financial institutions than the interest of common workers. Marxist theory provides one way to explain how these high concentrations of economic power have an impact on law and justice in a capitalist society.

However, examining the structure and operation of capitalist systems alone is not adequate enough to evaluate Marxist theory. Akers (1979) argues that, to substantiate their theory, Marxist criminologists must make the proper kinds of comparisons between real socialist and real capitalist societies. As yet, Marxists have been very reluctant to make such comparisons. Instead, they compare an idealized, future socialist utopia with the realities of historical and present-day capitalist democracies. This is not a valid method for determining the validity of a theory.

Serious doubt has been raised about the historical accuracy of Marxist explanations for the formation and operation of law in society. Marxists make reference to the inherent contradictions and injustices of capitalism as an economic system, under which a repressive legal system is seen as inevitable. But, in fact, while some capitalistic societies have indeed been ruled by authoritarian political systems that use the police, courts, and prisons to repress the population, the most open, free, and democratic societies in history have had capitalist economies. On the other hand, Marxist theory denigrates civil liberties and individual rights as "bourgeois democracy" and favors instead a dictatorship of the proletariat, in which there is no protection of human rights (Lipset, 1960).

In spite of adopting such names as "people's democratic republic," Marxist regimes have invariably been totalitarian or authoritarian. They have not progressed to the point of instituting a classless society with a non-repressive system of law and criminal justice. Instead, they have produced a command economy, in which a small group of rulers control the economy, the law, and the criminal justice system to repress political dissent and protect its own power.

If ever there was any further doubt about it, the collapse of the communist regimes around the world in the latter part of the 1980s has finally unveiled the repressive police-state law enforcement systems that existed in Marxist governments. Even before the failure of Marxist political-economic systems, comparisons of real societies could not support Marxist assertions that the law is inevitably a repressive tool of the elite in a capitalist society, while it is used to promote justice in a socialist society. The injustices attributed to Western capitalist democracies by Marxists better describe the now defunct systems in the former Soviet Union and eastern Europe and the current regimes in Cuba, China, Vietnam, and North Korea. In these systems, the privileged elite has coopted the criminal justice system to perpetuate its own interests.

This historical reality has been largely ignored in Marxist analyses of law and criminal justice. However, structural Marxists are more likely than instrumental Marxists to acknowledge some of the realities of socialist systems. Many American Marxist scholars disavowed the Soviet Union and similar regimes as not truly socialist even before their dissolution. Some did make negative reference to the problems of political repression and contradictions in the Soviet system (see Chambliss and Seidman, 1982; Greenberg, 1981a). Yet, these references seemed to be relatively muted afterthoughts given in a larger context of detailed, unrelenting critiques of law and social control in American society. While the problems in socialist systems were likely to be dismissed as unfortunate aberrations unreflective of true socialism, the problems in Western democracies were viewed as inherent and unavoidable in late-stage capitalism. Moreover, some Marxists simply denied that there were any problems of human rights and repression in communist societies (Chase-Dunn, 1980; Szymanski, 1981).

Although there are differences among modern Marxist criminologists, to a great extent all their theoretical analyses are subject to the same criticism that Austin Turk made of the early twentieth-century Marxist Willem Bonger.

> Succinctly put, the point is that Bonger's thought founders largely because he was unable to escape the confines of his Marxism, i.e., to see that the political, conflict processes through which definitions of deviance (criminality) are created and enforced are not peculiar to "capitalist" societies, but are generic to social life. (Turk, 1969b:14)

Marxist Theory of Crime

Karl Marx wrote virtually nothing about criminal behavior, and many Marxist criminologists have long recognized that there can be no purely Marxist theory of crime (Taylor et al., 1973; 1975). As do conflict theorists, Marxists concentrate on criminal law and the criminal justice system. They have less to say about the causes of criminal behavior.

Even when examining the causes of crime, Marxists tend to refer more to the control by the system than to the behavior of criminal offenders. For example, Steven Spitzer (1975) proposed a "Marxian theory of deviance" which is widely cited as an example of a Marxist explanation for crime. Spitzer's model, however, is largely devoted to how those who steal, participate in delinquent gangs, become involved in revolutionary activities, or become unemployed are defined and controlled by capitalists as "problem populations." Little attention is paid to the etiology of crime among these problem populations. Spitzer does no more than sketch out the general features of capitalism, such as its "contradictions," that may induce criminal behavior. Such general reference to capitalism as embodying the causes of crime is typical of Marxist explanations of crime.

Bonger: Early Marxist Theory of Crime

The first systematic application of Marxism to the etiology of crime was offered by the Dutch criminologist Willem Bonger (1876-1940), who hypothesized that crime is produced by the "capitalistic organization of society" (Bonger, 1969 [1916]; van Bemmelen, 1972). Private ownership of the means of production, as well as the profit motive found in capitalist society, induces "egoistic tendencies," encourages greed and selfishness, and fails to promote "social instincts" which would otherwise prevent "egoistic thoughts from leading to egoistic acts." Bonger further claimed, "We shall show that, as a consequence of the present [capitalist economic system], man has become very egoistic and hence more *capable of crime* than if the environment had developed the germs of altruism" (Bonger, 1969:40-41; emphasis in original).

All classes are affected by the egoism and greed produced by capitalism; but since the law is controlled by the bourgeoisie, it is the egoistic actions of the proletariat that are defined as criminal. The cause of crime in all classes, therefore, is the capitalist mode of economic organization by which one's class position in society is defined by one's relationship to the means of production. Adult crime and juvenile delinquency, the criminality of women, prostitution, alcoholism, and other aspects of crime are to be expected because of economic conditions under capitalism.

Consequently, crime will always be high in capitalist society, and there can be no solution to crime under capitalism. If socialism, a system of "having the means of production held in common," were substituted for the present capitalist mode of property ownership, "material poverty would be no longer known" (Bonger, 1969:198). The profit motive would be eliminated, concern for the general social welfare would dominate over selfish privilege and competitiveness, and crime would be reduced to negligible levels.

> Such a [socialist] society will not only remove the causes which now make men egoistic . . . there can be no question of crime properly understood. . . . There will be crimes committed by pathological individuals, but this will come rather within the sphere of the physician than that of the judge. (Bonger, 1969:200)

Quinney: Class, State, and Crime

Bonger's theory received little acceptance when it first appeared. By the 1940s, its single-factor economic explanation of crime and naive faith in socialism had been essentially discounted in American criminology (Gillen, 1945:152-157). Non-Marxist class analysis predominated, and economic factors were seen as just one set among a large number of causes of crime. Mainstream sociological theory of class and crime (e.g., anomie theory) prevailed over Marxist class analysis. There was strong emphasis on social class and the "root" causes of crime, but this did not include the notion that the capitalist social structure itself was the root cause of all crime.

Marxist theory enjoyed an intellectual boom in the 1970s, as it came to occupy a position of influence and respect in Western social science. When these neo-Marxists turned their attention to the issue of crime causation, however, they offered essentially the same explanation of crime that Bonger had given several decades earlier—capitalism is the central cause of crime.

Among them were the British scholars Ian Taylor, Paul Walton, and Jock Young (Taylor et al., 1973; 1975), who delivered a scathing critique of the ideological and theoretical shortcomings of such "traditional" sociological theories of crime as anomie, social disorganization, social control, labeling, and social learning. Yet, they offered little more than an outline of what a radical theory of crime should be and failed to provide a viable alternative to these other theories. According to Taylor et al., crime is one significant consequence of the exploitation and oppression of the working class under capitalism. Most proletariat lawbreakers are motivated to commit crimes of "accommodation" (e.g., professional crime, theft, prostitution, and organized crime). Their offenses have no relevance for the proletarian class struggle, because they are simply surviving the best they can in an unjust society without trying to change it. Other offenders, however, commit crimes of "rebellion," political crimes carried out as part of the revolutionary struggle against the capitalist system.

Richard Quinney (1980) upheld the same view of crime as an inevitable response to the material conditions of capitalism. Echoing Taylor et al., he proposed that the crimes of the working class are either "crimes of accommodation" or "crimes of resistance" to the capitalist system. Crimes of accommodation are predatory crimes, such as burglary and robbery, which simply "reproduce" the capitalist system of acquisition of property by expropriating the income and property of others. Violent crimes, such as murder, assault, and rape, are also crimes of accommodation committed by those who have been "brutalized" by the capitalist system. Similarly, Michalowski (1985) views both violent and property crimes as "crimes of the powerless." Crimes of resistance, according to Quinney, include both non-revolutionary, unconscious reactions against exploitation and crimes deliberately committed by the proletariat as acts of rebellion against capitalism.

Quinney's theory extends beyond the causes of crime among the proletariat: even the crimes committed by the ruling class are the result of the capitalist system. These are "crimes of domination and repression" committed by ruling capitalists to protect their interests. Corporate crime (e.g., bid rigging, price fixing, security and exchange violations) are forms of "economic domination" by the ruling class. "Crimes of control" are committed by criminal justice personnel, and "crimes of government" are committed by both appointed and elected officials. Even organized crime, according to Quinney, is part of the capitalist class's effort to ensure its continued domination in society. He also defined acts of sexism and racism, whether or not they violate the law, as crimes of the ruling class intended to maintain control over the working class. (For similar conceptions of crime, see Michalowski, 1985; Lynch and Groves, 1986.)

The policy recommendations of Quinney's theory are the same as those of Bonger in the earlier part of this century. Since both "crime control and criminality . . . are understood in terms of the conditions resulting from the capitalist appropriation of labor," it follows that:

> The only lasting solution to the crisis of capitalism is socialism. Under late, advanced capitalism, socialism will be achieved in the struggle of all people who are oppressed by the capitalist mode of production. . . . The *essential meaning* of crime in the development of capitalism is the need for a socialist society. (Quinney, 1980:67-68; emphasis added)

Quinney and others construct a typology of crimes found in any modern, industrial society, from ordinary street crimes to corporate crimes, then attribute the cause of each type to some feature of capitalism. But the addition of this typology does not advance their theory much beyond the basic Marxist assertion that crime is caused by capitalism.

Modifications of Marxist Theory

The Marxist theory of Quinney and others has been strongly criticized as simplistic, ideological, and utopian (Akers, 1979; Turk, 1979; Inciardi, 1980). On the other hand, Michael J. Lynch and W. Byron Groves (1986:45) contend that they and other radical criminologists have taken these critiques into account and propose explanations of crime that avoid any "oversimplified, 'unicausal' approach where the only source of crime is capitalism." These explanations stress the effects of economic inequality on crime through alienation, family disorganization, parental socialization practices, and other variables from strain and control theories. Vold and Bernard (1986:305-306) agree that the explanation of criminal behavior as simply a reaction to capitalist oppression is "now rejected by Marxists, who look for more complex explanations of crime within the context of the Marxist theory of history and of social change" (Vold and Bernard, 1986:305-306).

David Greenberg (1981a) also called for a modification of the Marxian explanation for crime:

> Marxists do not deny that social-psychological processes and face-to-face interactions may have some importance for understanding crime and criminal justice, but they try to see these as shaped by larger social structures. And in characterizing these structures, they give particular attention to the organization of economic activity, without neglecting the political and ideological dimensions of society. (Greenberg, 1981:18)

Although he covered a number of different areas and questions that a multi-dimensional Marxist theory of crime should address, Greenberg did not actually propose a Marxist theory of crime that could be distinguished from non-Marxist structural theories. But he came closer to presenting a specific theory of crime in his analysis of the age distribution of crime (1977), arguing that the disproportionate number of juveniles involved in crime "is not readily explained by current sociological theories of delinquency, but it can be readily understood as a consequence of the historically changing position of juveniles in . . . the long-term tendencies of a capitalist economic system" (Greenberg, 1977:189).

The assumption in Greenberg's theory is that juveniles in *all* social classes in capitalist societies are relatively deprived of access to the labor market. Faced with peer influences to possess certain material goods but without any parental ability or willingness to purchase these desired goods, juveniles must turn to other means to gain them. Since their adolescent status prevents them from integrating into the legitimate labor market, they turn to delinquent means. They will only do so, however, if they believe that the costs of crime, which are principally age-dependent, will not be too great. The younger they are, the less likely their criminal behavior will carry serious negative legal and social consequences. Hence, both the rewards and costs of crime in capitalist society are related to age. Greenberg notes that delinquency is also found in socialist societies, but he believes that it is decreasing and not as much of a problem as it is in capitalist societies (Greenberg, 1981b).

Whatever the empirical merits of Greenberg's theory of the age distribution of crime, it is difficult to see how it qualifies as a Marxist theory. Except for the assertion that juvenile age status is more likely to produce crime in capitalist than in socialist society, the theory basically utilizes concepts and propositions from non-Marxist theories, such as differential opportunity, social control, and social learning theories to account for age variations in crime.

Another explanation of delinquency that is frequently cited as a good example of an "integrated structural-Marxist" theory was subsequently proposed by Mark Colvin and John Pauly (1983). They argued that the practices of parents in the socialization and discipline of their children reflect the kind of control that the parents are themselves subjected to in the work place. White-collar workers experience control at work through the development of strong internal moral norms; in turn, they socialize their children in a positive way to develop strong moral bonds to the family. Other workers on the lower rungs of the economic structure are more subject to coercion and direct manipulation by employers and managers; thus, they carry over such work place subjugations into their disciplinary control over their own children. Blue-collar workers are controlled on the job by material rewards, so they tend to raise their children in the same utilitarian way by direct reward and punishment. Parents who hold very low-level, economically marginal jobs have little consistency in the work place and are coercively controlled by their bosses. Likewise, they are inconsistent, alternately permissive and punitive, in disciplining their children. Socialization patterns in the family produce delinquent or conforming behavior, and these same patterns reflect the parents' status in the work place. Not only are lower-class youth raised in a negative family environment, they are faced with negative school experiences and other social conditions related to delinquent behavior.

There is research showing some connection between school, family, and parental socialization practices, and delinquency. But there is little that shows how parents' disciplinary practices are determined by the type of job they hold. To date, there has been little empirical testing of this theory and what has been done reports positive but fairly weak empirical validity of the theory (Messner and Krohn, 1990; Simpson and Ellis, 1994). Simpson and Ellis (1994) tested the Colvin and Pauly theory by examining the effect on delinquent behavior of the class position of the parents, as measured by type of work in which they were employed, and the other family, school, and peer variables specified in the theory. They found that all the relevant variables in the theory combined accounted for little of the variation in the frequency of either violent (3 percent of variance explained) or property juvenile offenses (1 percent). Moreover, they report that the relationships are sometimes not in the predicted direction and that the type of parental work, the main variable in the theory, had the weakest effects. Moreover, the effects of class, family, and school variables differ somewhat by gender, a variable that is ignored in the Colvin and Pauly modification of Marxist theory.

Even if stronger research support for the Colvin and Pauly theory were to be found, it would still be difficult to distinguish this explanation from non-Marxist theory. Simply referring to the class position of parents and youth, especially when this is measured by occupational classifications similar to those used by non-Marxists, does not substantiate it as Marxist theory (see Akers, 1980). One could arrive at exactly the same propositions without any reference whatsoever to Marxist theory or to the class structure of capitalist society as defined by its relationship to the means of production. Those parts of the theory that give it some empirical credibility, such as its reference to family socialization and school experiences, are drawn from social bonding theory rather than from Marxist theory.

As these examples demonstrate, when Marxist theorists offer explanations of crime that go beyond simply attributing the causes of all crime to capitalism, they rely on concepts taken directly from the same "traditional" criminological theories of which they have been so critical and which they have declared to be inadequate. As Jensen (1980) points out, the specific factors used in modified Marxist theories to explain crime, such as economic and racial inequality, urban density, industrialization, family, and peers, are exactly the same factors proposed in mainstream, non-Marxist sociological theories. The more Marxist theory in criminology is modified to incorporate age, gender, socialization, strain, differential opportunity, and social learning patterns, the less it differs from non-Marxist theories. Except for nuances of emphasis and terminology, it becomes virtually indistinguishable from the main sociological theories of crime that it was meant to replace.

Is Crime the Result of a Capitalist Economy?

If the Marxist view of capitalist society as criminogenic is valid, then crime should be very low, if not non-existent, in all socialist societies. Conversely, it should be very high in all capitalist systems. The theory explains differences in the crime rate across types of society, but it does not explain differences in individual or group behavior within the same society. Therefore, any analysis of variations in crime solely within the same society cannot test the theory. The inherent, crime-generating contradictions of capitalism can only be tested by cross-national comparisons of crime in capitalist systems with crime in pre-capitalist and socialist systems.[2]

Marxist criminologists have shown little interest in such comparisons of real societies, preferring to compare existing capitalist society with ideal, future socialist systems. Many Marxists have long argued that none of the currently defunct socialist states of the Soviet Union and eastern Europe were truly socialist. These systems were state capitalism, collectivism, or at best imperfectly and improperly applied socialism (see Greenberg, 1981). During the time that countries such as Sweden moved from more capitalistic economies and voted in social democratic governments with policies that are often described as socialist, both violent and property crime rates have skyrocketed (Felson, 1994:12). But Marxists would not accept the political economy of these societies as truly socialist. This concept of socialist society as a future utopia that has yet to be established in reality renders Marxist theory untestable. If no such society based on Marxist principles exists or has ever existed, then there can be no empirical comparison of crime between capitalist and socialist systems; hence, it would be impossible to test the Marxist hypothesis that capitalism causes crime and socialism prevents crime. Such utopianism changes Marxism from a theoretical explanation of crime as it exists in reality into a moral philosophy about a crime-free ideal society.

Even when this utopian Marxism is rejected and real socialist systems are examined, effective comparisons are difficult, because the comparative data are usually not available. The former communist societies of the Soviet Union and eastern Europe were all closed systems in which the party-controlled government withheld information. Independent social science research was practically unknown. Valid and reliable official or unofficial data on crime either did not exist or was not openly reported. This is still the case in China, Cuba, and North Korea.

In spite of this, some relevant comparative observations can be made to allow at least a partial assessment of the validity of Marxist theory of crime. One variable to consider is the differences in *types* of crime between the two political systems. Any type of political dissent, forming independent labor unions, complaining about the government, or simply not having a job are all illegal under communist law. A whole range of activities, which in Western democracies are defined as legitimate variations in lifestyles or are protected by constitutional rights, are defined as criminal acts in socialist systems. (See Klockars, 1979; Nettler, 1984).

Therefore, the commission of these acts greatly increases the crime rate in communist societies, while the commission of the same acts would have no effect on the crime rate in Western democracies. In contrast, crimes by private corporations is a serious category of crime in capitalist society; but since there are no private corporations in communist societies, no such crime exists there. At the same time, black-market crimes in currency or ordinary merchandise run rampant in socialist economies but are relatively unknown or considered minor in capitalist systems. The range of acts outlawed in socialist societies are as great or greater than in capitalist systems, although many of the acts that are criminal in one system may not be criminal in the other.

The lack of data on crime in communist societies makes it extremely difficult to determine if there is more or less crime when comparing acts that are defined as criminal in *both* types of societies, such as the "ordinary" street crimes of violence, theft, fraud, and property damage. However, the little research that was done on the causes of crime in socialist states before the recent democratic changes found that the same socio-economic and social-psychological variables were related to crime there as they were to crime in the United States (see Chalidze, 1977; Shelley, 1980).

There have been reports of dramatic increases in crime in the major cities of Russia and other component republics of the former Soviet Union since the transition from communist control to more open-market, free-enterprise economies. Whether this is the result of the change from a socialist to a capitalist system is debatable, because it may be attributable to an economic and social breakdown and to the destruction of a once highly restrictive law-enforcement system. One finds few reports of similar crime increases in former East Germany, which because of its unification with West Germany may have been better able to maintain public order and avert the social disorganization that followed the dismantling of the Soviet Union.

The United States, Japan, Germany, Great Britain, and virtually all other industrialized nations, including the social welfare capitalism such as that found in the Scandinavian countries, as well as most of the developing nations, are more or less capitalist. Yet, they have widely varying crime rates, some of which are lower and others of which are higher than the crime rates that prevailed under communist rule. If there is something inherently criminogenic in a capitalist mode of production, then all capitalist societies should have similar crime rates and these rates should all be higher than those found in any socialist system. Historically, this has not been found to be true.

Critical Criminology

As we have seen, the Marxist label became highly visible in American criminology in the middle of the 1970s as an outgrowth of conflict theory. In the process, many criminologists used the terms "critical" and "radical" as code names and synonyms for Marxist theory. These terms have continued to be used over the years to identify perspectives that resonate well with Marxist theory and share with it a "critical" stance toward capitalist society, toward law and justice in Western democracies, and toward "mainstream" criminology. These critiques are often coupled with what are defined as "radical" policy analyses and proposals. In the Marxist boom in academic circles of the 1970s and 1980s, these terms tended to be seen less often and the Marxist label became dominant. But the Marxist label in criminological articles and books has been seen less often in the 1990s; radical, critical, leftist, and other designations are more often found. However, critical and radical criminology has never been fully synonymous with Marxist criminology, and in the past decade the former labels have come in for renewed attention, while broadening their identity beyond Marxist theory to feminist, left realist, and a variety of other viewpoints. Therefore, much of what comes under the heading of critical criminology is not Marxist. Assessing the content and validity of critical criminology, however, is made more difficult, because what does come under this heading is not clear, at least not to criminologists who are readers rather than authors of critical criminology. As Don Gibbons (1994:60) states:

> A sizable body of theorizing, in the broad sense, has accumulated in recent years and can be identified as critical criminology, but this work does not form a coherent whole, that is, a shared body of broad propositions or generalizations and supporting evidence. Indeed, critical criminology is an intellectual posture around which a variety of criminological endeavors have been pursued.

Critical/Constitutive Criminology

This lack of clarity as to what is critical criminology is shown in an overview of critical criminology by Stuart Henry and Dragan Milovanovic (1991). They suggest that, instead of critical criminology, the term "constitutive criminology" be used and that this umbrella label be used to encompass social constructionism, left realism, socialist feminism, and post-structuralism. Einstadter and Henry (1995) add anarchist, peacemaking, and postmodernist criminology to this list.

Although Henry and Milovanovic claim that constitutive criminology is not "oppositional," they continue the tradition in critical criminology of not only opposing but rejecting mainstream criminology. Indeed, Gibbons (1994) argues that constitutive criminology appears to recommend abandoning criminology altogether. Henry and Milovanovic explicitly reject the search for causes of crime, but they are silent regarding accepting or rejecting the search for causes of the law and criminal justice system. Instead, they assert that crime is a "discursive production" that somehow comes about when "agents act out criminal patterns, when others seek to control criminal behavior, and when yet others attempt to research, philosophize about, and explain crime" (Henry and Milovanovic, 1991:293).

At one level, this is an unexceptional, descriptive statement about crime, criminal justice, and criminology that is self-evident or true by definition. It simply says that some people commit crime (offenders who act out criminal patterns), others seek to control that crime (criminal justice agencies), and others (criminologists and other social scientists) seek to explain it. Both this description and the assertion by Henry and Milovanovic (1991:295) that crime is the outcome of human interaction are mundane statements that would be immediately accepted by virtually all criminologists. On another level, however, such statements seem to take an extreme position that denies that crime as such really exists. Crime exists only because it is a "discursive production," that is, a product not only of the interaction of offenders, control agents, criminologists, or other people, but also simply by their talking about it. "Discursive practices" that refer to various kinds of "talk," such as control talk, organizational talk, and law talk, constitute the narrative medium through which "codetermination" of crime, victims, and control take place. This implies that there is no such thing as crime as an objective behavioral reality to be explained; crime, criminal justice, social structure, and institutions are merely the products of talk, text, and discursive practices (Henry and Milovanovic, 1991:299). Does this mean that criminal behavior would not exist if we did not talk about it?

It is not clear that Henry and Milovanovic mean an affirmative answer to this question, because their statements also imply that crime does exist as something that is "codetermined" in this process—a process that includes the very acts of talking about it, trying to explain it, and attempting to control it. Thus, there may be some internal logical inconsistencies in constitutive criminology. If the search for causes must be abandoned, as clearly stated by Henry and Milovanovic, or if crime does not exist as an objective reality in the discursive process as they may imply, then how can crime be "enabled and constrained" (i.e., caused or prevented) and at the same time have reciprocal "shaping" effects on social structure. Victims and control agents are also real entities in the process. It would seem that constitutive criminology has not really abandoned the search for causes, because crime, victims, and control are "shaped" by both micro-level events, "individual choice or predisposition" and by macro-level structural arrangements. In turn, crime and control, or at least talk about them, "shape" both individual actions and social structure.

> Advocates decline the seduction that either human agents, through choice or predisposition, or structural arrangements at institutional and societal levels have priority in shaping crime, victims, and control. . . . [T]hey see social structure and its constituent control institutions as the emerging outcome of human interaction that both constrains and enables criminal action and recognizes that those structures are simultaneously shaped by the crime and crime control talk that is part of its reproduction. Constitutive criminology is not an exercise in polemics, in which human agency is separated from the structures that it makes.
> Constitutive criminology, then, is concerned with identifying the ways in which the interrelationships among human agents constitute crime, victims, and control as realities. Simultaneously, it is concerned with how these emergent realities themselves constitute human agents." (Henry and Milovanovic, 1991:295)

The concept of "transpraxis" is introduced by Henry and Milovanovic to heighten awareness of unintended consequences in this process and to go beyond the Marxist concept of "praxis," deliberate action taken for social change. Building on labeling theory's notion of the unintended consequences of societal labeling and control in producing deviance, Henry and Milovanovic argue that praxis often legitimizes the very capitalist control structures that it is meant to oppose. Thus, actions both by control agents and by those whom they attempt to control can produce unintended outcome. Whatever the truth of these assertions, there is little in this application of the concept of unintended consequences that constitutes a special or new insight of constitutive criminology. This is an old concept that has been applied in sociology to the full range of human behavior and social structures.

Henry and Milovanovic also claim that criminologists exclude the informal control system and do not understand that mutual obligations, loyalties, gratitude, and other processes in the informal system that constitute "symbolic violence" undergirding "ideological domination." Criminologists overlook this, do not understand it, or consign it to the past as "custom" rather than "law." Again, one would have to object to this characterization of criminology. It is simply not true that the informal control system or informal mechanisms in the criminal justice system are excluded from the purview of traditional, mainstream criminology. In fact, with the possible exception of classical deterrence theory and old-style biological theory, processes of informal interaction and control are recognized in virtually every criminological theory.

Henry and Milovanovic (1991:307) conclude as follows:

> Our position calls for abandoning of the futile search for causes of crime because that simply elaborates the distinctions that maintain crime as a separate reality while failing to address how it is that crime is constituted as part of society. We are concerned, instead, with the ways in which human agents actively coproduce that which they take to be crime."

To be "concerned" about how people coproduce what they construe to be crime only states the question; it does not offer an answer. It does not offer an explanation of crime. Although these authors discuss "talking about" crime and criminal justice and how they are "codetermined" both by human agents and social structure, constitutive criminology has not yet offered a testable explanation of either crime or criminal justice. Indeed, it rejects the very effort to explain or do anything about crime since these actions themselves constitute part of the process by which crime is produced. This presents a problem for the theory. If crime or criminal justice is not what constitutive criminology intends to explain, then what *is* it intended to explain? Constitutive criminology, as well as other varieties of critical criminology, focus more on a critique of the shortcomings of other criminologists than on offering an alternative explanation of crime. According to this critique, criminologists who are uninformed about constitutive criminology do not realize that they are actually participating in the production of crime by talking about it, studying it, and recommending policies to control it. But critical criminology can be criticized, in turn, for not offering viable theoretical alternatives and for being unrealistic about the crime problem. In fact, versions of critical criminology have been criticized on these very grounds by another group of critical/radical criminologists who call themselves "left realists."

Left Realism

Left realism refers primarily to the writings of a group of British criminologists, some of whom, such as Jock Young, were in the forefront of radical criminology in the 1970s in Great Britain. Left realism was developed by Young (1987) and others largely in reaction to what they call "left idealism," extreme positions that radical/critical criminology had come to take regarding crime and criminal justice. They were also responding to the rising tide of criminal victimization in British society, to the political changes that had taken place in the rise to power of political conservatism, and to the development of "right realism" (Matthews and Young, 1992).

By "left idealism," these authors mean the tendency in many radical/Marxist critiques of capitalist society and its oppressive criminal justice system to overlook the reality of pain and suffering generated by criminal offenders who victimize their fellow human beings, usually the poor and powerless. Left idealists view street crime "either as a diversion from class struggle, or as a vehicle for marketing news, and treat crime as an epiphenomenon, with the criminal—conceived of as a sort of socialist homunculus or proto-revolutionary—being viewed as determined and blameless, punishment as unwarranted or amplificatory" (Lowman, 1992:141). Left realists point out that neither the street-level criminal offender nor the white-collar offender is a revolutionary soldier in the class struggle.

The growing crime problem in society and the ascendancy of conservative government in Great Britain and the United States with very strong public support for get-tough, punitive criminal justice policies to control crime produced what the left realists thought was a "crisis" in criminology. This crisis called for a reappraisal of the radical, as well as the traditional liberal, approaches to crime. They were concerned that "conservative" criminology or "realism of the right," represented by biological and rational choice perspectives, would overwhelm radical views that had become sterile critiques of existing society with little direct relevance for alleviating the genuine problems of crime for ordinary members of society.

[Left realists criticize left idealists and orthodox Marxists for believing that crime is nothing but a fiction created by the ruling class to maintain its hegemony, that the criminal justice system does nothing but repress the population without providing any real control of crime, and that the only proper fate for the criminal justice system is to be totally dismantled. On the other hand, they propose that the inequities of the criminal justice system be rectified and that the system be made more effective, efficient, and just] Political repression can be reduced while improving governmental services to the poor and the working class. Matthews and Young (1992) reject the view that crime is an arbitrary social category that can be modified at will through verbal construction and narrative discourse. Left realists assert that street crime is real, relevant, important, and serious; moreover, there is a real consensus in society on the core of criminal law, and criminal justice reform and crime prevention are the most important immediate goals toward which criminologists and policy makers should strive (Lowman, 1992). In promoting this reform, left realists have toned down critiques of police and have provided vocal support for such policies as crime prevention, victim services, restitution, community service, community policing, and minimal use of prison sentences (Gibbons, 1994; Curran and Renzetti, 1994; Einstadter and Henry, 1995).

Left realists differentiate themselves from other critical criminologist by going beyond criticizing the punitive, conservative approaches of right realists to criticizing the unrealistic approaches of the left idealists. But there is little in the positions taken by left realists to differentiate them from advocates of mainstream liberal crime-control policies. Left realism "argues that only socialist intervention will fundamentally reduce the causes of crime rooted as they are in social inequality, that only the universality of crime prevention will guard the poor against crime, that only a genuinely democratic control of the police force will ensure that community safety is achieved" (Matthews, 1992:6). It is difficult to tell what "socialist intervention" means here. Nevertheless, exhortations to deal with the root causes of crime, promote crime prevention, institute victim restitution, reform punitive crime control and sentencing policies, and control police excesses to make the criminal justice both more effective and more just are found in the mainstream policy and reform proposals of the past half-century.

In short, left realists are former radical or critical criminologists who have recognized the reality of crime, have softened their critique of capitalist society and the criminal justice system, and are now advocating less radical and more ameliorative reform. Curran and Renzetti (1994:284) state that "[w]hile the left realist perspective is provocative, its empirical validity has yet to be established." The question is what theory of crime and/or criminal justice is proposed by left realists that can be validated? Reactions to the idealism of the left and proposals for more realistic reform of the system are not theoretical explanations; they are philosophical and political statements about what society should be and how the system ought to operate. Do left realists go beyond these statements to offer a new testable explanation of crime or of criminal justice as an alternative to existing theory? The answer is, not yet.

The 'Square of Crime'

This does not mean that there is nothing in left realist criminology relevant to explaining crime. There is the potential for formulating a theory of crime in the concept of the "square of crime," on which much left realist analysis rests. This concept of the square of crime refers to the four elements of *state, society, offender,* and *victim* that are said to operate in time and space to produce crime. It provides a list of elements or categories of variables that one can analyze, raise questions about, and explain; but in my view, there is nothing yet in the way in which left realists describe the square of crime that provides a set of propositions that would constitute a new testable explanation of crime or criminal justice. In fact, it does not seem to be proposed by left realists as an explanation, but simply as "four *definitional* elements of crime: a victim, an offender, formal control [the state] and informal control [society or the public]" (Young, 1992:27; emphasis added). These four elements, then, define crime and are not proposed as the causes of crime. Rather, each is itself a dependent variable or something to be explained according to the principle of multiple causation, lack of informal control, changes in exposure to victimization, and ineffective formal sanctions (Young, 1992). These multiple causes are not specified, but when the square of crime is applied to crime, it tends to be an eclectic analysis that leans heavily on variables specified in other criminological theories, such as labeling, relative deprivation, anomie, and deterrence (Lea, 1992). Or the analysis tends toward programmatic and non-explanatory statements such as:

> Realist criminology indicates that crime rates are a product of two forces: changes in behavior and changes in definitions of what is seriously criminal.
> Thus we can talk of (1) the background causes of crime; (2) the moral context of opting for criminal behavior; (3) the situation of committing crime; (4) the detection of crime; (5) the response to the offender; (6) the response to the victim. Criminal careers are built up by an interaction of the structural position the offender finds him or herself in and the administrative responses to his or her various offenses (Young, 1992:28-29).

The left realist movement in criminology is more a realistic reappraisal of critical criminology and a movement back toward the middle ground of intellectual discourse in the field. It has inspired victimization surveys and other kinds of research in Great Britain, promoted reform in the police, and exposed deficiencies in critical perspectives in criminology. However, just as was true for the earlier radical "new" criminology of Taylor, Walton, and Young (1972) in England twenty-five years ago, Young's left realism of today stops with an outline of categories of variables and sketches out what a sound theory should do. It does not actually offer a new theory of either criminal justice or crime. The four elements of the square of crime identify social phenomena around which discussion of issues in crime and criminal justice can be fruitfully organized. But the four are ordinary, well-known social categories and none of them singly, nor the notion that they are interrelated, is new or original with left realism. Left realism is really defined by its reaction to left idealism, its stance on the issues of social change, the significance of crime in society, and its attitude toward criminal justice policy. Its implications for these seem clear, but it is not at this time a testable theory that can be empirically validated.

Peacemaking Criminology

The left realists' concern for the real suffering created by crime is also reflected in what is known as "peacemaking" criminology, chief proponents of which are Harold E. Pepinsky and Richard Quinney (1991). They liken crime and its control to war and declare that it is time to try peace between offenders and victims, police, and the community. Peacemaking criminology advocates mediation, conflict resolution, reconciliation, and reintegration of the offender into the community in an effort to "alleviate suffering and thereby reduce crime" (Pepinsky and Quinney, 1991:ix). Peacemaking criminology is described as emerging out of religious, humanist, feminist, and critical/Marxist traditions (Pepinsky, 1991).

As we have seen, Quinney's previous theoretical views were first conflict and, later, Marxist. But his peacemaking criminology is religious (primarily Christian but with elements of Buddhism). It is a spiritual, transcendental, and visionary preaching of nonviolence and a plea to end suffering. Since Quinney defines crime itself as a form of suffering, his central contention is tautological—if suffering can be ended, crime will be ended. In his view, the criminal justice system as currently organized is based on the principle of violence. This must be done away with and replaced with the principles of love and nonviolence as the only solution to crime. "When our hearts are filled with love and our minds with willingness to serve, we will know what has to be done and how it is to be done. Such is the basis of a nonviolent criminology" (Quinney, 1991:12).

Others take more secular approaches to peacemaking criminology. For instance, Anderson (1991) argues that both Gandhian and Marxist humanism offer guidelines for peaceful resolution of the problems of crime. Harris (1991:88) claims that feminist theory values harmony and "felicity" above all else and that "feminists stress the themes of caring, sharing, nurturing, and loving." This is contrasted with the "power/control," "rights/justice" male perspective that dominates criminological thinking and government actions in the war on crime. Thus, the incorporation of this feminist perspective will lead to a resolution of conflict and peace in the criminal justice system.

Peacemaking criminology does not offer a theory of crime or of the criminal justice system that can be evaluated empirically. Explanations of crime and the criminal justice system might or might not be consistent with the religious and other precepts espoused by peacemaking criminologists, but these precepts do not themselves constitute a testable theory. It may be possible to construct a testable, parsimonious, and valid theory from peacemaking criminology, but at this point it remains a philosophy rather than a theory. It has a utopian vision of society that calls for reforming and restructuring to get away from war, crime, and violence and to institute a society with a justice system characterized by nonviolence, the peaceful resolution of conflict, and the restoration of offenders to the community. This is a highly laudable philosophy of criminal justice, but it does not offer an explanation of why the system operates as it does or why offenders commit crime. It can be evaluated on other grounds but not on empirical validity.

Although not all religious beliefs and practices are nonviolent and religion is not the only basis for nonviolence, the notion that the religious values of some of the criminologists underpin their peacemaking perspective is quite understandable. Christianity honors the commandment to love your neighbor as yourself and to love those who spitefully use you. It preaches nonviolence, forgiveness, reconciliation, and redemption. Although wrongdoing is not to be condoned, one does not cast stones at the wrongdoers. Rather, one restores them and admonishes them to sin no more. In Christianity, righteousness is based on serving others, not gaining power or control over them. Long before the peacemaking criminology label was adopted by Pepinsky, Quinney, and others, the in-prison religious programs and the many prison ministries run by churches and lay groups were practicing peacemaking; they have long applied the tenets of love and peaceful reformation of offenders, by persuading them toward a religious commitment and lifestyle incompatible with committing crime and causing suffering. The kind of coalition of churches and synagogues to provide aid, comfort, and shelter to transients and the homeless described by Barak (1991) for one city has long been duplicated in thousands of other communities around the country. Buddhist and other religious traditions also preach nonviolence and reconciliation. Ghandian and other philosophies, religious and secular, also preach nonviolent social change.

Nevertheless, on other counts, peacemaking criminology has some internal inconsistencies and contradictions that are difficult to reconcile. For instance, it seems to be contradictory to claim Marxist/critical criminology as one of the main foundations for peacemaking criminology. It is true, as Anderson (1991) shows, that there are humanistic elements in Marx's own writing. But are they enough to overcome the major thrust of Marxist theory that capitalist society is based on irreconcilable class conflict and Marx's own endorsement of violent revolution? Whether from the original Marx or some variety of neo-Marxism, the major policy recommendation of this theoretical tradition has long been to meet power with power, violence with violence to overthrow capitalist society. Further, how does one reconcile the peacemaking image with the characteristics of governments based on Marxist principles—the violent repression of citizens, intolerance of dissent, punitive control of deviance, and rule by terror? Certainly there is nothing particularly violent about non-Marxist varieties of critical criminology, but at the same time there is very little about them that is conciliatory and peacemaking. By its very name, it is critical and oppositional; it is not known for advocating peacemaking with those who are the subjects of its criticisms. There also seem to be some logical inconsistency in claiming feminist theory as a foundation for peacemaking criminology. The distinction that Harris (1991) makes between the peacemaking orientation of women and the control orientation of men may be valid. She cites research that shows that women do tend to support nurturing and caring values more than men who tend to endorse power relationships. But this celebration of the nurturing, caring, loving, and peaceful orientation of women is not a significant part of the feminist tradition (see Chapter 10). Indeed, it is more identified with the traditional "feminine" role of "acting like a woman." Feminists have long rejected this role as itself a reflection of the patriarchal system of oppression of women. How, then, does its incorporation into peacemaking criminology or into criminal justice practice represent feminist theory?

The assertion by peacemaking criminologists that no "traditional" criminologist or no one in the criminal justice system recognizes the real suffering created by crime, or that none has advocated peaceful, nonviolent ways of dealing with crime, is simply inaccurate. None of the policy implications of peacemaking criminology is unique to those who self-consciously identify themselves with this perspective. All these

policies, such as nonpunitive treatment of offenders, mediation, restitution, offender reintegration, rehabilitation, and so on, have long been
mainstays of the policy recommendations coming from mainline "liberal" criminologists. More to the point, they are already common practices in the criminal justice system. As Don Gibbons (1994) points out,
peacemaking criminologists have not shown how to get beyond those
policies already in place to the large-scale structural changes in society
that they claim are needed to perpetuate nonviolent and peaceful crime
control.

Summary

Marxist theory explains the law and criminal justice system as being
controlled by and serving the interests of the ruling capitalist elite.
Instrumental Marxists view all aspects of the political state, including
its law and justice system, as inevitably and always an instrument of
the ruling class. Structural Marxists modify this somewhat by arguing
that, in the short term, the political state is relatively independent of
the ruling class and may reflect the interests of the proletariat.

In Marxist theory, capitalism itself is the major cause of crime. Ownership of the means of production by the capitalist ruling class produces
a society that is inherently criminogenic. Some Marxists propose that
all forms of crime simply reflect the crime-producing system of capitalism. The crimes of the working class are either "crimes of accommodation" or "crimes of resistance" to the capitalist system. Crimes
committed by the ruling class are "crimes of domination and repression" that are committed to protect and promote the interests of the
ruling class. Other Marxist theorists have departed from this oversimplified approach. However, the more complex models that they offer
essentially rely on concepts and explanations from non-Marxist theories.

Since Marxist theory focuses on the inherent contradictions of capitalist society as a source of law and criminal justice, as well as crime,
it cannot be tested by examining only capitalist systems. Whether the
more simplified or complex Marxist theories are valid can be adequately
judged only on the basis of direct comparisons of real capitalist with
real socialist societies. When such comparisons are made, Marxist theory does not fare well as an explanation of the law and operation of the
criminal justice system, and such comparisons do not offer much empirical validation of the primary Marxist argument that crime is a problem in capitalism but not a problem in socialism.

Constitutive criminology, left realism, and peacemaking criminology
have all been identified as varieties of critical criminology. All offer a
critique of criminology as practiced by others and a critique of society

and the criminal justice system. Constitutive criminology rejects the search for causes of crime as an objective reality and views it as the product of "discursive practices" among offenders, controllers, and victims. Left realism rejects this kind of reasoning as unrealistic and proposes reform in the criminal justice system to deal with the real pain and suffering of crime in society. Peacemaking criminology draws on religious, humanist, feminist, and Marxist traditions to advocate a nonviolent, restitutive, and reconciling approach to the crime problem. None of these varieties of critical criminology offers a testable theory of crime or the criminal justice system.

Notes

1. For references to these reviews, critiques, and differentiations made among the models denoted by these terms, see Meier (1977), Inciardi (1980), and Bohm (1982).
2. As we have seen in Chapter 7 on social disorganization and anomie theories, the question of the unequal class distribution of crime has not yet been empirically resolved. But even if research finds a concentration of crime in an "under-class" or among the "truly disadvantaged" (Wilson, 1987), it is unclear how this would support Marxist theory. The research and theory on the class distribution of crime has developed out of a non-Marxist sociology.

CHAPTER 10

FEMINIST THEORIES

Introduction

The primary aim of feminist theory, according to Kathleen Daly and Meda Chesney-Lind (1988:490), is to draw upon women's "ways of knowing" in contrast to criminological theory "rooted in men's experience." Its objective is to eliminate "androcentric science" and produce a distinctly feminist approach to crime and criminal justice. Knowledge is assumed to be determined by experiences conditioned by one's gender (as well as one's race, class, and ethnicity). Since criminology has been dominated by males, existing criminological theory is seriously flawed by the "masculinist" perspective. Both the questions asked and the answers given in criminology are the "product of white, economically privileged men's experiences" (Daly and Chesney-Lind, 1988:506). Feminist theory is designed to counter this bias and to produce a new, deeper understanding of gender relations in society and how they affect both crime and criminal justice.

There is no single feminist theory. Rather, there are liberal, radical, Marxist, socialist, and other varieties of feminist thought. Yet, all these variations share a feminist perspective on gender issues that is not captured by mainstream criminological theories (Daly and Chesney-Lind, 1988; Simpson, 1989; Gelsthorpe and Morris, 1990; Chesney-Lind and Shelden, 1992).

> There is no one specific feminism, just as there is no one specific criminology. True, some positions and perspectives will be seen as more "right on" than others but . . . [W]hether or not there was or could be a "feminist criminology" . . . is not of importance. All that is necessary to say here . . . is that holding a feminist perspective means accepting the view that women experience subordination on the basis of their sex and working towards elimination of that subordination. (Gelsthorpe and Morris, 1990:2)

Feminist Theory of Criminal Justice

Feminist theory identifies the major blind spot in traditional "male-stream" criminological theory as the failure to understand the profound significance of gender and sex roles in society (Gelsthorpe and Morris, 1990). For some, this significance is reflected in the ongoing differential in sex roles and gender inequality. For others, the inequalities run deeper: "patriarchy" is a fundamental principle of societal organization. A patriarchal society, in which the rights and privileges of males are superior and those of females are subordinated, characterizes the vast majority of societies throughout history and the world. Although patriarchy is not universal and varies in intensity, it reigns in capitalist and socialist systems and in industrialized and non-industrialized societies. Conflict and labeling theory of criminal justice recognizes male-female differences in power; however, feminist theory proposes that the power differential between men and women is at least as important as, if not more important than, the power differentials by race, class, and age. Marxists view class as the fundamental, bifurcating force in capitalist society. Feminist theory posits that patriarchy is equally as important as class and may even override class in the division of society into the dominant and the subordinate. Feminist theories explain criminal justice decisions as reflecting this male dominance and functioning to support patriarchy by discriminating against women and reinforcing traditional female sex and family roles.

Empirical Validity of Feminist Theory of Criminal Justice

At one level, to examine the empirical validity of feminist theory of criminal justice entails the same kind of historical cross-societal comparisons of patriarchal and non-patriarchal societies as in the evaluation of Marxist theory by comparison of socialist and capitalist societies. However, its empirical validity can be judged more directly by research on the male-female disparities in criminal justice decisions in American society.

If those in less powerful social statuses are treated more harshly in the criminal justice system as conflict and labeling theory would predict, then, since women are less powerful than men, adolescent girls and adult women should receive harsher treatment in the system for the same offense than boys and men. Research evidence does not confirm this hypothesis; it shows instead that, when legally relevant variables are taken into account, there is little disparity by sex, age, race, or class in the criminal and juvenile justice systems. (See Bridges and Myers, 1994, and the research reviewed in Chapter 8.) Indeed, when sex differences are found, the system is almost always harder on men and more lenient with women (Daly, 1994b). "What is intriguing about the statistical sentencing literature is that gender differences, favoring women, are more often found than race differences, favoring whites" (Daly, 1989:137). This tendency to be tougher on men has existed for a long time and led many years ago to the "chivalry" hypothesis (Pollack, 1950). This hypothesis proposes that predominantly male police, prosecutors, and judges have a traditional, chivalrous attitude toward women and extend this attitude even to women offenders; therefore, they treat them with more leniency than men. Some contend that this pattern of sex disparity in the system supports the chivalry hypothesis (Moulds, 1980), while others argue that it does not (Bowker with Chesney-Lind and Pollock, 1978).

Because the chivalry hypothesis predates feminist theory and does not take a feminist stance on sex roles and the oppression of male dominance, feminist theorists tend to dismiss it as unfounded or valid only as an expression of "paternalism." Paternalism is not the same as chivalry, they argue, because it does not necessarily result in a more lenient treatment of female criminals or delinquents. Paternalism may result in less severe sanctions on females, but it can just as readily impose harsher penalties on them to serve the greater purpose of maintaining women in their submissive roles (Chesney-Lind, 1988; 1989).

> "Paternalism" generally implies that women who behave in ways that are congruent with traditional female roles of purity and submission receive preferential or lenient treatment, whereas women who violate those standards do not receive this benefit and may be dealt with more severely than males committing the same offense. (Horowitz and Pottieger, 1991)

One way that this paternalism can be expressed is in the differential handling by which "girls have . . . been the recipients of a special, and discriminatory, form of justice" (Chesney-Lind, 1988). A higher proportion of girls than of boys are brought into juvenile court for status offenses, such as running away from home, truancy, and incorrigibility. Moreover, girls are more likely than boys to be incarcerated for status offenses, although less likely for serious offenses. Chesney-Lind (1988; 1989; Chesney-Lind and Shelden, 1992) contends that girls are treated more harshly for minor offenses than boys, because the system "sexualizes" their offenses as a threat to traditional sex-role expectations. This is one example of how male-dominated society maintains control over women. Other research also finds that young adult women tend more often to be imprisoned for less serious offenses than men (Horowitz and Pottieger, 1991).

However, these findings do not necessarily support the paternalism hypothesis, because the difference may simply result from factors other than sex bias. For instance, prostitution may result in more frequent convictions and incarcerations, simply because it is easier to charge and prove in court and less likely than other charges to be dismissed. Also, women are very unlikely to be charged with major felonies, but more likely than men to be charged with petty theft. Yet, these male-female differences may reflect something other than gender bias in arrest and adjudication, such as the lower "visibility" of females involved in such "male" offenses as major felonies (Horowitz and Pottieger, 1991).

Corley et al. (1989) contrast the chivalry/paternalism hypothesis of more lenient treatment toward female offenders with the labeling/conflict hypothesis that the subordinate position of women in society results in harsher sanctions for the same offense. They investigated these hypotheses with research data on the delinquent behavior of non-institutionalized and incarcerated adolescents. The girls in the study perceived parents as more strongly disapproving of their disobedience and delinquent behavior than that of boys. But the actual parental sanctions reported were about the same for boys and girls, controlling for level of delinquent involvement. Males were more often punished for misconduct by school officials, but that is primarily because, in fact, they committed more serious offenses than females. Furthermore, age and race had no effect when seriousness of delinquency was controlled. Boys were more likely to be arrested by the police; but, when controlling for levels of delinquency involvement, there was little difference found in police action, and judicial sanctions were the same for both boys and girls. Neither the chivalry nor labeling/conflict hypotheses were supported because:

> [T]he findings suggest that judicial sanctions operate independently of sex, race, and age. The research offers support for the legal model in which legal variables such as the seriousness of the offense are important factors in judicial sanctions. (Corley et al., 1989:553)

Donna Bishop and Charles Frazier (1992) report similar findings in a Florida study of screening, detention, court referral, adjudication, and judicial disposition for delinquency cases and court referral and disposition for status offenses. The strongest effects on case workers' and juvenile court judges' decisions at each step in the process came from offense seriousness, contempt status, prior record, and prior disposition, not from gender. Juvenile males were more likely to be treated harshly for delinquent offenses, but there were no gender differences for "status offenses." However, Bishop and Frazier did locate a category of offense, contempt of court, for which juvenile females were clearly treated more harshly than males. When juveniles were brought before the judge on the non-delinquent status offense of "runaway," it was common for the judge to issue an order that they be returned home and remain there without running away again. Those juveniles who did run away from home in violation of this order were brought back into juvenile court, where they were very likely to be found in contempt of court as a separate offense from the original or new running-away episodes. While the original status offense carried no possibility of incarceration, juveniles could be incarcerated for contempt of court. In these contempt of court cases, the girls were much more likely than the boys to be sentenced to secure detention.

Daly (1989) claims that neither the conflict/labeling nor paternalism hypotheses properly account for the findings on gender variations in court decisions. She hypothesizes that judicial discretion in pre-trial releases and sentencing are very much influenced by the family status and relations of the defendants. Her research found that these family variables affect judges' decisions for both male and female defendants (as well as for different racial and ethnic groups). Judges tended to be more lenient with defendants, men and women, who had stronger family ties and obligations to children. Women with familial ties were treated more leniently than men with such ties. Since such ties characterize more female than male defendants, the judges gave more frequent pre-trial releases and lenient sentences to women. Daly's findings from two court systems showed that such legal variables as the offense charged and prior record were the key ingredients in judicial decisions. But her findings also supported the hypotheses that these legal variables interact with the family situation, so that "familied" defendants were given more lenient treatment. Therefore, the "initially significant sex effects can be explained by differences in treatment of some familied women and familied men" (Daly, 1989:152).

If judges' considerations of such factors as family status is an example of applying double-standard, sex-role expectations, then the findings are consistent with feminist theory. However, the fact that the same family factors were considered for both male and female defenders undercuts this feminist interpretation. The finding that judges based their decisions on offenses, prior records, and family variables equally for men and women runs counter to the theory.

Daly (1994a; 1992) has also reported the findings from a unique study of felony court cases. She conducted a statistical analysis of a "wide sample" of 300 felony court cases. Then she combined that with a qualitative analysis of pre-sentence reports and court transcripts for a "deep sample" of 40 female defendants matched by crime, prior record, age, and race with 40 male defendants. Although men were much more likely to receive prison sentences than women for convictions within the same offense category, upon closer examination of the matched pairs of defendants, she found that the men, ostensibly with the same criminal charge, actually had committed a more serious offense.

> I set out to determine whether men and women accused and convicted of statutorily similar crimes committed offenses of the same seriousness. Of the forty deep-sample pairs, I judged 48 percent to be comparably serious, but for 40 percent the men's offenses were more serious, and for 12 percent, the women's were. (Daly 1994a:110)

Thus, what appeared to be harsher penalties for men for the same crime could be justified by the characteristics of individual cases. Therefore, there are few cases in which the outcome was based mainly on gender. Although the felony court judges viewed women as more reformable than men, the justifications for sentencing used by the judges were the same for men and women.

Feminist theory expects criminal justice decisions to be based solely or primarily on considerations of gender or sex roles, yet this has not gained much support from the research literature. The fact that delinquent girls run a higher risk of confinement for status offenses, and that a higher proportion of women convicts serve time for lesser offenses, may reflect society's preference that women live up to certain sexual and family roles. But it is not solid evidence for the hypothesis it is a patriarchally dominated system in which decisions are exercised to the detriment of women, because the same system severely punishes a higher proportion of men over women for serious offenses. It is difficult to sustain the argument that minor offenses by women violate social rules of femininity but that serious felonies do not. In addition, the high proportion of women serving time for lesser offenses may simply indicate a low proportion of female offenders committing serious offenses. The probability of serving time is about equal for men and women convicted of the same offense and with the same prior record.

This is the same conclusion reached in a study by Darrell Steffensmeier and others (1993) of the prison sentences meted out to men and women by judges in Pennsylvania. Their review of past research on gender disparities in sentencing decisions shows that, when prior record and offense severity are controlled, most studies have found little or no gender bias. Their findings show that Pennsylvania judges are slightly more likely to sentence men to prison for serious offenses, but even this difference is based on the relevant considerations of offense circumstances, offenders' blameworthiness, and family responsibilities. Women receive slightly longer sentences for minor offenses and slightly shorter sentences for serious offenses. However, when other factors are held constant, gender has only a very small effect on decisions to impose a jail sentence rather than probation (men are more likely to receive a jail sentence than women for the same offense) and gender has no effect on either the decision to imprison or the length of the prison sentence imposed.

> We found (net of other variables) that the primary determinants of judges' imprisonment decisions are the type or seriousness of the crime committed and the defendant's prior record, not the defendant's gender (or, for that matter, age, race, or other background/contextual variables). Steffensmeier et al., 1993:435)

Similarly, George Bridges and Gina Beretta (1994) found that the factors that determine the imprisonment rate for men are the same factors that determine the imprisonment rate for women. Martha Myers (1995) found gender similarity, not gender disparity, in the history of imprisonment in one southern state. The rate of imprisonment for men was greater than for women for the whole period (1870-1940), but "the rate at which they [women] were admitted tracked comparable rates for men," and "within the constraints set by race, the social control of women was imbedded within the same general context as the social control of men" (Myers, 1995:38).

Research thus far shows that the independent effects of gender on criminal justice actions are weak or absent. The overall conclusion from research on gender disparities in juvenile and adult justice decisions is similar to the conclusion in Chapter 8 about the effect of other extra-legal variables in the criminal justice system. The strongest effect on criminal justice decisions comes from legally relevant, non-discriminatory factors, such as the seriousness of the charged offenses and the criminal characteristics of the offenders. Gender disparities favoring women exist, but they have less effect than legally relevant variables. When these variables are controlled, the remaining gender disparities are inconsequential.

Feminist Theories of Crime

Just as gender is the central issue in feminist explanations of criminal justice, it is at the center of feminist explanations of crime. Daly and Chesney-Lind (1988) identify two main gender-related issues that have engaged the attention of feminist theories of crime (see also Simpson, 1989; Chesney-Lind and Shelden, 1992). These are not the only concerns or the exclusive domain of feminist theory, but they are critical to understanding the feminist perspective on crime. The first issue is the "generalizability problem" that asks, "Do the theories of men's crime apply to women" (Daly and Chesney-Lind, 1988:514)? Were existing theories of crime and delinquency developed only with male offenders in mind, and do they hold up only when tested with male populations? One answer offered is that, although some extant theories do have relevance for both men and women, as a whole the traditional body of criminological theory inadequately accounts for female crime. The second issue is the "gender ratio problem" that poses the question, "Can extant theory explain the well-known gender difference in crime?" Why do women commit so much less crime than males? Again, different answers are provided, but feminist theorists tend to criticize those offered by existing theory and hypothesize that gender-specific variables explain and predict inter-gender differences in crime.[2]

This dissatisfaction with all "traditional" theories of crime and delinquency as too male-centered is a distinguishing feature of proponents of feminist theory. The common theme is that all current etiological theories, such as biological, psychological, anomie, control, differential association, conflict, labeling, social disorganization, and social learning theories were designed to explain only male criminality and have been tested only with male populations (Einstadter and Henry, 1995). There may be certain parts of these theories that are useful, but neither one single theory nor all the theories combined are capable of explaining female criminality or the male/female differences in crime (Leonard, 1982).[3] Even when traditional theories seem to apply, it is "more often 'Yes, but.' Yes, youth in groups often leads to delinquency, but if we are talking about girls' groups, that may not be so. Yes, school failure contributes to the delinquency of boys, but sometimes it is more important in the delinquency of girls" (Chesney-Lind and Shelden, 1992:213).

Some feminist theorists, however, disagree with this general critical assessment of all traditional criminological theories. For instance, Allison Morris (1987) contends that, though biological, psychiatric, and women's liberation theories are mistaken, traditional sociological explanations of crime have the potential of explaining female crime and why it occurs less frequently than male crime:

> Special theories for women's crimes have not been particularly successful. . . . One implication of this . . . is that we need to reconsider the relevance to women of general criminological theories. [T]here is no reason to suppose that explanations for women's crime should be fundamentally different from explanations for men's crime, though gender must play a part in any such explanation. . . . There are a number of criminological theories, however, which, though not originally developed for women, do contribute to our understanding of women's crime . . . . (Morris, 1987:75)

She finds special relevance in anomie, differential association, and social bonding theories and concludes, "Differential opportunity structure, associations, socialization, and social bonding can aid our understanding of crimes committed both by men and women and can take account of differences in the nature and extent of their crimes" (Morris, 1987:76).

There is not yet a well-developed, uniquely feminist explanation of crime and delinquency that can answer the generalizability or gender ratio questions. However, feminist theorists have approached the task of constructing such a theory by paying close attention to the dimensions of gender and sex roles that they believe other theories have ignored or misunderstood. This includes not only different sex-role expectations, but the significance of the underlying patriarchal structure that permeates all aspects of society.

> It is increasingly clear that gender stratification in patriarchal society is as powerful a system as is class. A feminist approach to delinquency means construction of explanations of female behavior that are sensitive to its patriarchal context. Feminist analysis of delinquency would also examine ways in which agencies of social control . . . act in ways to reinforce women's place in male society. (Chesney-Lind, 1989:19)

Women's Liberation and Female Crime

Freda Adler and Rita Simon address the issues of generalizability and sex ratio in crime from a "liberation" perspective. Their basic proposition is that, as social change occurs to advance male and female roles and behavior toward greater equality in the conforming contexts of education, occupation, family, politics, the military, and the economy, they become more similar in their deviant, delinquent, or criminal contexts as well.

Adler (1975) begins by showing a faster rate of increase in female arrests than in male arrests. She concludes that the differences in male and female criminality are decreasing rapidly. Her theoretical explanation for this is that the women's movement has brought about changes in traditional sex roles, greater equality for women, and an increase in the female labor force. An unintended consequence of this availability to women of a wider range of social roles previously reserved only for men is their greater involvement in another arena traditionally dominated by men—crime.

> But women, like men, do not live by bread alone. Almost every other aspect of their life has been similarly altered. The changing status of women as it affects family, marriage, employment, and social position has been well documented by all types of sociologists. But there is a curious hiatus: the movement for full equality has a darker side which has been slighted even by the scientific community. . . .
>
> In the same way that women are demanding equal opportunity in fields of legitimate endeavor, a similar number of determined women are forcing their way into the world of major crimes . . . formerly committed by males only. . . . Like her sisters in legitimate fields, the female criminal is fighting for her niche in the hierarchy [of crime]. . . . (Adler, 1975:13-14)

Simon (1975) offers a similar theory, referring to the changes in women's status in labor-force participation, education, professions and income. She shows that female property offenses have increased, for which more women are being arrested and incarcerated, while violent offenses by women have not increased. Her prediction is that white-collar, occupationally related crimes by women will increase even more as women take on more positions in the work force, allowing them greater opportunities to commit such crimes.

This liberation hypothesis has not received much empirical support (Mann, 1984). It has not yet been demonstrated that female equality has increased dramatically during the time of changing female crime rates, or that the two are somehow connected. Steffensmeier (1980) and others have shown that the increases in female crime predate the women's liberation movement. Furthermore, male-to-female ratios of crime have decreased somewhat, but the changes have not narrowed the gap all that much. Crime is still overwhelmingly a male phenomenon and recent trends do not show much change in the female rate of crime or in the ratio of male to female offenders (Steffensmeier and Streifel, 1992). Patterns of female delinquency and its relationship to male delinquency have remained little changed for a long time, and there is no relationship between feminist attitudes or ideology and female delinquency (Chesney-Lind and Shelden, 1992). Contrary to Simon's thesis, increases in female crime have been reported in non-white collar types of offenses, such as shoplifting (Datesman and Scarpitti, 1980).

Power-Control Theory of Gender and Delinquency

John Hagan's (1987; 1989a; Boritch and Hagan, 1990) "power-control theory" incorporates elements of feminist theory, conflict theory, and control theory. It accounts for the difference between male and female rates of delinquency by relating family structure (patriarchal/egalitarian) to the capitalistic economic system (class position) and to differences in the social control of males and females. According to power-control theory, "family class structure . . . derive[s] from the positions these spouses occupy in their work inside and outside the home." Family structure "shapes the social reproduction of gender relations, and in turn the social distribution of delinquency" (Hagan, 1989a:145).

Socialization within the family controls girls more, teaching boys to be risk-takers and girls to be risk-averse. This gender-based socialization and control is hypothesized to be stronger in "patriarchal" than in "egalitarian" families. Patriarchal families are those wherein the father's occupation places him in a "command" position, giving orders to others, and the mother either does not work outside the home or works in a job where she occupies an "obey" position, taking orders from supervisors. In egalitarian families, the father is absent or both mother and father work in jobs in which they have authority over others. Boys will be more delinquent than girls in any type of family, but:

> power-control theory predicts that patriarchal families will be charac-
> terized by large gender differences in common delinquent behaviour,
> while egalitarian families will be characterized by smaller gender dif-
> ferences in delinquency. (Hagan, 1989:158)

Hagan's own Canadian data tend to support this theory, but findings from other research have been less supportive. The class and gender differences, the low involvement of fathers in exercising parental control, and other internal family variables have no or very weak effects on delinquency. The gender difference in delinquency is about the same for patriarchal and egalitarian families (Morash and Chesney-Lind, 1991; Jensen and Thompson, 1990; Singer and Levine, 1988). Furthermore, the effects of family control variables on delinquent behavior are equally weak for both males and females (Hill and Atkinson, 1988).

Patriarchal Society and Crime

Although counted by some as "liberal feminism," the women's liberation theories of Adler and Simon are not considered to be feminist theories by Daly and Chesney-Lind (1988). Chesney-Lind (1989:19) refers to them rather as examples of "flawed theory building" that have been "more or less discredited." These authors also do not consider power-control theory to be feminist theory either, but simply a variation on the liberation hypothesis, because it is "arguing that mothers' work force participation . . . leads to daughters' delinquency." In effect, then, "mother's liberation causes daughter's crime" (Chesney-Lind, 1989:20).

If liberation and power-control theories are not feminist explanations of male and female crime, then what is?

> It is not easy to know when a work or action is feminist. . . . Neither
> a scholar's gender nor the focus of scholarship . . . can be used to dis-
> tinguish feminist, non-feminist, or even anti-feminist works. Research
> on women or on gender differences, whether conducted by a male or
> female criminologist, does not in itself qualify it as feminist. . . . [F]emin-
> ist inquiry is not limited to topics about women, it focuses on men as
> well." (Daly and Chesney-Lind, 1988:503)

In spite of this uncertainty about the distinguishing features of feminist theory, its theoretical development has apparently moved away from themes of female liberation and sex-role differentiation in family socialization. The themes emphasized in current feminist theory of crime are the pervasiveness of male dominance in patriarchal society and its impact on crimes committed both by and against women. This emphasis on patriarchy would seem to distinguish feminist theory of criminal behavior from non-feminist theory more clearly than the emphasis on women's liberation or family structure to account for gender differences in crime. It does not, however, represent a total departure from mainstream criminological theory. For instance, the primary dimension of power relations in feminist theory is no different than the power dimension in traditional, male-formulated conflict and Marxist theories. The difference lies in what *type* of power is placed at the center. In conflict theory, the dominant theme is the conflict between various powerful and powerless groups; while in Marxism, ruling class power dominates the proletariat. In feminist theory, male power over women is the dominant theme.

James Messerschmidt (1986), for example, modifies the Marxist position that capitalism is criminogenic because it exploits the working class to incorporate the feminist focus on patriarchy. His theory is that crime is caused by the combination of a male-dominated, patriarchal social structure and a capitalist economic system. To Messerschmidt, the criminality of women and the violent crime of lower-class men both result from their powerlessness, while corporate crimes and sexual crimes against women, especially rape, are the result of male power.

This patriarchal dominance is not only useful in understanding the gender differential in the rates of crime, according to feminist theory, it can also lead to a better understanding of such gender-specific offenses as prostitution by women and the commission of rape by men against women. Nowhere is the gender ratio more skewed toward male offenders than in the universality of males as perpetrators and the rarity of males as victims of rape. Closely related to this is the great disparity of males as offenders and females as victims of sexual and domestic abuse. Explaining rape and abuse is hardly unique to feminist theory, and differing feminist views have not yet coalesced into a coherent theory of rape and violence against women. Nevertheless, feminist research, theoretical, and policy agendas have brought attention to the issue of the extremely disadvantaged role of women as victims of rape and abuse. This issue has been defined not only in terms of female victimization and survivorship, but also in terms of the treatment of rape victims in the criminal justice system (Daly and Chesney-Lind, 1988).

Chesney-Lind (1989) has spelled out one possible process by which the patriarchal system, the family, physical and sexual abuse, "survival strategies" (e.g., running away from home), and other gender-relevant factors may cause female delinquency. Status offenses and minor delinquencies by girls are ways of responding to conflict in the family. The enforcement of a double standard of conduct for sons and daughters, even in non-traditional families, is one common source of this conflict. Sexual and physical abuse by stepfathers and others in the home is another. Girls who run away to the streets and engage in prostitution, theft, and other crimes are more likely than the boys who run away to have been victims of abuse. Thus, serious juvenile delinquency and, by extension, adult criminal careers are linked to the survival response of leaving home. These processes are similar for abused boys, but, "unlike boys, girls' victimization and their response to that victimization is specifically shaped by their status as young women" (Chesney-Lind, 1989:23). She argues that there are dramatic differences in childhood and adolescence for boys and girls. They live in very different worlds with very different choices. Even when boys and girls share similar circumstances these are filtered by gender. Therefore, family abuse, while also affecting boys, is especially important in the etiology of female delinquency and crime (Chesney-Lind and Shelden, 1992).

Empirical Validity of Feminist Theory

As shown above, the liberation hypothesis and power-control theory have been tested directly, but they have encountered non-supportive and contrary evidence. Both of these, however, are defined as non-feminist theories by some feminist theorists. Known variations in male and female patterns of crime and delinquency can be related to formulations such as Chesney-Lind's on female delinquency, but it is still difficult to find direct empirical tests of feminist hypotheses. Indirect tests by feminist theorists have found no or weak support for the hypothesis of major differences in the etiology of male and female crime. The same variables that are related to male offending are also related to female offending; gender modulates, but does not dramatically alter, the effects of these variables (Simpson and Ellis, 1995).

A generalized reliance on patriarchal social structure, such as Messerschmidt's (1986), as an explanation of all types of crime has the same problem as the Marxist explanation that "capitalism causes crime." Unless there is some way to measure degrees of patriarchy in different parts of society, any research within that same society will not allow for any variation in the independent variable. To test this theory, one would have to conduct cross-cultural comparisons of societies with greater or lesser patriarchy and examine the differences in male and female crime patterns. Some cross-national research has been done, in which the degree of gender inequality is measured in different societies. For example, Steffensmeier et al. (1989) compared the female percentage of arrests for homicide, major property crimes, and minor property crimes across a wide range of societies. They found that the ratio of female-to-male arrestees in different societies was related neither to their measure of "gender inequality" nor to "female economic marginality," but rather to the formalization of social control and greater access by women to consumer goods. Findings such as these, however, do not lend much support to the theory that the gender ratio in crime reflects patriarchal inequalities. It will take considerably more research than this study to measure more directly the concept of patriarchy in order to provide better tests of the theory.

Summary

Feminist theory focuses on the patriarchal system as the root division in society between the dominant and subordinate groups. Privileged males rule, make the rules, and enforce the rules. In this system, women are more disadvantaged, restricted, and controlled. Male dominance is maintained, and women are kept in their place in part by sex-role expectations that are enforced by both the informal and formal control systems. Gender disparities in the criminal justice system reflect male dominance and restrictive female sex roles. Women may be treated paternalistically by more lenient judgment in the system or punished more harshly for certain offenses that go strongly against traditional female sex-role expectations. Research on male-female differences in criminal justice decisions for offenders provides some data consistent with feminist theory, but for the most part, the gender of the offender has little or no effect on the outcome of criminal justice.

Feminist theory of criminal behavior has addressed two basic issues: whether or not explanations of law violations committed by males also apply to those committed by females, and what accounts for the high ratio of male-to-female crime rates. Earlier feminist theory postulated that committing crime and delinquency is a consequence of learning the male role; therefore, as women's liberation has increased the equality between men and women, female crime has risen to greater equality with male crime. Power-control theory proposed that the patriarchal family system creates more delinquent boys and less delinquent girls. Both these theories have had trouble in the face of empirical evidence and have been repudiated by many feminist theorists, who explain crime by reference to the basic patriarchal structure of society. No distinctive feminist theory on the etiology of crime has yet been formulated, but feminist theorists have utilized patriarchy to analyze rape and other sexual and physical violence by men against women and offenses by females. Feminist theory is still in formation, and the paucity of direct tests of its hypotheses has not yet provided a clear evaluation of its empirical validity.

Notes

1. Bowker with Chesney-Lind and Pollock (1978), Mann (1977), Messerschmidt (1986), Morris (1987), Daley and Chesney-Lind (1988), Simpson (1989; 1991), Daley (1989), Chesney-Lind (1988; 1989), and Gelsthorpe and Morris (1990), Chesney-Lind (1992), Daly (1992; 1994a; 1994b).

2. Virtually all criminologists recognize that in the past, the subject of female crime has been less studied than male crime. A theory that limits its scope only to male crime is certain to be viewed as non-feminist, but even those theories that have traditionally been proposed as general explanations of all crime, both male and female, are defined as non-feminist theory. Further, simply concentrating on female crime or explaining female versus male crime rates is insufficient to define feminist theory. Almost all of the research and theory on female crime and delinquency from the time of Lombroso to the 1970s has been defined as non-feminist theory (see, for instance, Chesney-Lind and Shelden, 1992). A theory that offers a specific explanation for female crime by modifying and extending extant theory (e.g. Ogle et al., 1995) will not be interpreted as a feminist theory. If a "traditional" theory is used to explain the gender ratio in crime, especially if the theory leans on biological differences between male and female, it is very unlikely to be defined as a feminist theory.

3. Leonard (1982) contends that all "traditional" theories are incapable of explaining female crime, but her critique mainly repeats the same empirical and logical flaws in the traditional theories that have long been identified by non-feminist critics. Contrary to her original assumption about the inadequacies of traditional theories, Leonard's analysis shows that some non-feminist theories, especially differential association and social learning, are quite capable of providing some explanation for both male and female crime. In fact, her suggestions for moving "toward a feminist theory of crime" are primarily selections of certain concepts and variables from the same traditional theories she has been criticizing for their insensitivity to feminist issues.

CHAPTER 11

INTEGRATING CRIMINOLOGICAL THEORIES

Theory Competition Versus Theory Integration

There are three principal ways by which theories can be evaluated and developed. The first is to consider each theory on its own. To the extent that the theory's predictions are confirmed by the data, it can be accepted; to the extent that they are disconfirmed by the evidence, it can be modified or discarded. The second way is to subject two or more theories to "theory competition" (Liska et al., 1989). Theory competition is the logical, conceptual, or empirical comparisons of two or more theories to determine which offers the better or best explanation of crime. In the previous chapters, the focus was on single-theory explication and assessment, during which some attention was given to the comparison of theories.

Evaluation of the evidence on a single theory seldom leads to a complete rejection of that theory. A modicum of truth can usually be found in each theory. At the other extreme, no theory has been able to explain all variations in crime. The evidence in support of, or counter to, most theories lies in between these two extremes.

The question remains, how well does each theory do in comparison with other theories? Criticism of one theory from the perspective of another is common, and direct competitive testing of two or more rival theories is often reported in the literature. Without going into all the details, if one were to compare the various theories introduced and evaluated in this book according to relative amount of empirical support, the result could be stated fairly succinctly. The evidence on law formation favors pluralistic conflict theory more than consensus or Marxist models. None of the theories (conflict, labeling, Marxist, or feminist) fits well with the data on disparities in the administration of criminal justice. The older biological theories of criminality have largely been discredited. Even the more recent and sophisticated biological theories of criminal behavior fare poorly in comparison with sociological theories. Psychological approaches that rely on emotional disturbance or personality traits do not perform as well as sociological or social-psychological explanations. Among the latter, strain and labeling theories have the weakest empirical support. Evidence in favor of deterrence and control/bonding theories range from weak to moderate. Social learning theory has received the strongest and most consistent empirical support. Structural theories of crime rates are seldom tested directly, but the research that has been conducted favors social disorganization/anomie, and the relationships found in this research range from moderate to strong.

The third way to assess and construct theory is by theoretical integration. Having made brief reference to theoretical integration in previous chapters, I will now return to it in some detail in this concluding chapter. The goal of theory integration is to identify commonalities in two or more theories to produce a synthesis that is superior to any one theory individually. Farnworth (1989) defines theoretical integration as:

> [T]he combination of two or more pre-existing theories, selected on the basis of their perceived commonalities, into a single reformulated theoretical model with greater comprehensiveness and explanatory value than any one of its component theories. (Farnworth, 1989:95)[1]

Theoretical integration often involves such deliberate attempts to fuse together two closely related theories, but it may also stem from theory competition. Upon closer examination, two opposing theories may not be as incompatible as thought. All of the theories reviewed in previous chapters have been subjected, to some degree, both to competition and to integration with other theories. When each theory was first formulated, it more or less leaned upon prior theories and drew from a number of different sources. Moreover, all these theories have been revised in some fashion after their original statements. These revisions almost always borrow from the insights and explanations found in other theories and constitute at least a partial integration of theories. (For example, see the revisions suggested for deterrence theory in Chapter 2, for strain theory in Chapter 7, and for labeling theory in Chapter 6.) At the same time, the proponents of each theory implicitly or explicitly compare its explanatory power with alternative explanations. Both theory competition and integration have been vigorously defended (see the various contributors to Messner et al., 1989). Hirschi and Gottfredson (Hirschi, 1979; 1989; Gottfredson and Hirschi, 1990) are strong proponents of the oppositional strategy of pitting theories against one another, while Elliott advocates theoretical integration (Elliott, 1985; Elliott et al., 1979; Elliott et al., 1985). Hirschi argues that what passes for theoretical integration in criminology usually involves ignoring crucial differences between the theories undergoing integration. He points out that some "integrated theories are merely oppositional theories in disguise, theories that pretend to open-mindedness while in fact taking sides in theoretical disputes" (Hirschi, 1989:41-42):

> I do not favor efforts to link theories together unless it can be shown that they are for all intents and purposes the same theory. . . .
> The first purpose of oppositional theory construction is to make the world safe for a theory contrary to currently accepted views. . . . Therefore, oppositional theorists should not make life easy for those interested in preserving the status quo. They should instead remain at all times blind to the weaknesses of their own position and stubborn in its defense. Finally, they should never smile. (Hirschi, 1989:44-45)

Akers (1989) agrees with Hirschi that the integration of theories, if done without regard to incompatibilities, can result in useless "theoretical mush." On the other hand, a strictly oppositional strategy often overlooks important compatibilities between theories.

> [T]he insistence on keeping theories separate and competing carries . . . the risk of ignoring similarities and overlap between two theories even when they are different. . . .
> If concepts and propositions from two or more theories are essentially the same, why pretend they are different and ignore the similarity merely for the sake of retaining separate theories? Such an attitude results in theories that are different in name only. (Akers, 1989:24-25)

Bernard and Snipes (1995) argue that Hirschi's opposition to integration is based on his characterization of theories as falling into three main categories: "control," "strain," and "cultural deviance." Hirschi believes that these are inherently incompatible theories resting on irreconcilable assumptions. Bernard and Snipes maintain that Hirschi reaches this conclusion because he has misinterpreted and distorted both strain and cultural deviance theory (see also Akers, 1996). When strain and cultural deviance theories are properly interpreted, they are not incompatible with control theory and the theories can be integrated.

Thornberry (1989) suggests "theoretical elaboration" as a strategy for theory building that lies somewhere between integration and outright opposition. In theoretical elaboration one begins with a particular theory and extends it as far as one can "to build a more and more comprehensive model by the logical extension of the basic propositions" (Thornberry, 1989:56). In the process of elaborating on the basic theory, the theorist may or may not incorporate compatible propositions and concepts from other theories.

Varieties of Theoretical Integration in Criminology

Liska et al. (1989) identify different types of theoretical integration. One type is *conceptual* integration, by which concepts from one theory are shown to overlap in meaning with concepts from another theory. *Propositional* integration relates propositions from different theories. This can be accomplished by showing how two or more theories make the same predictions about crime, even though each begins with different concepts and assumptions (e.g., both anomie theory and conflict theory would predict higher crime rates in the lower class). Propositional integration can also be done by placing the explanatory variables from different theories into some kind of casual or explanatory sequence. The sequence starts with the variables from one theory (e.g., social disorganization) to explain the variations in variables from another theory (e.g., attachment to family), which in turn can be used to explain delinquency. Theoretical integration can also be *within-level* (only micro-level or only macro-level) or *cross-level* (structural-processual).

The literature contains many examples of conceptual and propositional integration, within-level integration, and cross-level integration: *biological and psychosocial* theories (Jeffery, 1977; Gove and Hughes, 1989; Wellford, 1989); *anomie, labeling, and control* theories (Aultman and Wellford, 1979); *deterrence and social bonding* theories (Minor, 1977; Hawkins and Williams, 1989; Williams and Hawkins, 1989); *conflict and control theories* (Hagan, 1989a; 1989b); *Marxist and control/learning* theories (Colvin and Pauly, 1983); *Marxist and feminist theory* (Messerschmidt, 1986); *labeling, anomie, and social learning* theories (Braithwaite, 1989); and other theories (Farrell, 1989).[2]

To explicate all the instances of theoretical integration would take us beyond the purposes of this book. Instead, a few are presented here to illustrate integration of criminological theories. The illustrations given below involve social learning theory in one way or another, and most of them also encompass social bonding theory. There are two reasons for this. First, since I am a social learning theorist (see Chapter 4), I am more familiar with social learning integrations, including, of course, my own. Second, social learning and social bonding concepts and hypotheses are those most frequently used in the theoretical integrations found in the literature.[3]

Conceptual Integration

Akers: Integration by Conceptual Absorption

Akers (1973; 1977) long ago showed the ways in which social learning theory concepts and propositions overlap with and complement social bonding, labeling, conflict, anomie, and deterrence theories. Later, he proposed that integration could be achieved by "conceptual absorption." Conceptual absorption means subsuming concepts from one theory as special cases of the phenomena defined by the concepts of another (Akers and Cochran, 1985; Akers, 1989).

For instance, in social bonding theory, the concept of "belief" refers to general moral beliefs which, if strongly adhered to, constrain delinquency. The belief concept can be absorbed into the more general social learning concept of "definitions" favorable or unfavorable to crime and delinquency. This broader concept incorporates both general and specific beliefs and attitudes that constrain criminal and delinquent behavior, and that approve of or justify the behavior under certain circumstances. Strong adherence to conventional beliefs, therefore, is only one type of definition unfavorable to deviance, just as weak adherence to conventional moral beliefs is only one type of definition favorable to deviance. There is nothing in "beliefs" that is not included in "definitions," but definitions includes phenomena left out of the belief concept.

Akers contends that the social bonding concept of "commitment" can also be absorbed by social learning concepts. Commitment refers to the costs of criminal activity, e.g., the loss of investments made in conventional lines of activity. This identifies only one part of a more general social learning process referred to in the concept of "differential reinforcement." Differential reinforcement refers to the reward/punishment balance for both conforming and deviant activity. Commitment identifies only one specific item (loss of investment) in a larger classification of costs. Furthermore, that item enters into differential reinforcement on only one side of the overall reinforcement balance. There is nothing in commitment that is not already wholly contained in differential reinforcement.

The social bonding concept of "attachment" refers to the closeness of relationships and affectional ties with parents, peers, and others. According to Akers, this can be subsumed under the concept of the modalities of differential association as one measure of "intensity" of association specified in social learning theory. Attachment also means identification with others as role models, obviously subsumable under the general concept of imitation in social learning theory.

Akers notes that these areas of conceptual commonalities do not necessarily lead to the same propositions about delinquency. Conceptual integration does not by itself produce propositional integration. For example, while social bonding theory predicts that strong attachment to others will inhibit delinquency, even if that attachment is to delinquent friends, social learning theory predicts the opposite outcome—that delinquency will be *facilitated* by intense association or attachment with or to delinquent friends.

Thornberry (1989) contends that this subsuming of concepts from theories under social learning concepts, while interesting, stops well short of a fully integrated model. Understandably, Hirschi (1989) objects to this kind of conceptual absorption, because it is social bonding concepts that are absorbed. Conceptual absorption also runs the risk of becoming reductionist (Akers, 1968). These reservations about conceptual integration are well taken, because Akers has not shown that conceptual absorption produces anything more than what is already contained in social learning theory. If absorption simply means that concepts from other theories are subsumed under existing social learning concepts, then social learning has not been integrated with the other theories. It has simply executed a hostile takeover.

Pearson and Weiner: Conceptual Integrative Framework

The most comprehensive effort at conceptual integration is made by Frank S. Pearson and Neil A. Weiner (1985), by which they propose to integrate concepts from *all* the major macro and micro theories of criminal behavior into one "integrative framework." This integrative framework results from identifying "concepts common to particular theories and framing these concepts in a common vocabulary" (1985:119). Social learning theory is the principal foundation of the Pearson-Weiner model.

From social learning theory they identify eight general concepts or sets of variables. First, six of these concepts refer to antecedent factors in the ongoing learning process: (1) *utility* (reward/punishment), (2) *behavior skill* (the behavioral techniques of committing crime learned from reinforcement and imitation), (3) *signs of favorable opportunities* to commit crime (discriminative stimuli), (4) *behavioral resources*, (5) *rules of expedience* (learned guidelines for maximizing rewards, avoiding negative sanctions, and imitating successful role models), and (6) *rules of morality* (rules that define behavior as right or wrong). Second, Pearson and Weiner define two feedback mechanisms in the learning process. These are consequences of an act that have an impact on its future occurrence: (7) *utility receptions* (acquisition of rewards and punishments by the behavior) and (8) *information acquisition* (knowledge received about the behavior that may be used in a decision to repeat the act).

Pearson and Weiner then show how the principal concepts of all the other major theories can be seen as variations on, or subtypes of, these eight general concepts. For instance, they contend that attachment (from social bonding theory) to others entails imitating them and that these others are sources of positive utility in the form of emotional satisfaction. Similarly, the concept of commitment fits under the general concept of utility demand and reception. Concepts from deterrence and rational choice theories can be subsumed under utility demand, rules of expedience, signs of favorable opportunities, utility reception and information acquisition. Strain theory concepts of utilizing illegitimate means and adapting to the lack of opportunities are incorporated into the concepts of utility demand, rules of expedience, and signs of favorable opportunities. Finally, Pearson and Weiner add macro-level concepts to the framework as social-structural sources of the production and distribution of utilities, opportunities, and the rules of expedience and morality.

The scope of Pearson's and Weiner's (1985) conceptual integration of many different theories into a consistent, coherent framework is impressive. To my knowledge, however, it has not received much attention in criminological discourse (but see Bernard and Snipes, 1995, for recent attention to the framework). Moreover, just as in Akers' conceptual absorption strategy, the Pearson-Weiner model only demonstrates definitional and operational similarities among different concepts; it does not, by itself, produce new testable propositions.

Propositional Integration

Elliott's Integrative Model of Strain, Bonding, and Learning

Delbert S. Elliott and his associates have proposed the best known theoretical integration of strain, control, and social learning theories. As shown in the figure below, their integrated model proposes that (1) strain (in the family and school) weakens (2) social bonds to conventional society, which in turn promotes (3) strong bonds to delinquent peers (delinquent definitions, reinforcement, modeling and association from social learning theory). It is these strong bonds to delinquent peers, therefore, that are principal factors in (4) the commission of delinquent behavior.

Figure 11.1

Elliott's Integrated Theory of Delinquent Behavior			
(1)	(2)	(3)	(4)
Strain →	Weak Conventional Bonding →	Strong Bonding to Delinquent Peers →	Delinquent Behavior
Discrepancy in aspirations/achievements and other strain in the family and school	Family and school involvement, commitment, and attachment	Exposure to deviant peers compared to non-deviant peers; social reinforcement for delinquent behavior; peers' and ones' own attitudes Favorable to delinquency	Self-reported

Adapted from Elliott et al. (1985:94 and 146)

Elliott et al. argue that strain, control, and learning theories share some basic assumptions, propositions, and implications for social policy. However, they recognize some differences in assumptions which must be reconciled before propositional integration can be done. For instance, control theory starts with the assumption of a disposition by everyone to deviate from the law, so that the only source of variation in criminal or delinquent behavior is how strongly or weakly social control prevents deviant behavior. Strain theory, on the other hand, makes no assumptions about the inherent motives shared by all of us to commit crime. It makes no reference to the strength of social controls and hypothesizes that persons exposed to strain are more highly motivated to commit deviant acts than those who are not. Social learning theory proposes variation in motivation both to commit and refrain from offenses.

In social bonding theory the content and direction of socialization is always conventional; deviance results only from weaknesses or failures of socialization. In social learning theory, the direction in which the individual is socialized may be conforming or deviant. Delinquency is learned in the same way that conforming behavior is learned, and socialization may be more or less successful or unsuccessful in either direction.

Elliott et al. reconcile these positions by essentially taking the side of strain and learning theory. They do away with the assumption of a natural or uniform motivation to crime, allowing for bonding to produce either conventional or deviant outcomes, depending on the involvement with conforming or deviant peers. Not surprisingly, Hirschi (1989) has objected to this method of reconciling the differences among the theories. He contends that it is not integration at all, but simply a rejection of the assumptions of social bonding theory in favor of those of the other two theories.

Elliott et al. (1985) provide a rationale for building the assumptions of strain and learning theory into their integrated model, while retaining social bonding terminology and propositions. They point out that Hirschi and other control theorists have themselves previously recognized that the assumption of no variation in the positive motivation to commit crime is not tenable. They see no logical or empirical necessity for the assumption of uniform criminal motivation. (See the discussion of this issue in Chapter 5.) Therefore, their integrated model begins with the assumption that there is variation in motivations both to deviate and to conform.

Since family and school are the major conventionally socializing agencies in society, the model hypothesizes that any strong attachment to them promotes the learning of non-delinquent behavior. The attitudes, models, and rewards in these groups are more conducive to conforming than to delinquent behavior. By the same process, strong bonds to delinquent peers promote the learning of delinquent behavior more so than conventional behavior. Conventional socialization begins in the home, but it may be inadequate; therefore, weakened bonds to the family will enhance bonding to peers. The weaker the bond to conventional peers and the stronger the bond to delinquent peers, the greater the probability of delinquent behavior.

Elliott et al. tested this model with longitudinal data from their National Youth Survey and found that the integrated model was strongly supported by the findings. The original model proposed that the main direct effect on delinquent behavior would come from bonding to delinquent/non-delinquent peers. Most of the effect of strain and conventional bonding on delinquent behavior should come about indirectly through the effect that strain and bonding has on peer bonding. However, the hypothesis in the integrated theory, that bonding and strain variables have direct effects on delinquent behavior separate from their relationship with peer bonding, was not supported by the data. Strain and conventional bonding had *no* direct effect on delinquent behavior. Only bonding to delinquent peers had a strong, direct effect. This was the most predictive variable in the model. All the other variables had only indirect effects by their relationship with delinquent peer bonds. The rest of the variables added very little to the explanation of delinquency beyond that given by the direct effect of delinquent peer variables.

Elliott et al. recognized that the final integrated model that best fits the data could be stated as a social learning theory, but they chose instead to use the language of social bonding theory in the integrative model. They did this because:

It is not clear that a social learning model would have predicted a conditional relationship between conventional bonding (restraints) and deviant bonding (rewards). . . . The predictive efficiency resulting from adding the interaction effects to the linear regression model was relatively small (a 4 percent relative increase . . .) but statistically significant and substantively important. (Elliott et al. 1985:137)

In my opinion, even with the addition of the interactive effects of conventional bonding, the final model reported by Elliott et al. is more a variation on social learning theory (with bonding modifications) than it is a variation on social bonding theory (with learning modifications). The concepts and measures of differential attachment and involvement with family and school (under (2) in the model above) and differential involvement with non-delinquent or delinquent peers (under (3) in the model) correspond much more closely with concepts in social learning theory, and the way in which these concepts have been measured in previous research, than with social bonding concepts. Indeed, the measures of deviant peer bonds used by Elliott et al. are essentially measures of the main variables in social learning theory—differential associations, reinforcement, modeling, and definitions.

Most importantly, the findings on the relationship of peer bonding to delinquency in the model agree with predictions from social learning, rather than predictions from social bonding. Agnew's (1993) re-analysis of the data from the National Youth Survey confirms this conclusion. It is precisely on this issue that social learning and social bonding make opposing predictions. Social learning theory predicts that delinquent behavior is related to involvement with deviant peers, and conforming behavior is related to involvement with conventional peers. The social bonding proposition that strong attachment to others prevents delinquent behavior, even when that attachment is to unconventional peers, is not supported. It cannot be sustained either in a pure social bonding theory or a theory integrating bonding and learning. Thus, in any empirically valid integration of bonding and learning theory, only the learning theory proposition can survive. Any resulting integration would not be acceptable to social bonding theorists.

Krohn's Network Analysis

Marvin D. Krohn (1986) has proposed an explanation of delinquency that draws on both social learning and social bonding theory. His network theory is also a cross-level integration that connects the structural characteristics of social networks and interactional processes. His theory does not represent a full integration of the two theories, but rather represents what Krohn refers to as a "bridging" of theoretical propositions regarding the delinquency-enhancing effects of differential association and the delinquency-constraining effects of social bonds.

A social network is a set of actors, individuals or groups linked by friendship or some other relationship. A personal network refers to an individual's set of linkages to others (e.g., family, friends, church, and school). Consistent with social control theory, Krohn hypothesizes that "a social network constrains individual behavior . . . and the probability of behavior consistent with the continuance of their network relationships will increase" (Krohn, 1986:S82-S83). He makes the same decision as Elliott et al., rejecting the social bonding hypothesis that this constraint will lead only to conformity to conventional norms. Instead, consistent with social learning theory, his network analysis hypothesizes that "the network could be formed around participation in deviant activities and, as a consequence, the constraining effect of the network would be toward deviant behavior" (Krohn, 1986:S83).

Krohn identifies two major structural characteristics of social networks—multiplexity and density. Multiplexity is the *number* of different relationships or contexts that two or more persons have in common. For instance, two boys may be friends, live in the same neighborhood, go to the same church, belong to the same scout troop, attend the same school in the same grade, and so on. The greater the network multiplexity, the greater the constraint on the individual's behavior. The direction of this constraint is usually to lower delinquent behavior, but this is only because the multiplexity is most likely to be within family, school, and other conventionally oriented contexts, rather than within delinquent contexts. This recognizes both "what individuals' associates do (differential association) and the kind of activities in which they are mutually involved (commitment and/or involvement)" (Krohn, 1986:S84).

Network density refers to the *ratio* of existing social relationships to the maximum total number of possible relationships in a network. A small community in which everyone knows and interacts with everyone else would have a high network density. The higher the network density, the lower the delinquency rate. Network density is inversely related to population density (the number of persons within a given geographical area). The higher the population density, the lower the network density; therefore, the higher the delinquency rate.

Thornberry's Interactional Theory

Terence P. Thornberry (1987; Thornberry et al., 1991) integrates elements of social structure, social bonding, and social learning theory into an "interactional theory" of delinquency. Social class, race, community, and neighborhood characteristics affect both the elements of the social bond and social learning variables. The underlying cause of delinquency is the weakening of the bonds to society. But this weakening simply renders a youngster a more likely candidate for delinquency.

Delinquent acts will not occur until they have been learned through association, reinforcement, and definitions. To the extent that this continues over time, delinquency will become a stable part of a person's behavioral patterns.

These influences are not static but vary by age and at different stages of onset, continuation, or cessation of delinquency. Moreover, the relationships among bonding, learning, and delinquency do not all run in one direction. For instance, a lower attachment to parents can lead to a lowered commitment to school, which in turn can reduce the attachment to parents. Similarly, lowered commitment and attachment lead to delinquent behavior; this involvement in delinquency, in turn, will tend to interfere with the attachment to parents and the commitment to school.

Thornberry et al. (1991) found no support for the hypotheses about the reciprocal effects of parental attachment and school commitment. They did find reciprocal effects, by which the effect of delinquency on attachment and commitment were greater than the effects of attachment and commitment on delinquency. However, all the relationships were weak. Later, Thornberry et al. (1994) reported reciprocal effects of social learning variables and delinquency. Theirs and other research have found that the social learning variable of differential association has significant influence in all phases of delinquency (Smith et al., 1991).

Kaplan's Self-Derogation Theory

Howard B. Kaplan (1975) proposed a self-esteem/derogation theory of adolescent deviance that brings together deviant peer influences (social learning theory), family and school factors (control theory), dealing with failure to live up to conventional expectations (strain theory), and self-concept (symbolic interactionism and labeling theory). In this theory, delinquency and drug use are viewed as the response of certain adolescents to feelings of low self-esteem or self-derogation. According to Kaplan, each person has a "self-esteem motive" to take actions that minimize negative self-attitudes and maximize positive perceptions of self. For most people, experiences in conventional groups and conformity to their expectations produce positive self-concepts. But those adolescents for whom this is not true will turn to deviant groups and activities in an effort to get rid of self-derogatory attitudes and develop self-esteem.

If the inability to conform to conventional standards and interaction with others in the family, school, and peer groups is self-devaluing, then the social control exercised in these conventional groups becomes less effective. An individual's motivation to conform is lessened, and the motivation to deviate is increased. Conventionality becomes associated with self-derogation. As the adolescent becomes aware of delinquent alternatives, he or she will gravitate to those deviant groups that are perceived as offering an enhancement of self-esteem and as countering self-derogatory attitudes. Persistence and escalation of delinquency and drug use and greater involvement in deviant groups will occur to the extent that such actions continue to satisfy the need for positive self-evaluation. Positively conforming to the standards of a new reference group by committing deviant acts, as well as the reactions of deviant peers, allows a person to develop a positive, albeit deviant, identity. At the same time, the deviant affiliations enable that person to escape from the stress of self-derogation brought on by the failure to live up to the conventional expectations of family and school.

Kaplan and his associates have conducted a series of research projects to test out this general model, primarily involving adolescent substance abuse, and find some support for it. The overall model accounts for moderate amounts of variation in delinquent behavior. However, the strongest effects in the model come from peer associations, while the self-attitude measures are not as strongly related to delinquent outcomes (Kaplan et al., 1982; 1986).

Bernard's Unified Conflict Theory of Criminal Behavior and Criminal Law

Conflict, Marxist, and feminist theories each account for law-making and law-enforcing, rates of crime, and criminal behavior by reference to general societal factors and patterns of dominance in society—group conflict, capitalism, and patriarchy respectively (see Chapters 8, 9, and 10). When these theories move from using these general factors to explain criminal law and crime rates to using them to account for criminal behavior, they incorporate variables from other theories (see Quinney, 1970; Colvin and Pauly, 1983).

This is also what Thomas Bernard (Vold and Bernard, 1986:286-287) does in his "unified conflict theory of crime." He accounts for rates of crime, variations in individual criminal behavior, and criminal law and justice by integrating conflict propositions from Vold, Quinney, and others with Akers' view of social structure and social learning. The unified theory is stated in five main sets of propositions. Bernard claims that these statements produce:

> [A] theory of criminal law . . . since it explains the differences in official crime rates in terms of differences in the enactment and the enforcement of criminal laws. It includes and is based on a theory of criminal behavior, a social learning theory that argues that criminal behavior is normally learned behavior responding to different reinforcement schedules operating in different social structural locations. (Vold and Bernard, 1986:288)

Members of complex societies are members of different groups and, therefore, experience differences in the schedules of reinforcement and other social learning variables that produce behavior patterns that differ systematically across the groups. Since their values are the ones least protected by criminal law, members of less powerful groups have a higher risk of learning behavior that runs counter to the law. Even when members of the more powerful groups do commit law violations, law enforcement agencies find it more difficult or are more reluctant to apprehend and process them than they would law violators from less powerful groups. Thus, there will be a differential enforcement of the law and higher official rates of crime among the less powerful groups. The component parts of the theory, social learning and group conflict, have been studied, but Bernard does not report any direct empirical tests of the unified theory.

Tittle's Control Balance Theory

Charles Tittle proposes a "synthetic integration" in which "control balance" is the unifying causal process in criminal and deviant behavior.[4] Control balance is defined as the ratio of how much the individual is liable to control to how much he or she is able to control. This control balance is implicated in both motivation and inhibition of deviant behavior.

> The central premise of the theory is that the amount of control to which people are subject relative to the amount of control they can exercise affects their general probability that they will commit specific types of deviance. Deviant behavior is interpreted as a device, or maneuver, that helps people escape deficits and extend surpluses of control.
>
> An unbalanced control ratio, in combination with a desire for autonomy and fundamental bodily and psychic needs, predisposes an individual to act deviantly. (Tittle, 1995: 142, 147-148)

Control balance operates in the context of four main variables: *predisposition* (deviant motivation), *provocation* (positive and negative situational stimulation), *opportunity* (to commit specific types of deviance), and *constraint* (actual or perceived likelihood that one will be subject to restraining reactions by others). These incorporate concepts from social learning, anomie, deterrence/rational choice, and social bonding theory. The probability of deviance occurring is higher when the control ratio is imbalanced, either negatively or positively, and is lower when control is balanced. Those individuals experiencing "control deficits" will be predisposed toward predatory, defiant, or submissive deviance, while those with "control surpluses" will be predisposed toward "exploitative" or "decadent" deviance. "The theory contends that deviant behavior is undertaken mainly to alter the deviant's control ratio, even if temporarily" (Tittle, 1995:192). The predisposed individual must perceive that a deviant act will alter the balance of control, be in a situation that affords the opportunity to commit the act, and expect that the chance of countercontrol is not enough to overwhelm the balancing expected to be produced by the deviant act. The major sources of motivation and constraints on behavior, as well as opportunity and situational variables, are incorporated in a sequence of events leading to the commission of crime and deviance, in which balance control is the central process.

Control balance theory has not yet been tested. Tittle reviews the known relationships of crime and delinquency to a series of sociodemographic variables (age, gender, race, marital and parental status, urban living, and class) and offers an explanation of each by reference to control balance or imbalance. But he recognizes that this does not provide a direct test of the theory. "Firmer judgment about the empirical credibility of the theory must wait for tests with more precise and directly applicable data, which existing data sets do not permit" (Tittle, 1995:261).

How Successful Has Theoretical Integration Been in Criminology?

The weight of opinion in criminology favors the search for parsimonious, empirically valid integrated explanations of crime and criminal justice. The efforts reviewed in this chapter and references to other integrations in previous chapters demonstrate that theoretical integration has been given some priority in the development of criminological theory. The momentum toward theoretical integration was given a boost by a major conference held at the State University of New York in Albany (Messner et al., 1989), and integration of theories continues to be a prime topic at criminological meetings and in the criminological literature.[5]

Notwithstanding the value of theoretical integration as an ideal, in practice integrated models in criminology have met with mixed success and acceptance. Some have received empirical support, while others have received little or no testing. Many have been ignored. Within the overall favorable climate of opinion in criminology toward theoretical integration, there continues to be a considerable indifference and a healthy skepticism toward integration as a theory-building strategy.

Indeed, in spite of my own long-standing orientation to integration and my search for commonalities among theories, I see some value in the oppositional strategy. I have used the competitive approach in pitting social learning against alternative explanations of criminal and deviant behavior (Akers and Cochran, 1985; Krohn et al., 1984; Boeringer and Akers, 1993). The social learning integration of principles of differential association and reinforcement has been successful, empirically sustained, and has received considerable attention in criminology.[6] Nonetheless, I still have reservations about the future of theoretical integration (Akers, 1989). The issue of theory competition versus theory integration has not yet been, and perhaps should not necessarily be, fully resolved.

Summary

Theoretical development takes place through explicating, testing, and modifying a single theory, through competition of rival theories, and through theoretical integration. Theoretical integration can be conceptual and/or propositional. It entails either theories at the same level of explanation or theories from different explanatory levels. Social learning theory, in one way or another, is a main component of integrative models in criminology, along with social bonding and strain theories.

Pearson and Weiner present a framework for integrating concepts from *all* the major macro and micro theories of criminal behavior, utilizing learning concepts. Akers proposes the absorption of concepts from other theories by social learning concepts. Elliott proposes a theory of delinquency that integrates propositions of strain, control, and social learning theories. Krohn draws upon bonding and social learning theory in social network theory. Thornberry integrates structural, bonding, learning, and other variables in an interactive theory. Kaplan uses self-esteem as the central variable that ties learning, bonding, and labeling effects together. Bernard proposes an integration of conflict and social learning theory to account for both criminal behavior and criminal law. Tittle offers a general integrative theory that relies on the concept of control balance. Although there has been much integrative activity and a positive orientation toward theoretical integration in criminology, there remains controversy and skepticism about the value of building theory by melding together different explanations of crime and delinquency.

Notes

1. See the similar definition by Thornberry (1989:52). Liska et al. (1989:2) define theoretical integration more loosely as "the formulation of linkages among different theoretical arguments."

2. For excellent introductory reviews of other theoretical integrations, see Siegel and Senna (1991) and Shoemaker (1990). For recent scholarly reviews and discussions of issues in theoretical integration see Bernard and Snipes (1995) and Tittle (1995).

3. There are many other examples of partial or full integration with social learning besides those given here, several of which have been discussed or alluded to in previous chapters. See Cloward and Ohlin (1961), differential association and differential opportunity; Voss (1969), containment and differential association; Conger (1976), social bonding and social learning; Johnson (1979), social bonding, learning, and strain; Braukman et al. (1980), social bonding and learning; Anderson et al. (1977) and Grasmick et al. (1980), deterrence, social learning, and social bonding; Kandel and Adler (1982), social bonding and learning; Massey and Krohn (1986), social bonding and social learning; Hawkins and Lishner (1987), social bonding, learning, and strain; and Agnew (1991), strain and social learning.

4. Jack Gibbs (1989) proposes "control" as the central unifying notion for sociology. Frances Cullen (1994), proposes that "social support" can be used as the central organizing concept around which all of criminology can be unified. He offers several propositions that link "differential social support" to crime, victimization, law, criminal justice, and prevention.

5. The program listings at meetings of the American Society of Criminology and of the Academy of Criminal Justice Sciences nearly always include papers or whole sessions on theoretical integration.

6. However, even successful integrations are often ignored. The integration of the principles of differential association and differential reinforcement was first proposed almost thirty years ago. During that time, it has become one of the most visible theories in criminology and is considered standard fare in criminology, delinquency, and deviance textbooks. In spite of this, one still sees references in the literature to differential association theory without any mention whatsoever of its integration into social learning theory or any references to differential association and social learning, as if they were unrelated or even rival theories.

REFERENCES
and
INDEXES

REFERENCES

Adler, Freda

1975 Sisters in Crime: The Rise of the New Female Criminal. New York: McGraw-Hill.

Adler, Patricia and Peter Adler

1978 "Tinydopers: a case study of deviant socialization," Symbolic Interaction 1:90-105.

Agnew, Robert

1985a "Social control theory and delinquency: a longitudinal test," Criminology 23:47-62.

1985b "A revised strain theory of delinquency," Social Forces 64:151-167.

1991a "The interactive effect of peer variables on delinquency," Criminology 29:47-72.

1991b "A longitudinal test of social control theory and delinquency," Journal of Research of Crime and Delinquency 28:126-156.

1992 "Foundation for a general strain theory of crime and delinquency," Criminology 30:47-88.

1993 "Why do they do it? An examination of the intervening mechanisms between 'social control' variables and delinquency," Journal of Research in Crime and Delinquency 30:245-266.

1994 "The techniques of neutralization and violence," Criminology 32:555-580.

1995 "Determinism, indeterminism, and crime: an empirical exploration," Criminology 33:83-110.

Agnew, Robert and Helene Raskin White

1992 "An empirical test of general strain theory," Criminology 30:475-500.

Aichhorn, August

1963 Wayward Youth. New York: Viking

Akers, Ronald L.

1964 "Socio-economic status and delinquent behavior: a re-test," Journal of Research in Crime and Delinquency 1:38-46.

1965 "Toward a comparative definition of law," Journal of Criminal Law, Criminology, and Police Science 56:301-6.

1968 "Problems in the sociology of deviance: social definitions and behavior," Social Forces 46:455-65.

1973 Deviant Behavior: A Social Learning Approach. Belmont, CA: Wadsworth.

1977 Deviant Behavior: A Social Learning Approach. Second Edition. Belmont, CA: Wadsworth.

1979 "Theory and ideology in Marxist criminology," Criminology 16:527-544.

1980 "Further critical thoughts on Marxist criminology: Comment on Turk, Toby, and Klockars," pp. 133-138 in James A. Inciardi, ed., Radical Criminology: The Coming Crises. Beverly Hills, CA: Sage.

1985 Deviant Behavior: A Social Learning Approach. Third Edition Belmont, CA: Wadsworth. Reprinted 1992. Fairfax, VA: Techbooks.

1990 "Rational choice, deterrence, and social learning theory: the path not taken," Journal of Criminal Law and Criminology 81:653-676.

1991 "Self-control as a general theory of crime," Journal of Quantitative Criminology 7:201-211.

1992a "Linking sociology and its specialties: the case of criminology," Social Forces 71:1-16.

1992b Drugs, Alcohol, and Society: Social Structure, Process and Policy. Belmont, CA: Wadsworth.

Akers, Ronald L., Robert L. Burgess, and Weldon Johnson

1968 "Opiate use, addiction, and relapse," Social Problems 15:459-69.

Akers, Ronald L. and John K. Cochran

1985 "Adolescent marijuana use: a test of three theories of deviant behavior," Deviant Behavior 6:323-346.

Akers, Ronald L. and Richard Hawkins

1975 Law and Control in Society. Englewood Cliffs, NJ:Prentice-Hall.

Akers, Ronald L., Marvin D. Krohn, Lonn Lanza-Kaduce, and Marcia Radosevich

1979 "Social learning and deviant behavior: a specific test of a general theory," American Sociological Review 44:635-55.

1980 "Social characteristics and self-reported delinquency: differences in extreme types," pp. 48-62 in Gary F. Jensen, ed., Sociology of Delinquency: Current Issues. Beverly Hills, CA: Sage.

Akers, Ronald L. and Anthony J. La Greca

1991 "Alcohol use among the elderly: social learning, community context, and life events," pp. 242-262 in David J. Pittman and Helene Raskin White, eds., Society, Culture, and Drinking Patterns Re-examined. New Brunswick, NJ: Rutgers Center of Alcohol Studies.

Akers, Ronald L., Anthony J. La Greca, John Cochran, and Christine Sellers

1989 "Social learning theory and alcohol behavior among the elderly," Sociological Quarterly 30:625-638.

Akers, Ronald L., Lonn Lanza-Kaduce, Paul Cromwell, and Roger Dunham

1994 "Hurricane Andrew: Exploring its impact on law and social control," Presented at the annual meetings of the American Society of Criminology, Miami, November.

Akers, Ronald L. and Gang Lee

1996 "A longitudinal test of social learning theory: adolescent smoking," Journal of Drug Issues, in press.

Akers, Ronald L. and Ross Matsueda

1989 "Donald Cressey: an intellectual portrait of a criminologist," Sociological Inquiry 29:423-438.

Alexander, Jeffrey C., Bernhard Giesen, Richard Munch, and Neil J. Smelser, eds.

1987 The Micro-Macro Link. Berkeley: University of California Press.

Alix, Ernest K.

1978 Ransom Kidnapping in America, 1874-1974: The Creation of a Capital Crime. Carbondale: Southern Illinois Press.

Andenaes, Johannes

1971 "The moral or educative influence of criminal law," Journal of Social Issues 24:17-31.

Anderson, Kevin

1991 "Radical criminology and the overcoming of alienation: perspectives from Marxian and Gandhian humanism," pp. 14-30 in Harold E. Pepinsky and Richard Quinney, eds., Criminology as Peacemaking. Bloomington, IN: Indiana University Press.

Anderson, Linda S., Theodore G. Chiricos, and Gordon P. Waldo

1977 "Formal and informal sanctions: a comparison of deterrent effects," Social Problems 25:103-112.

Andrews, Kenneth H. and Denise B. Kandel

1979 "Attitude and behavior: a specification of the contingent consistency hypothesis," American Sociological Review 44:298-310.

Aultman, Madeline and Charles F. Wellford

1979 "Towards an integrated model of delinquency causation: an empirical analysis," Sociology and Social Research 63:316-327.

Austin, Roy L.

1977 "Commitment, neutralization, and delinquency," pp. 121-37 in Theordore N. Ferdinand, ed., Juvenile Delinquency: Little Brother Grows Up. Beverly Hills, CA: Sage.

Balbus, Isaac D.

1977 "Commodity form and legal form: an essay on the 'relative autonomy' of the state," Law and Society Review 11:571-588.

Balkan, Sheila, Ronald J. Berger, and Janet Schmidt

1980 Crime and Deviance in America: A Critical Approach. Belmont, CA: Wadsworth.

Ball, John C.

1955 "The deterrent concept in criminology and the law," Journal of Criminal Law, Criminology, and Police Science 46:349-54.

Ball, Harry V. and George O. Simpson

1962 "Law and social change: Sumner reconsidered," American Journal of Sociology 67:532-40.

Ball, Richard A.

1968 "An empirical exploration of neutralization theory," pp. 255-65 in Mark Lefton, James K. Skipper, and Charles H. McCaghy, eds., Approaches to Deviance. New York: Appleton-Century-Crofts.

Bandura, Albert

1969 Principles of Behavior Modification. New York: Holt. Rinehart, and Winston.
1973 Aggression: A Social Learning Analysis. Englewood Cliffs, NJ: Prentice Hall.
1977 Social Learning Theory. Englewood Cliffs, NJ: Prentice Hall.
1986 Social Foundations of Thought and Action: A Social Cognitive Theory. Englewood Cliffs, NJ: Prentice-Hall.

Bandura, Albert and Richard H. Walters

1963 Social Learning and Personality Development. New York: Holt, Rinehart, and Winston.

Barak, Gregg

1991 "Homelessness and the case for community-based initiatives: the emergence of a model shelter as a short-term response to the deepening crisis in housing," pp. 47-68 in Harold E. Pepinsky and Richard Quinney, eds., Criminology as Peacemaking. Bloomington, IN: Indiana University Press.

Barlow, Hugh D. and Theodore N. Ferdinand

1992 Understanding Delinquency. New York: HarperCollins Publishers.

Beccaria, Cesare

1963 On Crimes and Punishments. Translated with an introduction by Henry Paolucci. New York: Macmillan Publishing Co.
1972 "On crimes and punishment," pp. 11-24 in Sawyer F. Sylvester, ed., The Heritage of Modern Criminology. Cambridge, MA: Schenkman Publishing Co.

Becker, Gary S.

1968 "Crime and punishment: an economic approach," Journal of Political Economy 76:169-217.

Becker, Howard S.

1963 Outsiders: Studies in the Sociology of Deviance. New York: Free Press.
1973 Outsiders: Studies in the Sociology of Deviance. Revised Edition. New York: The Free Press.

Becker, Howard S., ed.

1964 The Other Side. New York: Free Press.

Bedau, Hugo, ed.

1964 The Death Penalty in America. Garden City, NY: Anchor Books.

Beirne, Piers

1979 "Empiricism and the critique of Marxism on law and crime," Social Problems 26:373-385.

1991 "Inventing criminology: the 'science of man' in Cesare Beccaria's *dei delitte e delle pene* (1764)," Criminology 29:777-820.

Beirne, Piers and Richard Quinney, eds.

1982 Marxism and Law. New York: Wiley.

Benda, Brent B.

1994 "Testing competing theoretical concepts: adolescent alcohol consumption," Deviant Behavior 15:375-396.

Bennett, Trevor

1986 "A decision-making approach to opioid addiction," pp. 84-182 in Derek B. Cornish and Ronald V. Clarke, eds., The Reasoning Criminal. New York: Springer.

Benson, Michael L. and Elizabeth Moore

1992 "Are white-collar and common offenders the same? an empirical and theoretical critique of a recently proposed general theory of crime," Journal of Research in Crime and Delinquency 29:251-272.

Bentham, Jeremy

1948 An Introduction to the Principles of Morals and Legislation. Edited with an introduction by Laurence J. Lafleur. New York: Hafner Publishing Co.

Ben-Yehuda, Nachman, Richard A. Brymer, Steven C. Dubin, Douglass Harper, Rosanna Hertz, and William Shaffer

1989 "Howard S. Becker: a portrait of an intellectual's sociological imagination," Sociological Inquiry 59:467-489.

Bernard, Thomas J.

1983 The Consensus-Conflict Debate: Form and Content in Social Theories. New York: Columbia University Press.

1987 "Testing structural strain theories," Journal of Research in Crime and Delinquency 24:262-290.

1990 "Angry aggression among the 'truly disadvantaged,'" Criminology 28:73-96.

Bernard, Thomas J. and R. Richard Ritti

1991 "The Philadelphia birth cohort and selective incapacitation," Journal of Research in Crime and Delinquency 28:33-54.

Bernard, Thomas J. and Jeffrey B. Snipes

1995 "Theoretical integration in criminology," pp. 1-48 in Michael Tonry, ed., Crime and Justice. Chicago: University of Chicago Press.

Bishop, Donna M. and Charles E. Frazier

1988 "The influence of race in juvenile justice processing," Journal of Research in Crime and Delinquency 25:244-63.

1992 "Gender bias in juvenile justice processing: implications of the JJDP Act," Journal of Criminal Law and Criminology 82:1162-1186.

1996 "Race effects in juvenile justice decision-making: findings of a statewide analysis," Journal of Criminal Law and Criminology 86:392-414.

Black, Donald J.

1976 The Behavior of Law. New York: Academic Press.

Blumer, Herbert

1969 Symbolic Interactionism: Perspective and Method. Englewood Cliffs, NJ: Prentice-Hall.

Blumstein, Alfred

1982 "On the racial disproportionality of the United States prison population," Journal of Criminal Law and Criminology 73:1259-1281.

Blumstein, Alfred, Jacqueline Cohen, and Daniel Nagin

1978 Deterrence and Incapacitation: Estimating the Effects of Sanctions on the Crime Rate. Washington, DC: National Academy Press.

Blumstein, Alfred, David P. Farrington, and S. Moitra

1985 "Delinquency careers: innocents, desisters, and persisters," pp. 137-168 in Michael Tonry and Norval Morris, eds., Crime and Justice. Volume Six. Chicago: University of Chicago Press.

Boeringer, Scot

1992 Sexual Coercion Among College Males: Assessing Three Theoretical Models of Coercive Sexual Behavior. Ph.D. Dissertation. University of Florida.

Boeringer, Scot and Ronald L. Akers

1993 "Rape and rape proclivity: a comparison of social learning, social control, and relative deprivation models," unpublished paper, Department of Sociology, University of Florida.

Boeringer, Scot, Constance L. Shehan, and Ronald L. Akers

1991 "Social contexts and social learning in sexual coercion and aggression: assessing the contribution of fraternity membership," Family Relations 40:558-64.

Bohm, Robert M.

1982 "Radical criminology: an explication," Criminology 19:565-589.

Bonger, Willem

1969 Criminality and Economic Conditions. [1916.] Abridged with an Introduction by Austin T. Turk. Bloomington: Indiana University Press.

Booth, Alan and D. Wayne Osgood

1993 "The influence of testosterone on deviance in adulthood: assessing and explaining the relationship," Criminology 31:93-117.

Bordua, David J.

1967 "Recent trends: deviant behavior and social control," Annals 369:149-63.

Boritch, Helen and John Hagan

1990 "A century of crime in Toronto: gender, class, and patterns of social control, 1859 to 1955," Criminology 28:567-600.

Bowker, Lee H. with contributions by Meda Chesney-Lind and Joy Pollock

1978 Women, Crime, and the Criminal Justice System. Lexington, MA: Lexington Books.

Braithwaite, John

1989 Crime, Shame, and Reintegration. Cambridge: Cambridge University Press.

Brennan, Patricia A., Sarnoff Mednick, and Jan Volavka

1995 "Biomedical factors in crime," pp. 65-90 in James Q. Wilson and Joan Petersilia, eds., Crime. San Francisco: ICS Press.

Brezina, Timothy

1996 "Adapting to strain: an examination of delinquent coping responses," Criminology 34:39-60

Briar, Scott and Irving Piliavin

1965 "Delinquency, situational inducements, and commitment to conformity," Social Problems 13:35-45.

Bridges, George S. and Gina Beretta

1994 "Gender, race, and social control: toward an understanding of sex disparities in imprisonment," pp. 158-175 in George S. Bridges and Martha A. Myers, eds., Inequality, Crime, and Social Control. Boulder, CO: Westview Press.

Bridges, George and Robert Crutchfield

1988 "Law, social standing, and racial disparities in imprisonment," Social Forces 66:699-724.

Bridges, George S. and Martha A. Myers, eds.

1994 Inequality, Crime, and Social Control. Boulder, CO: Westview Press.

Brownfield, David and Ann Marie Sorenson

1993 "Self-control and juvenile delinquency: theoretical issues and an empirical assessment of selected elements of a general theory of crime," Deviant Behavior 14:243-264.

Bruinsma, Gerben J. N.

1992 "Differential association theory reconsidered: an extension and its empirical test," Journal of Quantitative Criminology 8:29-49.

Brunk, Gregory G. and Laura Ann Wilson

1991 "Interest groups and criminal behavior," Journal of Research in Crime and Delinquency 28:157-173.

Burgess, Robert L. and Ronald L. Akers

1966a "Are operant principles tautological?" Psychological Record 16:305-12.
1966b "A differential association-reinforcement theory of criminal behavior," Social Problems 14:128-47.

Burkett, Steven and Eric L. Jensen

1975 "Conventional ties, peer influence, and the fear of apprehension: a study of adolescent marijuana use," Sociological Quarterly 16:522-33.

Burkett, Steven and Bruce O. Warren

1987 "Religiosity, peer associations, and adolescent marijuana use: a panel study of underlying causal structures," Criminology 25:109-132.

Burkett, Steven and Mervin White

1974 "Hellfire and delinquency: another look," Journal for the Scientific Study of Religion 13:455-62.

Bursik, Robert J.

1988 "Social disorganization and theories of crime and delinquency: problems and prospects," Criminology 26:519-551.

Burton, Velmer S. and Francis T. Cullen

1992 "The empirical status of strain theory," Journal of Crime and Justice 15:1-30

Burton, Velmer, Frances Cullen, David Evans, and R. Gregory Dunaway

1994 "Reconsidering strain theory: operationalization, rival theories, and adult criminality," Journal of Quantitative Criminology 10:213-239.

Bynum, Jack E. and William E. Thompson

1992 Juvenile Delinquency: A Sociological Approach. Boston: Allyn and Bacon.

Cantor, David and Kenneth C. Land

1985 "Unemployment and crime rates in the post-World War II United States: a theoretical and empirical analysis," American Sociological Review 50:317-332.

Carey, Gregory

1992 "Twin imitation for antisocial behavior: implications for genetic and family environment research," Journal of Abnormal Psychology 101:18-2

Carroll, John and Frances Weaver

1986 "Shoplifters' perceptions of crime opportunities: a process-tracing study," pp. 20-38 in Derek B. Cornish and Ronald V. Clarke, eds., The Reasoning Criminal. New York: Springer.

Caspi, Avshalom, Terrie E. Moffitt, Phil A. Silva, Magda Stouthamer-Loeber, Robert F. Krueger, and Pamela S. Schmutte

1994 "Are some people crime-prone? Replications of the personality-crime relationship across countries, genders, races, and methods," Criminology 32: 163-196.

Castellano, Thomas C. and Edmund F. McGarrell

1991 "The politics of law and order: case study evidence for the conflict model of the criminal law formation process," Journal of Research in Crime and Delinquency 28:304-329.

Cernkovich, Stephen and Peggy Giordano

1992 "School bonding, race, and delinquency," Criminology 30:261-291.

Chadwick-Jones, J. K.

1976 Social Exchange Theory: Its Structure and Influence in Social Psychology. London: Academic Press.

Chalidze, Valery

1977 Criminal Russia: Crime in the Soviet Union. New York: Random House.

Chamlin, Mitchell and John K. Cochran

1995 "Assessing Messner and Rosenfeld's institutional anomie theory: a partial test," Criminology 33:411.

Chambliss, William J.

1964 "A sociological analysis of the law of vagrancy," Social Problems 12:67-77.

Chambliss, William J., ed.

1969 Crime and the Legal Process. New York: McGraw-Hill.
1975 Criminal Law in Action. Santa Barbara, CA: Hamilton.

Chambliss, William J. and Robert B. Seidman

1971 Law, Order, and Power. Reading, MA: Addison-Wesley.
1982 Law, Order, and Power. Second Edition. Reading, MA: Addison-Wesley.

Chase-Dunn, Christopher K.

1980 "Socialist states in the capitalist world-economy," Social Problems 27:505-525.

Chesney-Lind, Meda

1988 "Girls in jail," Crime and Delinquency 34:150-168.
1989 "Girls' crime and woman's place: toward a feminist model of female delinquency," Crime and Delinquency 35:5-29.

Chesney-Lind, Meda and Randall G. Shelden

1992 Girls, Delinquency, and Juvenile Justice. Pacific Grove, CA: Brooks/Cole.

Chiricos, Theodore

1991 "Unemployment and punishment: an empirical assessment," Criminology 29:701-724.

Chiricos, Theodore G. and Gordon P. Waldo

1970 "Punishment and crime: an examination of some empirical evidence," Social Problems 18:200-17.

Cloward, Richard

1959 "Illegitimate means, anomie, and deviant behavior," American Sociological Review 24:164-77.

Cloward, Richard and Lloyd Ohlin

1960 Delinquency and Opportunity. Glencoe, IL: Free Press.

Cochran, John K. and Ronald L. Akers

1989 "Beyond hellfire: an exploration of the variable effects of religiosity on adolescent marijuana and alcohol use," Journal of Research in Crime and Delinquency 26: 198-225.

Cohen, Albert K.

1955 Delinquent Boys. Glencoe, IL: Free Press.

Cohen, Albert K., Alfred R. Lindesmith, and Karl F. Schuessler, eds.

1956 The Sutherland Papers. Bloomington, IN: Indiana University Press.

Cohen, Lawrence E. and Marcus Felson

1979 "Social change and crime rate trends: a routine activities approach." American Sociological Review 44:588-608.

Cohen, Lawrence E., James Kluegel, and Kenneth Land

1981 "Social inequality and predatory criminal victimization: an exposition and test of a formal theory," American Sociological Review 46:505-524.

Colvin, Mark and John Pauly

1983 "A critique of criminology: toward an integrated structural-Marxist theory of delinquency production," American Journal of Sociology 89:513-551.

Conger, Rand

1976 "Social control and social learning models of delinquency: a synthesis," Criminology 14:17-40.

Conger, Rand D. and Ronald L. Simons

1995 "Life-course contingencies in the development of adolescent antisocial behavior: a matching law approach," pp. in Terrance P. Thornberry, ed., Developmental Theories of Crime and Delinquency," New Brunswick, NJ: Transaction Books.

Cooley, Charles Horton

1902 Human Nature and the Social Order. New York: Scribner.

Corley, Charles J., Stephen Cernkovich, and Peggy Giordano

1989 "Sex and the likelihood of sanction," Journal of Criminal Law and Criminology 80:540-556.

Cornish, Derek B. and Ronald V. Clarke, eds.

1986 The Reasoning Criminal: Rational Choice Perspectives on Offending. New York: Springer.

Creechan, James H.

1994 "A test of the general theory of crime: delinquency and school dropouts," pp. 233-256 in James H. Creechan and Robert A. Silverman, eds., Canadian Juvenile Delinquency. Canada: Prentice Hall.

Cressey, Donald R.

1953 Other People's Money. Glencoe, IL: Free Press.
1960 "Epidemiology and individual conduct: a case from criminology," Pacific Sociological Review 3:47-58.

Cressey, Donald R. and David Ward

1969 Delinquency, Crime, and Social Process. New York: Holt, Rinehart, and Winston.

Cromwell, Paul F., Roger Dunham, Ronald Akers, and Lonn Lanza-Kaduce

1995 "Routine activities and social control in the aftermath of a natural catastrophe," European Journal on Criminal Policy and Research 3:56-69.

Cromwell, Paul F., James N. Olson, and D'Aunn Wester Avary

1991 Breaking and Entering: An Ethnographic Analysis of Burglary. Newbury Park, CA: Sage.

Crouch, Robert L.

1979 Human Behavior: An Economic Approach. North Scituate, MA: Duxbury Press.

Cullen, Frances T.

1983 Rethinking Crime and Deviance Theory: The Emergence of a Structuring Tradition. Totowa, NJ: Rowman & Allanheld.

1994 "Social support as an organizing concept for criminology: presidential address to the Academy of Criminal Justice Sciences," Justice Quarterly 11: 528-559.

Curran, Daniel J. and Claire M. Renzetti

1994 Theories of Crime. Boston: Allyn and Bacon.

Dabney, Dean

1995 "Neutralization and deviance in the workplace: theft of supplies and medicines by hospital nurses," Deviant Behavior 16:313-331.

Daly, Kathleen

1989 "Neither conflict nor labeling nor paternalism will suffice: intersections of race, ethnicity, gender, and family in criminal court decisions," Crime and Delinquency 35:136-168.

1992 "Women's pathways to felony court: feminist theories of lawbreaking and problems of representation," Review of Law and Women's Studies 2:11-52

1994a Gender, Crime, and Punishment. New Haven: Yale U. Press.

1994b "Gender and punishment disparity," pp. 117-133 in George S. Bridges and Martha A. Myers, eds., Inequality, Crime, and Social Control. Boulder, CO: Westview Press.

Daly, Kathleen and Meda Chesney-Lind

1988 "Feminism and criminology," Justice Quarterly 5:497-538.

Datesman, Susan K. and Frank R. Scarpitti, eds.

1980 Women, Crime, and Justice. New York: Oxford University Press.

Davis, F. James

1962 "Law as a type of social control," pp. 39-61 in F. James Davis, Henry H. Foster, C. Ray Jeffery, and E. Eugene Davis, eds., Society and the Law: New Meanings for an Old Profession. New York: Free Press.

Davis, Kingsley

1966 "Sexual behavior," pp. 322-408 in Robert K. Merton and Robert A. Nisbet, eds., Contemporary Social Problems. Second Edition. New York: Harcourt Brace Jovanovich.

DeFleur, Melvin L. and Richard Quinney

1966 "A reformulation of Sutherland's differential association theory and a strategy for empirical verification," Journal of Research in Crime and Delinquency 3:1-22.

Dembo, Richard, Gary Grandon, Lawrence La Voie, James Schmeidler, and William Burgos

1986 "Parents and drugs revisited: some further evidence in support of social learning theory," Criminology 24:85-104.

Dickson, Donald T.

1968 "Bureaucracy and morality: an organizational perspective on a moral crusade," Social Problems 16:43-56.

Dinitz, Simon

1977 "Chronically antisocial offenders," in John P. Conrad and Simon Dinitz, eds., In Fear of Each Other. Lexington, MA: Lexington Books.

Dinitz, Simon, Frank R. Scarpitti, and Walter C. Reckless

1962 "Delinquency vulnerability: a cross-group and longitudinal analysis," American Sociological Review 27: 515-17.

Donnerstein, Edward and Daniel Linz

1995 "The media," pp. 237-266 in James Q. Wilson and Joan Petersilia, eds., Crime. San Francisco: ICS Press.

Dotter, Daniel L. and Julian B. Roebuck

1988 "The labeling approach re-examined: interactionism and the components of deviance," Deviant Behavior 9:19-32.

Driver, Edwin D.

1972 "Charles Buckman Goring, 1870-1919," pp. 429-442 in Hermann Mannheim, ed., Pioneers in Criminology. Second Edition Enlarged. Montclair, NJ: Patterson Smith.

Durkheim, Emile

1951 Suicide. [1897.] Translated by John A. Spaulding and George Simpson. New York: Free Press.

Einstadter, Werner and Stuart Henry

1995 Criminological Theory: An Analysis of Its Underlying Assumptions. Ft. Worth: Harcourt Brace College Publishers.

Elliott, Delbert S.

1985 "The assumption that theories can be combined with increased explanatory power," pp. 123-149 in Robert F. Meier, ed., Theoretical Methods in Criminology. Beverly Hills, CA: Sage.

1994 "Serious violent offenders: onset, developmental course, and termination," Criminology 32:1-22.

Elliott, Delbert S., David Huizinga, and Suzanne S. Ageton

1985 Explaining Delinquency and Drug Use. Beverly Hills: Sage.

Elliott, Delbert S. and Scott Menard

1991 "Delinquent friends and delinquent behavior: temporal and developmental patterns," The Institute of Behavioral Science, University of Colorado.

in press "Delinquent friends and delinquent behavior: temporal and developmental patterns, in David Hawkins, ed., Current Theories of Crime and Deviance. New York: Springer-Verlag.

Elliott, Delbert S. and Susan S. Ageton

1980 "Reconciling race and class differences in self-reported and official estimates of delinquency," American Sociological Review 45:95-110.

Elliott, Delbert S. and Harwin L. Voss

1974 Delinquency and Dropout. Lexington, MA: Lexington Books.

Empey, LaMar T.

1967 "Delinquency theory and recent research," Journal of Research in Crime and Delinquency 4:28-42.

Empey, LaMar T. and Mark Stafford

1991 American Delinquency: Its Meaning and Construction. Belmont, CA: Wadsworth.

Erikson, Kai T.

1964 "Notes on the sociology of deviance," pp. 9-23 in Howard S. Becker, ed., The Other Side. New York: Free Press.

Erlanger, Howard S.

1974 "The empirical status of the subculture of violence thesis," Social Problems 22:280-91.

1976 "Is there a 'subculture of violence' in the South? Journal of Criminal Law and Criminology 66:483-490.

Esbensen, Finn-Aage and David Huizinga

1993 "Gangs, drugs, and delinquency in a survey of urban youth," Criminology 31:565-590.

Eysenck, Hans J. and Gisli H. Gudjonsson

1989 The Causes and Cures of Criminality. New York: Plenum.

Fagan, Jeffrey and Sandra Wexler

1987 "Family origins of violent delinquents," Criminology 25:643-669.

Farnworth, Margaret

1989 "Theory integration versus model building," pp. 93-100 in Steven F. Messner, Marvin D. Krohn, and Allen E. Liska, eds., Theoretical Integration in the Study of Deviance and Crime. Albany: State University of New York Press.

Farnworth, Margaret and Michael J. Leiber

1989 "Strain theory revisited: economic goals, educational means, and delinquency," American Sociological Review 54:263-274.

Farrell, Ronald A.

1989 "Cognitive consistency in deviance causation: a psychological elaboration of an integrated systems model," pp. 77-92 in Steven F. Messner, Marvin D. Krohn, and Allen E. Liska, eds., Theoretical Integration in the Study of Deviance and Crime. Albany: State University of New York Press.

Farrington, David P.

1977 "The effects of public labeling," British Journal of Criminology 17:112-25.

Felson, Marcus

1994 Crime and Everyday Life: Insight and Implications for Society. Thousand Oaks, CA: Pine Forge Press.

Fishbein, Diana H.

1990 "Biological perspectives in criminology," Criminology 28:27-72.

Fox, Richard G.

1971 "The XYY offender: a modern myth?" Journal of Criminal Law, Criminology, and Police Science 62:59-73.

Friedlander, Kate

1947 The Psychoanalytic Approach to Juvenile Delinquency. London: Kegan Paul.

Friedman, Lawrence

1975 The Legal System. New York: Russell Sage.

Galliher, John F. and Harold E. Pepinsky

1978 "A meta-study of social origins of substantive criminal law," pp. 27-38 in Marvin D. Krohn and Ronald L. Akers, eds., Crime, Law, and Sanctions. Beverly Hill, CA: Sage.

Galliher, John F. and A. Walker

1977 "The puzzle of the origin of the Marijuana Tax Act of 1937. Social Problems 24:367-76.

Gastil, Raymond D.

1971 "Homicide and a regional culture of violence," American Sociological Review 36:412-427.

Gaylord, Mark S. and John F. Galliher

1988 The Criminology of Edwin Sutherland. New Brunswick: Transaction.

Geis, Gilbert

1972 "Jeremy Bentham 1748-1832," pp. 51-68 in Hermann Mannheim, ed., Pioneers in Criminology. Second Edition, Enlarged. Montclair, NJ: Patterson Smith.

Gelsthorpe, Loraine and Allison Morris, eds.

1990 Feminist Perspectives in Criminology. Philadelphia: Open University Press.

Gibbons, Don C.

1979 The Criminological Enterprise: Theories and Perspectives. Englewood Cliffs, NJ: Prentice Hall.

1994 Talking About Crime and Criminals: Problems and Issues in Theory Development in Criminology. Englewood Cliffs, NJ: Prentice Hall.

Gibbs, Jack P.

1966 "Conceptions of deviant behavior: the old and the new," Pacific Sociological Review 9:9-14.

1968 "Crime, punishment, and deterrence," Southwestern Social Science Quarterly 48:515-30.

1975 Crime, Punishment, and Deterrence. New York: Elsevier.

1986 "Punishment and deterrence: theory, research, and penal policy," pp. 319-368 in Leon Lipson and Stanton Wheeler, eds., Law and the Social Sciences. New York: Russell Sage Foundation.

1989 Control: Sociology's Central Notion. Urbana, IL: University of Illinois Press.

1990 "The notion of a theory in sociology," National Journal of Sociology 4:129-158.

Gillen, John L.

1945 Criminology and Penology. New York: Appleton-Century.

Glaser, Daniel

1956 "Criminality theories and behavioral images," American Journal of Sociology 61:433-44.

Glueck, Sheldon and Eleanor Glueck

1959 Predicting Delinquency and Crime. Cambridge, MA: Harvard University Press.

Goffman, Erving

1963 Stigma: Notes on the Management of Spoiled Identity. Englewood Cliffs, NJ: Prentice-Hall.

Goode, Erich

1975 "On behalf of labeling theory," Social Problems 22:570-83.

Gordon, Robert A.

1980 "Research on IQ, race, and delinquency: taboo or not taboo?" pp. 37-66 in Edward Sagarin, ed., Taboos in Criminology. Beverly Hills, CA: Sage.

1987 "SES versus IQ in the race-IQ delinquency model," International Journal of Sociology and Social Policy 7:29-96.

Goring, Charles

1913 The English Convict: A Statistical Study. Patterson Smith Reprint, 1972. Montclair, NJ: Patterson Smith.

Gottfredson, Denise C., Richard J. McNeil, III, and Gary Gottfredson

1991 "Social area influences on delinquency: a multilevel analysis," Journal of Research in Crime and Delinquency 28:197-226.

Gottfredson, Michael and Travis Hirschi

1990 A General Theory of Crime. Palo Alto, CA: Stanford University Press.

Gove, Walter R.

1982 "Labeling theory's explanation of mental illness: an update of recent evidence," Deviant Behavior 3:307-27.

Gove, Walter, ed.

1980 The Labeling of Deviance. Second Edition. Beverly Hills, CA: Sage.

Gove, Walter R. and Russell G. Carpenter, eds.

1982 The Fundamental Connection Between Nature and Nurture: A Review of the Evidence. Lexington, MA: Lexington Books.

Gove, Walter R. and Michael Hughes

1989 "A theory of mental illness: an attempted integration of biological, psychological, and social variables," pp. 61-76 in Steven F. Messner, Marvin D. Krohn, and Allen E. Liska, eds., Theoretical Integration in the Study of Deviance and Crime. Albany: State University of New York Press.

Grasmick, Harold G. and Robert J. Bursik

1990 "Conscience, significant others, and rational choice: extending the deterrence model," Law and Society Review 24:837-862.

Grasmick, Harold G., Robert J. Bursik, Jr. and Bruce Arneklev

1993 "Reduction in drunk driving as a response to increased threats of shame, embarrassment, and legal sanctions," Criminology 31:41-67.

Grasmick, Harold G. and Donald E. Green

1980 "Legal punishment, social disapproval, and internalization as inhibitors of illegal behavior," Journal of Criminal Law and Criminology 71:325-35.

Grasmick, Harold G., Charles R. Tittle, Robert J. Bursik, Jr., and Bruce J. Arneklev

1993 "Testing the core empirical implications of Gottfredson and Hisrchi's general theory of crime," Journal of Research in Crime and Delinquency 30:5-29.

Green, Donald E.

1989 "Measures of illegal behavior in individual-level research," Journal of Research in Crime and Delinquency 26: 253-275.

Greenberg, David F.

1977 "Delinquency and the age structure of society," Contemporary Crises: Crime, Law, and Social Policy 1:189-223.

1980 "Penal sanctions in Poland: a test of alternative models," Social Problems 28:199-204.

1981b "Delinquency and the age structure of society," pp. 118-139 in David F. Greenberg, ed., Crime and Capitalism. Palo Alto, CA: Mayfield.

Greenberg, David F., ed.

1981a Crime and Capitalism: Readings in Marxist Criminology. Palo Alto, CA: Mayfield.

Greenleaf, Richard G. and Lonn Lanza-Kaduce

1995 "Sophistication, organization, and authority-subject conflict: rediscovering and unraveling Turk's theory of norm resistance," Criminology 33:565-586.

Grimes, Ruth-Ellen M. and Austin T. Turk

1978 "Labeling in context: conflict, power, and self-definition," pp. 39-58 in Marvin D. Krohn and Ronald L. Akers, eds., Crime, Law, and Sanctions: Theoretical Perspectives. Berkeley, CA: Sage.

Hagan, John

1973 "Labeling and deviance: a case study in the 'sociology of the interesting,'" Social Problems 20:447-58.

1974 "Extra-legal attributes in criminal sentencing: an assessment of a sociological viewpoint," Law and Society Review 8:357-83.

1980 "The legislation of crime and delinquency: a review of theory, method, and research," Law and Society Review 14:603-28.

1989a Structural Criminology. New Brunswick, NJ: Rutgers University Press.

1989b "Micro- and macro-structures of delinquency causation and a power-control theory of gender and delinquency," pp. 213-228 in Steven F. Messner, Marvin D. Krohn, and Allen E. Liska, eds., Theoretical Integration in the Study of Deviance and Crime. Albany: State University of New York Press.

1989c "Why is there so little criminal justice theory? neglected macro- and micro-level links between organizations and power," Journal of Research in Crime and Delinquency 26:116-35.

Hagan, John and Jeffrey Leon

1977 "Rediscovering delinquency: social history, political ideology, and the sociology of law," American Sociological Review 42:587-98.

Hagan, John and Alberto Palloni

1990 "The social reproduction of a criminal class in working-class London, circa 1950-1980," American Journal of Sociology 96:265-299.

Hagan, John, John H. Simpson, and A. R. Gillis

1987 "Class in the household: a power-control theory of gender and delinquency," American Journal of Sociology 92:788-816.

Hakeem, Michael

1957 "A critique of the psychiatric approach to the prevention of juvenile delinquency," Social Problems 5:194-206

Hall, Jerome

1952 Theft, Law and Society. Revised Edition. Indianapolis: Bobbs-Merrill.

Halleck, Seymour L.

1967 Psychiatry and the Dilemmas of Crime. New York: Harper and Row.

Hamblin, Robert L.

1979 "Behavioral choice and social reinforcement: step function versus matching," Social Forces 57:1141-56.

Hanke, Penelope J.

1995 "Sentencing disparities by race of offender and victim: women homicide offenders in Alabama 1929-1985," Sociological Spectrum 15:277-298.

Harding, Richard W.

1990 "Rational-choice gun use in armed robbery: the likely deterrent effect on gun use of mandatory additional punishment," Criminal Law Forum 1:427-50.

Harris, M. Kay

1991 "Moving into the new millennium: toward a feminist vision of justice," pp. 83-97 in Harold E. Pepinsky and Richard Quinney, eds., Criminology as Peacemaking. Bloomington, IN: Indiana University Press.

Hathaway, Starke

1939 "The personality inventory as an aid in the diagnosis of psychopathic inferiors," Journal of Consulting Psychology 3:112-117.

Hathaway, Starke and Paul E. Meehl

1951 An Atlas for the Clinical Use of the MMPI. Minneapolis: University of Minnesota Press.

Hathaway, Starke and Elio Monachesi

1953 Analyzing and Predicting Juvenile Delinquency with the MMPI. Minneapolis: University of Minnesota Press.

Hathaway, Starke R. and Elio D. Monachesi

1963 Adolescent Personality and Behavior. Minneapolis, MN: University of Minnesota Press.

Hawkins, J. David and Denise M. Lishner

1987 "Schooling and delinquency," pp. 179-221 in Elmer Johnson, ed., Handbook on Crime and Delinquency Prevention. Westport, CT: Greenwood Press.

Hawkins, Richard and Gary Tiedeman

1975 The Creation of Deviance: Interpersonal and Organizational Determinants. Columbus, OH: Merrill.

Hawkins, Richard and Kirk B. Williams

1989 "Acts, arrests, and the deterrence process: the case of wife assault," Paper presented to the Society for the Study of Social Problems, Berkeley, CA.

Heimer, Karen and Ross Matsueda

1994 "Role-taking, role-commitment, and delinquency: a theory of differential social control," American Sociological Review 59:365-390.

Heineke, J. M., ed.

1978 Economic Models of Criminal Behavior. Amsterdam: North-Holland.

Henry, Stuart and Dragan Milovanovic

1991 "Constitutive criminology: the maturation of critical theory," Criminology 29:293-315.

Hewitt, John P. and Randall Stokes

1975 "Disclaimers," American Sociological Review 40:1-11.

Hill, Gary D. and Maxine P. Atkinson

1988 "Gender, familial control, and delinquency," Criminology 26:127-149.

Hills, Stuart L.

1971 Crime, Power, and Morality: The Criminal-Law Process in the United States. Scranton: Chandler Publishing.

Hindelang, Michael J.

1970 "The commitment of delinquents to their misdeeds: do delinquents drift?" Social Problems 17:502-509.
1973 "Causes of delinquency: a partial replication and extension," Social Problems 20:471-87.

Hindelang, Michael J., Travis Hirschi, and Joseph C. Weis

1979 "Correlates of delinquency: the illusion of discrepancy between self-report and official measures," American Sociological Review 44:995-1014.
1980 Measuring Delinquency. Beverly Hills, CA: Sage

Hirschi, Travis

1969 Causes of Delinquency. Berkeley, CA: University of California Press.
1973 "Procedural rules and the study of deviant behavior," Social Problems 21:159-73.
1979 "Separate and unequal is better," Journal of Research in Crime and Delinquency 16:34-38.
1989 "Exploring alternatives to integrated theory," pp. 37-49 in Steven F. Messner, Marvin D. Krohn, and Allen E. Liska, eds., Theoretical Integration in the Study of Deviance and Crime. Albany: State University of New York Press.

Hirschi, Travis and Michael Gottfredson

1993 "Commentary: testing the general theory of crime," Journal of Research in Crime and Delinquency 30:47-54.

Hirschi, Travis and Michael J. Hindelang

1977 "Intelligence and delinquency: a revisionist review," American Sociological Review 42:571-87.

Hirschi, Travis and Rodney Stark

1969 "Hellfire and delinquency," Social Problems 17:202-13.

Hollinger, Richard C.

1991 "Neutralizing in the workplace: an empirical analysis of property theft and production deviance," Deviant Behavior 12:169-202.

Hollinger, Richard and Lonn Lanza-Kaduce

1988 "The process of criminalization: the case of computer crime law," Criminology 26:101-126.

Holman, John E. and James F. Quinn
1992 Criminology: Applying Theory. St. Paul: West Publishing.

Holzman, Harold R.
1979 "Learning disabilities and juvenile delinquency: biological and sociological theories," pp. 77-86 in C. R. Jeffery, ed., Biology and Crime. Beverly Hills, CA: Sage.

Hooten, Earnest A.
1939 Crime and the Man. Cambridge: Harvard University Press.

Horowitz, Ruth and Anne E. Pottieger
1991 "Gender bias in juvenile justice handling of seriously crime-involved youths," Journal of Research in Crime and Delinquency 28:75-100.

Huff, C. Ronald, ed.
1990 Gangs, in America. Newbury Park, CA: Sage.

Hutchings, Barry and Sarnoff A. Mednick
1977a "A review of studies of criminality among twins," pp. 45-88 in Sarnoff A. Mednick and Karl O. Christensen, eds., Biosocial Bases of Criminal Behavior. New York: Gardner.
1977b "A preliminary study of criminality among twins," pp. 89-108 in Sarnoff A. Mednick and Karl O. Christensen, eds., Biosocial Bases of Criminal Behavior. New York: Gardner.
1977c "Criminality in adoptees and their adoptive and biological parents: a pilot study," pp. 127-142 in Sarnoff A. Mednick and Karl O. Christensen, eds., Biosocial Bases of Criminal Behavior. New York: Gardner.

Inciardi, James, ed.
1980 Radical Criminology: The Coming Crises. Beverly Hills: Sage.

Inciardi, James A., Ruth Horowitz, and Anne E. Pottiger
1993 Street Kids, Street Drugs, Street Crime: An Examination of Drug Use and Serious Delinquency in Miami. Belmont, CA: Wadsworth Publishing.

Jankovic, Ivan
1977 "Labor market and imprisonment," Crime and Social Justice 8:17-31.

Jarjoura, G. Roger and Josine Junger-Tas
1993 "Does dropping out of school enhance delinquent involvement? results from a large-scale national probability sample," Criminology 2:149-171.

Jeffery, C. Ray
1965 "Criminal behavior and learning theory," Journal of Criminal Law, Criminology, and Police Science 56:294-300.
1977 Crime Prevention Through Environmental Design. Second Edition. Beverly Hills, CA: Sage.
1980 "Sociobiology and criminology: the long lean years of the unthinkable and the unmentionable," in Edward Sagarin, ed., Taboos in Criminology. Beverly Hills, CA: Sage.

Jeffery, C. R., ed.
1979 Biology and Crime. Beverly Hills, CA: Sage.

Jensen, Gary F.
1969 "'Crime doesn't pay': correlates of a shared misunderstanding," Social Problems 17:189-201.
1970 "Containment and delinquency: analysis of a theory," Washington Journal of Sociology 2:1-14.
1972 "Parents, peers, and delinquent action: a test of the differential association perspective," American Journal of Sociology 78:63-72.
1973 "Inner containment and delinquency," Journal of Criminal Law and Criminology 64:464-70

Jensen, Gary F., ed.

1980 Sociology of Delinquency: Current Issues. Beverly Hills, CA: Sage.

Jensen, Gary F. and David Brownfield

1983 "Parents and drugs," Criminology 21:543-54.

1986 "Gender, lifestyle, and victimization: beyond routine activity," Violence and Victims 2:85-99.

Jensen, Gary F., Maynard L. Erickson, and Jack P. Gibbs

1978 "Perceived risk of punishment and self-reported delinquency," Social Forces 57:57-78.

Jensen, Gary F. and Dean G. Rojek

1992 Delinquency and Youth Crime. Second Edition. Prospect Heights, IL: Waveland Press.

Jensen, Gary F. and Ken Thompson

1990 "What's class go to do with it? a further examination of power-control theory," American Journal of Sociology 95:1009-23.

Jessor, Richard

1979 "Marijuana: a review of recent psychosocial research," pp. 337-56 in Robert I. Dupont, Avram Goldstein, and John O'Donnell, eds., Handbook on Drug Abuse. Washington, DC: U.S. Government Printing Office.

Jessor, Richard and Shirley L. Jessor

1977 Problem Behavior and Psychosocial Development. New York: Academic Press.

Jessor, Richard, Shirley Jessor, and John Finney

1973 "A social psychology of marijuana use: longitudinal studies of high school and college youth," Journal of Personality and Social Psychology 26:1-15.

Johnson, Richard E.

1979 Juvenile Delinquency and Its Origins: An Integrated Theoretical Approach. New York: Cambridge University Press.

Junger-Tas, Josine

1992 "An empirical test of social control theory," Journal of Quantitative Criminology 8:9-28.

Kandel, Denise

1980 "Drug and drinking behavior among youth," Annual Review of Sociology 1980:235-85.

Kandel, Denise B.

1978 "Homophily, selection, and socialization in adolescent friendships," American Journal of Sociology 84:427-36.

Kandel, Denise B. and Israel Adler

1982 "Socialization into marijuana use among French adolescents: a cross-cultural comparison with the United States," Journal of Health and Social Behavior 23:295-309.

Kandel, Denise and Mark Davies

1991 "Friendship networks, intimacy, and illicit drug use in young adulthood: a comparison of two competing theories," Criminology 29:441-469.

Kaplan, Howard B.

1975 Self-attitudes and Deviant Behavior. Pacific Palisades, CA: Goodyear.

Kaplan, Howard B., Steven S. Martin, Robert J. Johnson, and Cynthia A. Robbins

1986 "Escalation of marijuana use: application of a general theory of deviant behavior," Journal of Health and Social Behavior 27:44-61.

Kaplan, Howard B., Steven S. Martin, and Cynthia A. Robbins
1982 "Application of a general theory of deviant behavior: self-derogation and adolescent drug use," Journal of Health and Social Behavior 23:274-94.

Karmen, Andrew
1980 "Race, inferiority, and research taboos," pp. 81-113 in Edward Sagarin, ed., Taboos in Criminology. Beverly Hills, CA: Sage.

Keane, Carl, Paul S. Maxim, and James T. Teevan
1993 "Drinking and driving, self-control, and gender: testing a general theory of crime," Journal of Research in Crime and Delinquency 30:30-46.

Kempf, Kimberly and Roy L. Austin
1986 "Older and more recent evidence on racial discrimination in sentencing," Journal of Quantitative Criminology 2:29-48.

Kennedy, Leslie W. and David R. Forde
1990 "Routine activities and crime: an analysis of victimization in Canada," Criminology 28:137-152.

Kitsuse, John I.
1964 "Societal reaction to deviant behavior: problems of theory and method," pp. 87-102 in Howard S. Becker, ed., The Other Side. New York: Free Press.

Kleck, Gary
1985 "Life support for ailing hypothesis: summarizing the evidence on racial discrimination in sentencing," Law and Human Behavior 9:271-285.

Klein, Stephen, Susan Turner, and Joan Petersilia
1988 Racial Equity in Sentencing. Santa Monica, CA: Rand Corporation.

Klepper, Steven and Daniel Nagin
1989 "The deterrenct effect of perceived certainty and severity of punishment revisited," Criminology 27:721-746.

Klinger, David A.
1996 "More on demeanor and arrest in Dade County," Criminology 34:61-82

Klockars, Carl
1979 "The contemporary crisis of Marxist criminology," Criminology 16:477-515.

Krohn, Marvin D.
1974 "An investigation of the effect of parental and peer associations on marijuana use: an empirical test of differential association theory," pp. 75-89 in Marc Riedel and Terence P. Thornberry, eds., Crime and Delinquency: Dimensions of Deviance. New York: Praeger.
1986 "The web of conformity: a network approach to the explanation of delinquent behavior," Social Problems 33:S81-S93.

Krohn, Marvin D., Ronald L. Akers, Marcia J. Radosevich, and Lonn Lanza-Kaduce
1982 "Norm qualities and adolescent drinking and drug behavior," Journal of Drug Issues 12:343-59.

Krohn, Marvin D., Lonn Lanza-Kaduce, and Ronald L. Akers
1984 "Community context and theories of deviant behavior: an examination of social learning and social bonding theories," Sociological Quarterly 25:353-71.

Krohn, Marvin D. and James L. Massey
1980 "Social control and delinquent behavior: an examination of the elements of the social bond," Sociological Quarterly 21:529-43.

Krohn, Marvin D., William F. Skinner, James L. Massey, and Ronald L. Akers

1985 "Social learning theory and adolescent cigarette smoking: a longitudinal study," Social Problem 32:455-73.

LaFree, Gary, Kriss A. Drass, and Patrick O'Day

1992 "Race and crime in post-war America: determinants of African-American and white rates, 1957-1988," Criminology 30:157-188.

LaGrange, Randy L. and Helene Raskin White

1985 "Age differences in delinquency: a test of theory," Criminology 23:19-46.

Land, Kenneth C., Patricia L. McCall, and Lawrence E. Cohen

1990 "Structural covariates of homicide rates: are there any invariances across time and social space?" American Journal of Sociology 95:922-963.

Lander, Bernard

1954 Towards an Understanding of Juvenile Delinquency. New York: Columbia University Press.

Lanza-Kaduce, Lonn

1988 "Perceptual deterrence and drinking and driving among college students," Criminology 26:321-342.

Lanza-Kaduce, Lonn, Ronald L. Akers, Marvin D. Krohn, and Marcia Radosevich

1984 "Cessation of alcohol and drug use among adolescents: a social learning model," Deviant Behavior 5:79-96.

Lanza-Kaduce, Lonn, Marvin D. Krohn, Ronald L. Akers, and Marcia Radosevich

1979 "Law and Durkheimian order," pp. 41-61 in Paul J. Brantingham and Jack M. Kress, eds., Structure, Law, and Power: Essays in the Sociology of Law. Beverly Hills, CA: Sage.

Lasley, James R.

1988 "Toward a control theory of white-collar offending," Journal of Quantitative Criminology 4:347-359.

Laub, John H. and Robert J. Sampson

1993 "Turning points in the life course: why change matters to the study of crime," Criminology 31:301-26.

Lauer, Ronald M., Ronald L. Akers, James Massey, and William Clarke

1982 "The evaluation of cigarette smoking among adolescents: the Muscatine study," Preventive Medicine 11:417-28.

Lauritsen, Janet L.

1993 "Sibling resemblance in juvenile delinquency: findings from the national youth survey," Criminology 31:387-410.

Lea, John

1992 "The analysis of crime," pp. 69-94 in Jock Young and Roger Matthews, eds., Rethinking Criminology: The Realist Debate. London: Sage Publications.

Lemert, Edwin M.

1951 Social Pathology. New York: McGraw-Hill.
1967 Human Deviance, Social Problems, and Social Control. Englewood Cliffs, NJ: Prentice-Hall.
1974 "Beyond Mead: the societal reaction to deviance," Social Problems 21:457-68.

Leonard, Eileen B.

1982 Women, Crime, and Society: A Critique of Theoretical Criminology. New York: Longman.

Lieber, Michael J.

1994 "A comparison of juvenile court outcomes for Native Americans, African Americans, and Whites," Justice Quarterly, 11:257-279.

Lilly, J. Robert, Francis T. Cullen, and Richard A. Ball

1989 Criminological Theory: Context and Consequences. Newbury Park, CA: Sage.

Linden, Eric and James Hackler

1973 "Affective ties and delinquency," Pacific Sociological Review 16:27-46.

Lindner, Robert

1944 Rebel Without a Cause. New York: Grove Press.

Link, Burce, G., Francis T. Cullen, Elmer Struening, Patrick E. Shrout, and Bruce P. Dohrenwend

1989 "A modified labeling theory approach to mental disorders: an empirical assessment," American Sociological Review 54:400-23.

Lipset, Seymour M.

1960 Political Man: The Social Bases of Politics. Garden City, NY: Doubleday.

Liska, Allen E.

1969 "Uses and misuses of tautologies in social psychology," Sociometry 33:444-57.
1971 "Aspirations, expectations, and delinquency: stress and additive models," Sociological Quarterly 12:99-107.
1987 Perspectives on Deviance. Englewood Cliffs, NJ: Prentice Hall.

Liska, Allen E. and Mitchell B. Chamlin

1985 "Testing the economic production and conflict models of crime control," Social Forces 64:119-138.

Liska, Allen E., Marvin D. Krohn, and Steven F. Messner

1989 "Strategies and requisites for theoretical integration in the study of crime and deviance," pp. 1-20 in Steven F. Messner, Marvin D. Krohn, and Allen E. Liska, eds., Theoretical Integration in the Study of Deviance and Crime. Albany: State University of New York Press.

Liska, Allen E. and Mark Tausig

1979 "Theoretical interpretation of social class and racial differentials in legal decision-making for juveniles," Sociological Quarterly 20:197-207.

Loeber, Rolf and Thomas J. Dishion

1987 "Antisocial and delinquent youths: methods for their early identification," pp. 75-89 in J. D. Burchard and Sara Burchard, eds., Prevention of Delinquent Behavior. Newbury Park, CA: Sage.

Loeber, Rolf and Magda Stouthamer-Loeber

1986 "Family factors as correlates and predictors of juvenile conduct problems and delinquency," pp. 29-149 in Michael Tonry and Norval Morris, eds., Crime and Justice, Vol. 7. Chicago: University of Chicago Press.

Loeber, Rolf, Magda Stouthamer-Loeber, Welmoet Van Kammen, and David P. Farrington

1991 "Initiation, escalation, and desistance in juvenile offending and their correlates," Journal of Criminal Law and Criminology 82:36-82.

Loftin, Colin and R. Hill

1974 "Regional subculture and homicide," American Sociological Review 39:714-24.

Lombroso, Cesare

1876 The Criminal Man (L'uomo Delinquente). First Edition. Milan: Hoepli. Second Edition (1878) through Fifth Edition (1896). Turin: Bocca.
1912 Crime: Its Causes and Remedies. Patterson Smith Reprint, 1968. Montclair, NJ: Patterson Smith.

Lowman, John

1992 "Rediscovering crime," pp. 141-160 in Jock Young and Roger Matthews, eds., Rethinking Criminology: The Realist Debate. London: Sage Publications.

Lundman, Richard J.

1993 Prevention and Control of Juvenile Delinquency. Second Edition. New York: Oxford University Press.

Lyman, Stanford M. and Marvin B. Scott

1970 A Sociology of the Absurd. New York: Appleton-Century-Crofts.

Lynch, James and David Cantor

1992 "Ecological and behavioral influences on property victimization at home: implications for opportunity theory," Journal of Research in Crime and Delinquency 29:335-362.

Lynch, Michael J. and W. Byron Groves

1986 A Primer in Radical Criminology. New York: Harrow and Heston.

McCord, Joan

1991a "Family relationships, juvenile delinquency, and adult criminality," Criminology 29:397-418.

1991b "The cycle of crime and socialization practices," Journal of Criminal Law and Criminology 82:211-228.

McCord, William and Joan McCord

1959 Origins of Crime. New York: Columbia University. McGarrell, Edmund F. and Thomas C. Castellano.

1991 "An integrative conflict model of the criminal law formation process," Journal of Research in Crime and Delinquency 28:174-196.

McCord, Joan and John H. Laub, eds.

1995 Contemporary Masters in Criminology. New York: Plenum Press.

McGarrell, Edmund F.

1993 "Institutional theory and the stability of a conflict model of the incarceration rate," Justice Quarterly 10:7-28.

McGee, Zina T.

1992 "Social class differences in parental and peer influence on adolescent drug use," Deviant Behavior 13:349-372.

McIntosh, W. Alex, Starla D. Fitch, J. Branton Wilson, and Kenneth L. Nyberg

1981 "The effect of mainstream religious social controls on adolescent drug use in rural areas," Review of Religious Research 23:54-75.

Mahoney, Ann Rankin

1974 "The effect of labeling upon youths in the juvenile justice system: a review of the evidence," Law and Society Review 8:583-614.

Mak, Anita

1991 "Psychosocial control characteristics of delinquents and nondelinquents," Criminal Justice and Behavior 18:287-303.

Makkai, Toni and John Braithwaite

1994 "Reintegrative shaming and compliance with regulatory standards," Criminology 32:361-386.

Mankoff, Milton

1970 "Power in advanced capitalist society: a review essay on recent elitist and Marxist criticism of pluralist theory," Social Problems 17:418-430.

Mann, Coramae Richey

1984 Female Crime and Delinquency. University of Alabama Press.

Marcos, Anastasios, C., Stephen J. Bahr, and Richard E. Johnson
1986 "Testing of a bonding/association theory of adolescent drug use," Social Forces 65:135-61.

Marshall, Ineke H. and Charles W. Thomas
1983 "Discretionary decision-making and the juvenile court," Journal of Juvenile and Family Courts 34:47-59.

Massey, James L. and Marvin D. Krohn
1986 "A longitudinal examination of an integrated social process model of deviant behavior," Social Forces 63:106-34.

Massey, James, Marvin Krohn, and Lisa Bonati
1989 "Property crime and the routine activities of individuals," Journal of Research in Crime and Delinquency 26:378-400.

Matthews, Victor M.
1968 "Differential identification: an empirical note," Social Problems 14:376-83.

Matthews, Roger and Jock Young,
1992 "Reflections on realism," pp. 1-24 in Jock Young and Roger Matthews, eds., Rethinking Criminology: The Realist Debate. London: Sage Publications.

Matsueda, Ross L.
1982 "Testing control theory and differential association," American Sociological Review 47:489-504.
1992 "Reflected appraisals, parental labeling, and delinquency: specifying a symbolic interactionist theory," American Journal of Sociology 97:1577-1611.

Matsueda, Ross L. and Karen Heimer
1987 "Race, family structure, and delinquency: a test of differential association and social control theories," American Sociological Review 52:826-840.

Matza, David
1964 Delinquency and Drift. New York: Wiley.

Matza, David and Gresham M. Sykes
1961 "Juvenile delinquency and subterranean values," American Sociological Review 26:712-19.

Mead, George Herbert
1934 Mind, Self, and Society. Chicago: University of Chicago Press.

Mednick, Sarnoff A.
1977 "A biosocial theory of the learning of law-abiding behavior," pp. 1-8 in Sarnoff A. Mednick and Karl O. Christensen, eds., Biosocial Bases of Criminal Behavior. New York: Gardner.

Mednick, Sarnoff and Karl O. Christiansen, eds.
1977 Biosocial Bases of Criminal Behavior. New York: Gardner.

Mednick, Sarnoff, William Gabrielli, and Barry Hutchings
1984 "Genetic influences in criminal convictions: evidence from an adoption cohort," Science 224:891-94.

Mednick, Sarnoff A., Terrie E. Moffitt, and Susan A. Stack, eds.
1987 The Causes of Crime: New Biological Approaches. Cambridge: Cambridge University Press

Mednick, Sarnoff A., Terrie E. Moffitt, and Susan A. Stack, eds.
1987 "Biological factors in crime causation: the reactions of social scientists," pp. 1-6 in Sarnoff Mednick, Terrie E. Moffitt, and Susan A. Stack, eds., The Causes of Crime: New Biological Approaches. Cambridge: Cambridge University Press.

Mednick, Sarnoff; Vicki Pollack, Jan Volavka, and William F. Gabrielli
1982 "Biology and violence," pp. 21-79 in Marvin E. Wolfgang and Neil A. Weiner, eds., Criminal Violence. Beverly Hills, CA: Sage.

Mednick, Sarnoff and Giora Shoham, eds.
1979 New Paths in Criminology. Lexington, MA: Lexington Books.

Mednick, Sarnoff, Jan Volavka, William F. Gabrielli,and Turan M. Itil
1981 "EEG as a predictor of antisocial behavior," Criminology 19:219-229.

Meier, Robert F.
1977 "The new criminology: continuity in criminological theory," Journal of Criminal Law and Criminology 67:461-469.

Meier, Robert F. and Weldon T. Johnson
1977 "Deterrence as social control: the legal and extralegal production of conformity," American Sociological Review 42:292-304.

Melossi, Dario
1985 "Overcoming the crisis in critical criminology: toward a grounded labeling theory," Criminology 23:195-208.

Menard, Scott and Delbert S. Elliott
1990 "Longitudinal and cross-sectional data collection and analysis in the study of crime and delinquency," Justice Quarterly 7:11-55.
1994 "Delinquent bonding, moral beliefs, and illegal behavior: a three-wave panel model," Justice Quarterly 11:173-188.

Merton, Robert K.
1938 "Social structure and anomie," American Sociological Review 3:672-82.
1957 Social Theory and Social Structure. Glencoe, IL: Free Press.

Messerschmidt, James W.
1986 Capitalism, Patriarchy, and Crime: Toward a Socialist Feminist Criminology. Totowa, NJ: Rowman and Littlefield.

Messner, Steven F.
1988 "Merton's 'Social structure and anomie': The road not taken," Deviant Behavior 9:33-53.

Messner, Steven and Marvin Krohn
1990 "Class compliance structures and delinquency: assessing integrated structural-Marxist theory," American Journal of Sociology 96:300-328.

Messner, Steven F. and Richard Rosenfeld
1994 Crime and the American Dream. Belmont, CA: Wadsworth.

Messner, Steven F. and Kenneth Tardiff
1985 "The social ecology of urban homicide: an application of the 'routine activities' approach," Criminology 23:241-268.

Michalowski, Raymond J.
1985 Order, Law, and Crime. New York: Random House.

Miethe, Terance D.
1982 "Public consensus on crime seriousness: normative structure or methodological artifact?" Criminology 20:515-526.

Miethe, Terance D., Mark C. Stafford, and J. Scott Long
1987 "Social differentiation in criminal victimization: a test of routine activities lifestyle theories," American Sociological Review 52:184-194.

Miller, Susan L. and Lee Ann Iovanni
1994 "Determinants of perceived risk of formal sanction for courtship violence," Justice Quarterly 11:281-312.

Miller, Walter B.

1958 "Lower class culture as a generating milieu of gang delinquency," Journal of Social Issues 14:5-19.

Minor, W. William

1975 "Political crime, political justice, and political prisoners," Criminology 12:385-98.

1977 "A deterrence-control theory of crime," pp. 117-137 in Robert F. Meier, ed., Theory in Criminology. Beverly Hills, CA: Sage.

1980 "The neutralization of criminal offense," Criminology 18:103-20.

1981"Techniques of neutralization: a reconceptualization and empirical examination," Journal of Research in Crime and Delinquency 18:295-318.

Moffitt, Terrie E.

1993 "Adolescence-limited and life-course-persistent antisocial behavioral: a developmental taxonomy," Psychological Review 100:674-701.

Moffitt, Terrie E., Donald R. Lyman, and Phil A. Silva

1994 "Neuropsychological tests predicting persistent male delinquency," Criminology 32:277-300.

Monachesi, Elio

1972 "Cesare Beccaria, 1738-1794," pp. 36-50 in Hermann Mannheim, ed. Pioneers in Criminology. Second Edition Enlarged. Montclair, NJ: Patterson Smith.

Morash, Merry and Meda Chesney-Lind

1991 "A reformulation and partial test of the power control theory of delinquency," Justice Quarterly 8:347-378.

Morris, Allison

1987 Women, Crime, and Criminal Justice. New York: Basil Blackwell.

Moulds, Elizabeth F.

1980 "Chivalry and paternalism: disparities of treatment in the criminal justice system," pp. 276 in Susan K. Datesman and Frank R. Scarpitti, eds., Women, Crime, and Justice. New York: Oxford University Press.

Murray, Charles A.

1976 The Link Between Learning Disabilities and Juvenile Delinquency. Washington, DC: U.S. Government Printing Office.

Myers, Martha

1995 "Gender and Southern punishment after the civil war," Criminology 33:17-46.

Nagin, Daniel and David P. Farrington

1992a "The stability of criminal potential from childhood to adulthood," Criminology 30:235-260.

1992b "The onset and persistence of offending," Criminology 30:501-523.

Nagin, Daniel S., David P. Farrington, and Terrie E. Moffitt

1995 "Life-course trajectories of different types of offenders," Criminology 33:111-140.

Nagin, Daniel S. and Raymond Paternoster

1991a "On the relationship of past to future participation in delinquency," Criminology 29:163-189.

1991b "Preventive effects of the perceived risk of arrest: testing an expanded conception of deterrence," Criminology 29:561-85.

1993 "Enduring individual differences and rational choice theories of crime," Law and Society Review 27:201-230.

1994 "Personal capital and social control: the deterrence implications of a theory of individual differences in criminal offending," Criminology 32:581-606.

National Institute of Mental Health

1970 Report on the XYY Chromosomal Abnormality. Washington, DC: U.S. Government Printing Office.

Nettler, Gwyn

1984 Explaining Crime. Third Edition. New York: McGraw-Hill.

Nye, F. Ivan

1958 Family Relationships and Delinquent Behavior. New York: Wiley.

O'Brien, Robert M.

1991 "Sex ratios and rape rates: a power control theory," Criminology 29:99-114.

Ogle, Robbin S., Daniel Maier-Kaktin, Thomas J. Bernard

1995 "A theory of homicidal behavior among women," Criminology 33:173-194.

Orcutt, James D.

1983 Analyzing Deviance. Homewood, IL: Dorsey.

1987 "Differential association and marijuana use: a closer look at Sutherland (with a little help from Becker)," Criminology 25:341-358.

Palamara, Frances, Francis T. Cullen, and Joanne C. Gersten

1986 "The effects of police and mental health intervention on juvenile deviance: specifying contingencies in the impact of formal reaction," Journal of Health and Social Behavior 27:90-106.

Pallone, Nathaniel J. and James J. Hennessy

1992 Criminal Behavior: A Process Psychology Analysis. New Brunswick, NJ: Transaction Publishers.

Park, Robert E.K., Ernest W. Burgess, and Roderick D. McKenzie

1928 The City. Chicago: University of Chicago Press.

Paternoster, Raymond

1989a "Decisions to participate in and desist from four types of common delinquency: deterrence and the rational choice perspective," Law and Society Review 23:7-40.

1989b "Absolute and restrictive deterrence in a panel of youth: explaining the onset, persistence/desistance, and frequency of delinquent offending," Social Problems 36:289-309.

Paternoster, Raymond and Lee Ann Iovanni

1989 "The labeling perspective and delinquency: an elaboration of the theory and an assessment of the evidence," Justice Quarterly 6:379-394.

Paternoster, Raymond, Linda E. Saltzman, Gordon P. Waldo, and Theodore G. Chiricos

1983 "Perceived risk and social control: do sanctions really deter?" Law and Society Review 17:457-80.

Patterson, Gerald R.

1975 Families: Applications of Social Learning to Family Life. Champaign, IL: Research Press.

1995 "Coercion as a basis for early age of onset for arrest," pp. 81-105 in Joan McCord, ed., Coercion and Punishment in Long-Term Perspectives. Cambridge: Cambridge University Press.

1996 "Some characteristics of a development theory for early-onset delinquency," pp. 81-124 in Mark F. Lenzenweger and Jeffrey J. Haugaard, eds., Frontiers of Developmental Psychopathology. New York: Oxford University Press.

Patterson, G. R., J. B. Reid, R. Q. Jones, and R. E. Conger

1975 A Social Learning Approach to Family Intervention. Vol. 1. Eugene, OR: Castalia Publishing Co.

Patterson, G. R. and Patricia Chamberlain

1994 "A functional analysis of resistance during parent training therapy," Clinical Psychology: Science and Practice 1:53-70.

Patterson, Gerald R. and Thomas J. Dishion
1985 "Contributions of families and peers to delinquency," Criminology 23:63-79.

Patterson, Gerald R., John B. Reid, and Thomas J. Dishion
1992 Antisocial Boys. Eugene, OR: Castalia Publishing Co.

Pearson, Frank S. and Neil Alan Weiner
1985 "Toward an integration of criminological theories," Journal of Criminal Law and Criminology 76:116-50.

Pease, Kenneth, Judith Ireson, and Jennifer Thorpe
1975 "Modified crime indices for eight countries," Journal of Criminal Law and Criminology 66:209-14.

Pepinsky, Harold E. and Richard Quinney, eds.
1991 Criminology as Peacemaking. Bloomington, IN: Indiana University Press.

Pepinsky, Harold E.
1991 "Peacemaking criminology and criminal justice," pp. 299-327 in Harold E. Pepinsky and Richard Quinney, eds., Criminology as Peacemaking. Bloomington, IN: Indiana University Press.

Petersilia, Joan
1983 Racial Disparities in the Criminal Justice System. Santa Monica, CA: Rand Corporation.

Petersilia, Joan and Susan Turner
1987 "Guideline-based justice: the implications for racial minorities," pp. 151-182 in Don Gottfredson and Michael Tonry, eds., Prediction and Classification in Criminal Justice Decision Making. Chicago: University of Chicago Press.

Piliavin, Irving, Graig Thornton, Rosemary Gartner, and Ross L. Matsueda
1986 "Crime, deterrence, and rational choice," American Sociological Review 51:101-119.

Platt, Anthony M.
1969 The Child Savers: The Invention of Delinquency. Chicago: University of Chicago Press.
1977 The Child Savers. Second Edition Enlarged. Chicago: University of Chicago Press.

Platt, Anthony and Paul Takagi, eds.
1981 Crime and Social Justice. Totowa, NJ: Barnes and Noble.

Pollack, Otto
1950 The Criminality of Women. Philadelphia: University of Pennsylvania Press.

Quinney, Richard
1964 "Crime in political perspective," American Behavioral Scientist 8:19-22.
1970 The Social Reality of Crime. Boston: Little, Brown.
1974a Critique of the Legal Order. Boston: Little, Brown.
1979 "The production of criminology," Criminology 16:445-458.
1980 Class, State, and Crime. Second Edition. New York: Longman.
1991 "The way of peace: on crime, suffering, and service," pp. 3-13 in Harold E. Pepinsky and Richard Quinney, eds., Criminology as Peacemaking. Bloomington, IN: Indiana University Press.

Quinney, Richard, ed.
1969 Crime and Justice in Society. Boston: Little, Brown.
1974b Criminal Justice in America: A Critical Understanding. Boston: Little, Brown.

Radelet, Michael L.
1981 "Racial characteristics and the imposition of the death penalty," American Sociological Review 46:918-927.

Radelet, Michael L. and Glenn L. Pierce

1991 "Choosing those who will die: race and the death penalty in Florida," Florida Law Review 43:1-43.

Radosevich, Marcia, Lonn Lanza-Kaduce, Ronald L. Akers, and Marvin D. Krohn

1980 "The sociology of adolescent drug and drinking behavior: a review of the state of the field: part II," Deviant Behavior 1:145-69.

Rafter, Nicole Hahn

1992 "Criminal anthropology in the United States," Criminology 30:525-545.

Rankin, Joseph H. and Roger Kern

1994 "Parental attachments and delinquency," Criminology 32:495-516.

Reasons, Charles E. and Robert M. Rich

1978 The Sociology of Law: A Conflict Perspective. Toronto: Butterworth.

Reckless, Walter

1961 "A new theory of delinquency and crime," Federal Probation 25:42-46.
1967 The Crime Problem. New York: Appleton-Century-Crofts.

Reckless, Walter, Simon Dinitz, and Barbara Kay

1957 "The self-component in potential delinquency and potential non-delinquency," American Sociological Review 25:566-70.

Reckless, Walter, Simon Dinitz, and Ellen Murray

1956 "Self-concept as an insulator against delinquency," American Sociological Review 21:744-56.

Reiss, Albert J.

1951 "Delinquency as the failure of personal and social controls," American Sociological Review 16:196-207.

Ritzer, George

1992 Sociological Theory. Third Edition. New York: McGraw-Hill.

Roby, Pamela A.

1969 "Politics and criminal law: revision of the New York State penal law on prostitution," Social Problems 17:83-109.

Rogers, Joseph W. and M. D. Buffalo

1974 "Fighting back: nine modes of adaptation to a deviant label," Social Problems 22:101-18.

Rojek, Dean G.

1982 "Juvenile diversion: a study of community cooptation," pp. 316-322 in Dean G. Rojek and Gary F. Jensen, eds., Readings in Juvenile Delinquency. Lexington, MA: D. C. Heath.

Rose, Arnold

1954 Theory and Method in the Social Sciences. Minneapolis: University of Minnesota Press.
1967 The Power Structure. New York: Oxford University Press.

Rosenbaum, Jill L. and James R. Lasley

1990 "School, community context, and delinquency: rethinking the gender gap," Justice Quarterly 7:493-513.

Ross, Edward Alsworth

1901 Social Control. New York: Macmillan.

Ross, Lawrence H.

1982 Deterring the Drinking Driver: Legal Policy and Social Control. Lexington, MA: Lexington Books.

Ross, Lee

1994 "Religion and deviance: exploring the impact of social control elements," Sociological Spectrum 14:65-86.

Rossi, Peter H., Emily Waite, Christine E. Bose, and Richard Berk

1974 "The seriousness of crime: normative structure and individual differences," American Sociological Review 39:224-37.

Rotter, Julian

1954 Social Learning and Clinical Psychology. Englewood Cliffs, NJ: Prenctice-Hall.

Rowe, David C.

1985 "Sibling interaction and self-reported delinquent behavior: a study of 265 twin pairs," Criminology 23:223-240.

1986 "Genetic and environmental components of antisocial behavior: a study of 265 twin pairs," Criminology 24:513-532.

Rowe, David and Chester L. Britt, III

1991 "Developmental explanations of delinquent behavior among siblings: common factor vs. transmission mechanisms," Journal of Quantitative Criminology 7:315-332.

Rowe, David and Daniel Flannery

1994 "An examination of environmental and trait influences on adolescent delinquency," Journal of Research in Crime and Delinquency 31:374-389.

Rowe, David C. and Bill L. Gulley

1992 "Sibling effects on substance use and delinquency," Criminology 30:217-234.

Rowe, David C. and D. Wayne Osgood

1984 "Heredity and sociological theories of delinquency: a reconsideration," American Sociological Review 49:526-540.

Sampson, Robert J.

1995 "The community," pp. 193-216 in Wilson and Petersilia.

Sampson, Robert J. and W. Byron Groves

1989 "Community structure and crime: testing social-disorganization theory," American Journal of Sociology 94:774-802.

Sampson, Robert J. and John H. Laub

1993 Crime in the Making: Pathways and Turning Points Through Life. Cambridge: Harvard U. Press.

Scarpitti, Frank, Ellen Murray, Simon Dinitz, and Walter Reckless

1960 "The good boy in a high-delinquency area: four years later," American Sociological Review 23:555-558.

Schur, Edwin M.

1965 Crimes Without Victims. Englewood Cliffs, NJ: Prentice-Hall.

1971 Labeling Deviant Behavior. New York: Harper and Row.

1973 Radical Non-Intervention: Rethinking the Delinquency Problem. Englewood Cliffs, NJ: Prentice-Hall.

1979 Interpreting Deviance. New York: Harper and Row.

1984 Labeling Women Deviant: Gender, Stigma, and Social Control. New York: Random House.

Schrag, Clarence

1962 "Delinquency and opportunity: analysis of a theory," Sociology and Social Research 46:168-175.

Schreiber, Flora Rheta

1984 The Shoemaker: The Anatomy of a Psychotic. New York: New American Library.

Schwartz, Richard D.

1986 "Law and normative order," pp. 63-108 in Leon Lipson and Stanton Wheeler, eds., Law and the Social Sciences. New York: Russell Sage Foundation.

Schwendinger, Julia R. and Herman Schwendinger

1983 Rape and Inequality. Beverly Hills, CA: Sage. Schwendinger, Herman and Julia R. Schwendinger.

1985 Adolescent Subcultures and Delinquency. New York: Praeger.

Schuessler, Karl and Donald R. Cressey

1950 "Personality characteristics of criminals," American Journal of Sociology 55:476-484.

Sellers, Christine S. and Thomas L. Winfree

1990 "Differential associations and definitions: a panel study of youthful drinking behavior," International Journal of the Addictions 25:755-771.

Sellin, Thorsten

1958 Culture Conflict and Crime. New York: Social Science Research Council.

1959 The Death Penalty. Philadelphia: American Law Institute.

Shah, Saleem A. and Loren H. Roth

1974 "Biological and psychophysiological factors in criminality," pp. 101-174 in Daniel Glaser, ed., Handbook of Criminology. Chicago: Rand McNally.

Shannon, Lyle

1982 Assessing the Relationship of Adult Criminal Careers to Juvenile Careers. National Institute of Juvenile Justice and Delinquency Prevention. Washington, DC: U.S. Government Printing Office.

Shaw, Clifford and Henry D. McKay

1942 Juvenile Delinquency and Urban Areas. Chicago: University of Chicago Press.

1969 Juvenile Delinquency and Urban Areas. Revised Edition. Chicago: University of Chicago Press.

Shelley, Louise

1980 "The geography of Soviet criminality," American Sociological Review 45:111-122.

Sherman, Lawrence W., Patrick R. Gartin, and Michael D. Buerger

1989 "Hot spots of predatory crime: routine activities and the criminology of place," Criminology 27:27-56.

Shoemaker, Donald J.

1990 Theories of Delinquency: An Examination of Explanations of Delinquent Behavior. Second Edition. New York: Oxford University Press.

Shoham, S. Giora and John Hoffman

1991 A Primer in the Sociology of Crime. New York: Harrow and Heston.

Shoham, S. Giora and Mark Seis

1993 A Primer in the Psychology of Crime. New York: Harrow and Heston.

Short, James F.

1957 "Differential association and delinquency," Social Problems 4:233-39.

1958 "Differential association with delinquent friends and delinquent behavior," Pacific Sociological Review 1:20-25.

1960 "Differential association as a hypothesis: problems of empirical testing," Social Problems 8:14-25.

Short, James F. and Fred L. Strodtbeck

1965 Group Process and Gang Delinquency. Chicago: University of Chicago Press.

Siegel, Larry J. and Joseph J. Senna

1991 Juvenile Delinquency: Theory, Practice, and Law. Fourth Edition. St. Paul: West Publishing Co.

Simcha-Fagan, Ora and Joseph E. Schwartz

1986 "Neighborhood and delinquency: an assessment of contextual effects," Criminology 24:667-704.

Simmel, Georg

1950 The Sociology of Georg Simmel. Translation and Introduction by Kurt H. Wolff. Glencoe, IL: The Free Press.

Simon, Rita

1975 Women and Crime. Lexington, MA: Lexington Books.

Simons, Ronald L., C. Wu, Rand D. Conger, and F. O. Lorenz

1994 "Two routes to delinquency: differences between early and late starters in the impact of parenting and deviant peers," Criminology 32:247-276.

Simpson, Sally S.

1989 "Feminist theory, crime, and justice," Criminology 27:605-627.
1991 "Caste, class, and violent crime: explaining differences in female offending," Criminology 29:115-135.

Simpson, Sally S. and Lori Ellis

1994 "Is gender subordinate to class? An empirical assessment of Colvin and Pauly's Structural Marxist Theory of Delinquency," Journal of Criminal Law and Criminology 85:453-480.
1995 "Doing gender: sorting out the caste and crime conundrum," Criminology 33:47-82.

Singer, Simon I. and Murray Levine

1988 "Power-control theory, gender, and delinquency: a partial replication with additional evidence on the effects of peers," Criminology 26:627-48.

Skinner, B. F.

1953 Science and Human Behavior. New York: Macmillan.
1959 Cumulative Record. New York: Appleton-Century-Crofts.

Smith, Douglas A. and Robert Brame

1994 "On the initiation and continuation of delinquency," 32:607-632.

Smith, Douglas A. and Raymond Patenoster

1990 "Formal processing and future delinquency: deviance amplification as selection artifact," Law and Society Review 24:1109-1131.

Smith, Douglas A., Christy A. Visher, and G. Roger Jarjoura

1991 "Dimensions of delinquency: exploring the correlates of participation, frequency, and persistence of delinquent behavior," Journal of Research in Crime and Delinquency 28:6-32.

Smith, Linda G. and Ronald L. Akers

1993 "A research note on racial disparity in sentencing to prison or community control," unpublished paper, Department of Criminology, University of South Florida.

Snyder, James J. and Gerald R. Patterson

1995 "Individual differences in social aggression: a test of a reinforcement model of socialization in the natural environment," Behavior Therapy 26:371-391.

Sommer, Robert, Emily Burstein, and Sandy Holman

1988 "Tolerance of deviance as affected by label, act, and actor," Deviant Behavior 9:193-207.

Spear, Sherilyn and Ronald L. Akers
1988 "Social learning variables and the risk of habitual smoking among adolescents: the Muscatine Study," American Journal of Preventive Medicine 4:336-348.

Spergel, Irving
1964 Racketville, Slumtown, and Haulburg. Chicago: University of Chicago Press.

Spitzer, Steven
1975 "Toward a Marxian theory of deviance," Social Problems 22:638-651.

Spohn, Cassia
1994 "Crime and the social control of blacks: offender/victim race and the sentencing of violent offenders," pp. 249-268 in George S. Bridges and Martha A. Myers, eds., Inequality, Crime, and Social Control. Boulder, CO: Westview Press.

Stafford, Mark and Mark Warr
1993 "A reconceptualization of general and specific deterrence," Journal of Research in Crime and Delinquency 30:123-135.

Stahura, John M. and John J. Sloan
1988 "Urban stratification of places, routine activities, and suburban crime rates," Social Forces 66:1102-1118.

Stark, Rodney, Lori Kent, and Daniel P. Doyle
1980 "Religion and delinquency: the ecology of a 'lost' relationship," Journal of Research in Crime and Delinquency 19:4-24.

Steffensmeier, Darrell J.
1980 "Sex differences in patterns of adult crime, 1965-77," Social Forces 58:1080-1109.

Steffensmeier, Darrell, Emilie Allan, and Cathy Streifel
1989 "Development and female crime: a cross-national test of alternative explanations," Social Forces 68:262-283.

Steffensmeier, Darrell, John Kramer, and Cathy Streifel
1993 "Gender and imprisonment decisions," Criminology 31:411-446.

Steffensmeier, Darrell and Cathy Streifel
1992 "Trends in female crime: 1960-90," pp. in Concetta Culliver, eds., Female Criminality: The State of the Art. New York: Garland Publishing, 1992.

Stinchcombe, Arthur L.
1968 Constructing Social Theories. New York: Harcourt Brace and World.

Stitt, B. Grant and David J. Giacopassi
1992 "Trends in the connectivity of theory and research in Criminology," The Criminologist 17:1, 3-6.

Stumphauzer, Jerome S.
1986 Helping Delinquents Change: A Treatment Manual of Social Learning Approaches. New York: Hayworth.

Strodtbeck, Fred L. and James F. Short
1964 "Aleatory risks versus short-run hedonism in explanation of gang action," Social Problems 12:127-140.

Sumner, William Graham
1906 Folkways. Boston: Ginn.

Sutherland, Edwin H.
1924 Criminology. Philadelphia: J. B. Lippincott.
1934 Principles of Criminology. Second Edition. Philadelphia: J. B. Lippincott.
1937 The Professional Thief. Chicago: University of Chicago Press.
1939 Principles of Criminology. Third Edition. Philadelphia: J. B. Lippincott.
1940 "White Collar Criminality," American Sociological Review 5:1-12.

1947 Principles of Criminology. Fourth Edition. Philadelphia: J. B. Lippincott.
1949 White-collar Crime. New York: Holt, Rinehart, Winston.
1973 On Analyzing Crime. Edited with an Introduction by Karl Schuessler. Chicago: University of Chicago Press.

Sutherland, Edwin H. and Donald R. Cressey

1974 Criminology. Ninth Edition. Philadelphia: J. B. Lippincott.
1978 Criminology. Tenth Edition. Philadelphia: J. B. Lippincott.

Sutherland, Edwin H., Donald R. Cressey, and David F. Luckenbill

1992 Principles of Criminology. Eleventh Edition. Dix Hills, NY: General Hall.

Sykes, Gresham and David Matza

1957 "Techniques of neutralization: a theory of delinquency," American Journal of Sociology 22:664-70.

Szymanski, Albert

1981 "Socialist societies and the capitalist system," Social Problems 28:521-526.

Tangri, Sandra S. and Michael Schwartz

1967 "Delinquency research and the self-concept variable," Journal of Criminal Law, Criminology, and Police Science 58:182-90.

Tannenbaum, Frank

1938 Crime and the Community. Boston: Ginn.

Tarde, Gabriel

1912 Penal Philosophy. Translated by R. Howell. Boston: Little, Brown.

Taylor, Ian, Paul Walton, and Jock Young

1973 The New Criminology. New York: Harper and Row.
1975 "Marx and Engels on law, crime, and morality," pp. 203-230 in Paul Q. Hirst, ed., Critical Criminology. London: Routledge and Kegan Paul Ltd.

Taylor, Lawrence

1984 Born to Crime: The Genetic Causes of Criminal Behavior. Westport: Greenwood Press.

Thomas, Charles W., Robin J. Cage, and Samuel C. Foster

1976 "Public opinion on criminal law and legal sanctions: an examination of two conceptual models," Journal of Criminal Law and Criminology 67:110-16.

Thomas, Charles W. and Donna M. Bishop

1984 "The effects of formal and informal sanctions on delinquency: a longitudinal comparison of labeling and deterrence theories," Journal of Criminal Law and Criminology 75:1222-45.

Thornberry, Terence P.

1987 "Towards an interactional theory of delinquency," Criminology 25:863-891.
1989 "Reflections on the advantages and disadvantages of theoretical integration," pp. 51-60 in Steven F. Messner, Marvin D. Krohn, and Allen E. Liska, eds., Theoretical Integration in the Study of Deviance and Crime. Albany: State University of New York Press.

Thornberry, Terence P. and R. L. Christenson

1984 "Unemployment and criminal involvement," American Sociological Review 49:398-411.

Thornberry, Terence P. and Margaret Farnworth

1982 "Social correlates of criminal involvement," American Sociological Review 47:505-17.

Thornberry, Terence P., Melanie Moore, and R. L. Christenson
1985 "The effect of dropping out of high school on subsequent criminal behavior," Criminology 23:3-18.

Thornberry, Terence P., Alan J. Lizotte, Marvin D. Krohn, Margaret Farnworth, and Sung Joon Jang
1991 "Testing interactional theory: an examination of reciprocal causal relationships among family, school, and delinquency," Journal of Criminal Law and Criminology 82:3-33.
1994 "Delinquent peers, beliefs, and delinquent behavior: a longitudinal test of interactional theory," Criminology 32:47-84.

Tittle, Charles R.
1969 "Crime rates and legal sanctions," Social Problems 16:409-22.
1975 "Deterrents or labeling?" Social Forces 53:399-410.
1980 Sanctions and Social Deviance. New York: Praeger.
1995 Control Balance: Toward a General Theory of Deviance. Boulder, CO: Westview Press.

Tittle, Charles R. and Debra Curran
1988 "Contingencies for dispositional disparities in juvenile justice," Social Forces 67:23-58.

Tittle, Charles R. and Wayne J. Villemez
1977 "Social class and criminality," Social Forces 56:474-503.

Tittle, Charles R., Wayne J. Villemez, and Douglas A. Smith
1978 "The myth of social class and criminality: an empirical assessment of the empirical evidence," American Sociological Review 43:643-656.

Tittle, Charles R. and Robert F. Meier
1990 "Specifying the SES/delinquency relationship," Criminology 28:271-299.

Toby, Jackson
1957 "Social disorganization and stake in conformity: complementary factors in the predatory behavior of hoodlums," Journal of Criminal Law, Criminology, and Police Science 48:12-17.
1964 "Is punishment necessary?" Journal of Criminal Law, Criminology, and Police Science 55:332-37.

Trevino, A. Javier
1996 The Sociology of Law: Classical and Contemporary Perspectives. New York: St. Martin's Press.

Triplett, Ruth and Roger Jarjoura
1994 "Theoretical and empirical specification of a model of informal labeling," Journal of Quantitative Criminology 10:241-276.

Troyer, Ronald J. and Gerald F. Markle
1983 Cigarettes: The Battle Over Smoking. New Brunswick, NJ: Rutgers University Press.

Tunnell, Kenneth D.
1990 "Choosing crime: close your eyes and take your chances," Justice Quarterly 7:673-90.
1992 Choosing Crime: The Criminal Calculus of Property Offenders. Chicago: Nelson-Hall.

Turk, Austin T.
1964 "Prospects for theories of criminal behavior," Journal of Criminal Law, Criminology, and Police Science 55:454-461.
1966 "Conflict and criminality," American Sociological Review 31:338-52.
1969a Criminality and the Legal Order. Chicago: Rand-McNally.
1969b "Introduction" to Willem A. Bonger, Criminality and Economic Conditions. Bloomington, IN: Indiana University Press.

1977 "Class, conflict, and criminalization," Sociological Focus 10:209-220.
1979 "Analyzing official deviance: for non-partisan conflict analyses in criminology," Criminology 16:459-476.

Udry, J. Richard
1988 "Biological predisposition and social control in adolescent sexual behavior," American Sociological Review 53:709-722.

van Bemmelen, J. M.
1972 "Willem Adriaan Bonger," pp. 443-457 in Hermann Mannheim, ed., Pioneers in Criminology. Second Edition Enlarged. Montclair, NJ: Patterson Smith.

Vila, Bryan
1994 "A general paradigm for understanding criminal behavior: extending evolutionary ecological theory," Criminology 32:311-360.

Vold, George B.
1958 Theoretical Criminology. New York: Oxford University Press.
1979 Theoretical Criminology. Second Edition. Prepared by Thomas J. Bernard. New York: Oxford University Press.

Vold, George B. and Thomas J. Bernard
1986 Theoretical Criminology. Third Edition. New York: Oxford University Press.

Voss, Harwin
1969 "Differential association and containment theory: a theoretical convergence," Social Forces 47:381-91.

Voss, Harwin L. and David M. Petersen, eds.
1971 Ecology, Crime, and Delinquency. New York: Appleton-Century-Crofts.

Waldo, Gordon P. and Theodore G. Chiricos
1972 "Perceived penal sanction and self-reported criminality: a neglected approach to deterrence research," Social Problems 19:522-40.

Waldo, Gordon and Simon Dinitz
1967 "Personality attributes of the criminal: an analysis of research studies, 1950-65," Journal of Research in Crime and Delinquency 4:185-202.

Walker, Samuel, Cassia Spohn, and Miriam DeLonc
1996 The Color of Justice: Race, Ethnicity, and Crime in America. Belmont, CA: Wadsworth Publishing.

Walters, Glenn D.
1992 "A meta-analysis of the gene-crime relationship," Criminology 30:595-613.

Walters, Glenn D. and Thomas W. White
1989 "Heredity and crime: bad genes or bad research," Criminology 27:455-486.

Warner, Barbara D. and Glenn L. Pierce
1993 "Reexamining social disorganization theory using calls to the police as a measure of crime," Criminology 31:493-518.

Warr, Mark
1993a "Parents, peers, and delinquency," Social Forces 72:247-264.
1993b "Age, peers, and delinquency," Criminology 31:17-40.
1996 "Organization and instigation in delinquent groups," Criminology 34:11-38.

Warr, Mark and Mark Stafford
1991 "The influence of delinquent peers: what they think or what they do?" Criminology 4:851-866.

Weber, Max
1964 Max Weber on Law in Economy and Society. Edited by Max Rheinstein. Translated by Edward Shils and Max Rheinstein. Cambridge: Harvard University Press.

Weisburd, David, Elin Waring, and Ellen Chayet
1995 "Specific deterrence in a sample of offenders convicted of white-collar crimes," Criminology 587-607.

Wellford, Charles
1975 "Labeling theory and criminology," Social Problems 22:313-32.
1989 "Towards an integrated theory of criminal behavior," pp. 119-128 in Steven F. Messner, Marvin D. Krohn, and Allen E. Liska, eds., Theoretical Integration in the Study of Deviance and Crime. Albany: State University of New York Press.

Wells, Edward and Joseph H. Rankin
1988 "Direct parental controls and delinquency," Criminology 26:263-285.

White, Helen Raskin, Marsha E. Bates, and Valerie Johnson
1991 "Learning to drink: familial, peer, and media influences," pp. 177-197 in David J. Pittman and Helene Raskin White, eds., Society, Culture, and Drinking Patterns Reconsidered. New Brunswick, NJ: Rutgers Center of Alcohol Studies.

White, Helene R., Valerie Johnson, and A. Horowitz
1986 "An application of three deviance theories for adolescent substance use," International Journal of the Addictions 21:347-366.

White, Helene Raskin, Robert J. Pandina, and Randy L. LaGrange
1987 "Longitudinal predictors of serious substance use and delinquency," Criminology 25:715-740.

Wiatrowski, Michael D., David B. Griswold, and Mary K. Roberts
1981 "Social control theory and delinquency," American Sociological Review 46:525-41.

Wilbanks, William
1987 The Myth of a Racist Criminal Justice System. Monterey, CA: Brooks/Cole.

Wilkins, Leslie
1964 Social Deviance: Social Policy, Action, and Research. Englewood Cliffs, NJ: Prentice-Hall.

Williams, Franklin P. III
1980 "Conflict theory and differential processing: an analysis of the research literature," pp. 213-232 in James Inciardi, ed., Radical Criminology: The Coming Crises. Beverly Hills, CA: Sage.

Williams, Frank P. III and Marilyn D. McShane
1988 Criminological Theory. Englewood Cliffs, NJ: Prentice Hall.

Williams, Frank P., III and Marilyn McShane, eds.
1993 Criminology Theory: Selected Classic Readings. Cincinnati, OH: Anderson Publishing.

Williams, Kirk R. and Richard Hawkins
1989 "The meaning of arrest for wife assault," Criminology 27: 163-181.

Wilson, James Q. and Richard J. Herrnstein
1985 Crime and Human Nature. New York: Simon and Schuster.

Wilson, James Q. and Joan Petersilia, eds.
1995 Crime. San Francisco: ICS Press.

Wilson, William Julius
1987 The Truly Disadvantaged: The Inner-City, the Underclass and Public Policy. Chicago: University of Chicago Press.

Winfree, L. Thomas, and Curt T. Griffiths
1983 "Social learning and marijuana use: a trend study of deviant behavior in a rural middle school," Rural Sociology 48:219-39.

Winfree, L. Thomas, Curt T. Griffiths, and Christine S. Sellers

1989 "Social learning theory, drug use, and American Indian youths: a cross-cultural test," Justice Quarterly 6: 395-417.

Winfree, L. Thomas, Jr., G. Larry Mays, and Teresa Vigil-Backstrom

1994 "Youth gangs and incarcerated delinquents: exploring the ties between gang membership, delinquency, and social learning theory," Justice Quarterly 11:229-256.

Winfree, L. Thomas, Christine Sellers, and Dennis L. Clason

1993 "Social learning and adolescent deviance abstention: Toward understanding reasons for initiating, quitting, and avoiding drugs," Journal of Quantitative Criminology 9:101-125.

Witkins, H. A.

1977 "XYY and XXY men: criminality and aggression," pp. 165-97 in Sarnoff A. Mednick and Karl O. Christensen, eds., Biosocial Bases of Criminal Behavior. New York: Gardner.

Wolfgang, Marvin E.

1972 "Cesare Lombroso (1835-1909)," pp. 232-291 in Hermann Mannheim, ed., Pioneers in Criminology. Second Edition Enlarged. Montclair, NJ: Patterson Smith.

Wolfgang, Marvin B. and Franco Ferracuti

1982 The Subculture of Violence. Beverly Hills, CA: Sage.

Wolfgang, Marvin E., Robert M. Figlio, and Thorsten Sellin

1972 Delinquency in a Birth Cohort. Chicago: University of Chicago Press.

Wolfgang, Marvin E, Robert M. Figlio, Paul E. Tracy, and Simon I. Singer

1985 The National Survey of Crime Severity. Bureau of Justice Statistics. Washington, DC: U.S. Government Printing Office.

Wolfgang, Marvin E., Terence P. Thornberry, and Robert M. Figlio

1987 From Boy to Man, from Delinquency to Crime. Chicago: University of Chicago Press.

Wood, Peter B., John K. Cochran, Betty Pfefferbaum, and Bruce J. Arneklev

1995 "Sensation-seeking and delinquent substance use: an extension of learning theory," Journal of Drug Issues 25:173-193.

Worden, Robert E. and Robin L. Shepard

1996 "Demeanor, crime, and police behavior: a reexamination of the police services study data," Criminology 34:83-106.

Wright, Richard A.

1993a "A socially sensitive criminal justice system," pp. 141-60 in John W. Murphy and Dennis L. Peck, eds., Open Institutions: The Hope for Democracy. Westport, CT: Praeger.

1993b In Defense of Prisons. Westport, CT: Greenwood Press.

Young, Jock

1987 "The tasks facing a realist criminology," Contemporary Crises 11:337-356.

1992 "Ten points of realism," pp. 24-68 in Jock Young and Roger Matthews, eds., Rethinking Criminology: The Realist Debate. London: Sage Publications.

Young, Jock and Roger Matthews, eds.

1992 Rethinking Criminology: The Realist Debate. London: Sage Publications.

Zatz, Marjorie

1987 "The changing forms of racial/ethnic biases in sentencing," Journal of Research in Crime and Delinquency 24:69-92.

Zhang, Lening and Steven F. Messner

1995 "Family deviance and delinquency in China," Criminology 33:359-388.

Zimring, Franklin E.

1971 "Perspectives on deterrence," NIMH Monograph Series on Crime and Delinquency Issues. Washington, DC: U.S. Government Printing Office.

Zimring, Franklin and Gordon Hawkins

1968 "Deterrence and marginal groups," Journal of Research in Crime and Delinquency 5:100-115.

1973 Deterrence. Chicago: University of Chicago Press.

Author Index

Subject Index